D1596646

Ritual and Myth
in Odawa Revitalization

Ritual and Myth in Odawa Revitalization

Reclaiming a Sovereign Place

Charles Meyers

By Melissa A. Pflüg

With a Foreword by Lee Irwin

University of
Oklahoma Press
Norman

Published with the assistance of the National Endowment for the Humanities, a federal agency which supports the study of such fields as history, philosophy, literature, and language.

Library of Congress Cataloging-in-Publication Data

Pflüg, Melissa A.
  Ritual and myth in Odawa revitalization : reclaiming a sovereign place / by Melissa A. Pflüg ; with a foreword by Lee Irwin.
      p.   cm.—
  Includes bibliographical references and index.
  ISBN 0-8061-3007-5
    1. Ottawa Indians—Religion.   2. Ottawa Indians—Ethnic iden-
  tity.   I. Title.   II. Series.
E99.O9P45   1998
299'.783—dc21   97-27798
                                                            CIP

Text design by Cathy Carney Imboden. Text set in the typeface California, which is similar to Caledonia.

1 2 3 4 5 6 7 8 9 10

To my mother, Marjorie Patterson,
and to the memory of my father, John Andrew,
both of whom made this work possible.

What is this
I promise you?
The skies shall be bright and clear for you
This is what I promise you.

Midéwiwin prayer

Contents

Foreword
By Lee Irwin

This is a book rich in ethnography, religious practices, and the moral and spiritual values of the Odawa people. Furthermore, it illustrates the importance of contemporary research in giving a more nuanced view of the complex relationships found in every living human community. Melissa Pflüg has very successfully maintained long-term relationships with diverse members of the Odawa communities of the Great Lakes region, and her inclusion of so many Native voices in her work shows clearly the dynamic tensions that are intrinsic to ongoing social transformations. Pflüg organizes these multiple voices from her own perspective as both a friend of contemporary Odawas and a social-anthropological theorist. However, unlike many ethnographers working in Native communities, Pflüg shows the distinctness of the voices of specific Odawa people in her narrative as they describe how they validate and maintain the traditional roots of their cultural heritage.

While Melissa Pflüg's primary concern is how myths act as creative narratives for social change through ritual enactment, she also is deeply concerned to show how, in the course of social upheaval and dramatic, often destructive changes, the Odawa have maintained their inherited ethical values. These values, like those held by so many other Native communities, revolve around the issue of how to maintain a distinct and cohesive communal identity while being forced to enact inherited values in the midst of the continual pressure to accommodate and adapt to a larger cultural imperium. In the face of large-scale Euro-American cultural demands and expectations, Odawa resistance has been strongly articulated by persons who identify themselves with a traditional cultural orientation. And yet, these members of Odawa society often are marginal or liminal to those more accommodated to contemporary American life.

As in most Native communities today, the range of Odawa values spans a full spectrum from the emphatically traditional, through outward espousal of general American values (which nonetheless are often reinterpreted according to Native ways of thinking and acting) to values that may be fully shaped by accommodation to a non-Odawa way of life. The focus in *Ritual and Myth in Odawa Revitalization* is on how traditional Odawa values have been reasserted in ways congruent with the earlier prophetic models established by such Native religious leaders as Neolin, The Trout, Tenskwatawa, and Handsome Lake. In an ethical system of religious beliefs and practices, the rituals of reciprocal gift giving, when allied with a strong appeal to live according to a specific tradition (that is, in resistance to non-Natives), provides a context not only for resistance to what is alien and destructive, but also for the affirmation of communal identity and a sense of place in that community.

The prophetic call for the maintenance of communal identity is further strengthened by the collective nature of mythic narratives and by their enactment in ritual events that also foster an empowered sense of ethnicity, well-being, and health. Such linkage provides, it seems to me, a very cohesive framework for understanding the relation of myth and ritual to dynamic, often life-threatening, social transformations. The traditional Odawa emphasis on *pimadaziwin* (that is, good health and a moral life mediated by communal values) has its roots in sacred stories and the ways in which those stories lend themselves to expression in ritualized behaviors. These behaviors and the revered narratives, enacted in the meaningful context of ritual, constitute a bulwark against cultural erosion and loss of identity. Pflüg's careful delineation of such relationships is highly admirable and shows real mastery of the complex of historical transformations that the Odawa have resisted through the reinterpretation of such narratives and application of them to current events. She dives deep, like an Odawa earth diver, into the vital spiritual heart of cultural preservation and shows clearly how myth and ritual are crucial to the process of cultural survival and affirmation.

The overall process view of this work also touches on another significant point. As Melissa Pflüg demonstrates, Odawa affirmation of tradition follows a general pattern: first, as social liminalization or marginality increases, myth and ritual are gradually reinterpreted and reapplied to present circumstances; then that process leads to social changes, renewed status, and the affirmation of group solidarity and cultural autonomy. The process is modulated not only by large-scale historical events involving cultural contact and oppression, but also by general turbulences of American society at large, as well as infractions and tensions of adaptation within Odawa society. Clearly, at significant intersections, historical circumstances are mediated by mythic narratives, spiritual values, and religious actions that are fully in the world and yet clearly demonstrate how engaged and observant Odawa persons are in relation to existential needs. The Odawa exist not in a "timeless" world of myth, but in an engaged praxis where real-life concerns are paramount in determining how traditional values are understood.

Ritual and Myth in Odawa Revitalization is also remarkable because its contents are highly interdisciplinary: although Melissa Pflüg's primary orientation is strongly toward social anthropology, she makes very substantive use of theoretical perspectives from history, comparative religion, literature, and law. The interdisciplinary range of her work shows clearly what is expected in doing ethnography in a contemporary setting; studies in Native American religion, myth, and ritual can no longer be held within a single disciplinary frame without severely constricting the richness and complexity of any specific community. In a diverse and transformative world, this book stands out as an excellent contribution demonstrating how necessary it is to draw on a plurality of disciplinary perspectives to approximate the complexity in the real lives of human beings, many of whom are creatively engaged in understanding the present through reinterpretations of the past. Pflüg's critique of revitalization theories is particularly salient and shows clearly the weaknesses of those theories insofar as they often miss the core values, beliefs, and behaviors that have reaffirmed communal identity.

The traditional seven ways of being Odawa are to seek purity of body, heart, and mind while practicing humility, honesty, love, and respect. At the center of this set of revered values is the importance of showing compassion through acts of giving to others. The return of those gifts ensures a harmonious ongoing exchange that seeks to maintain itself in the face of threat and denial by a largely indifferent and often self-absorbed non-Native majority. Melissa Pflüg shows clearly the complexity of Odawa interactions based on the seven primary values and how the values are contextualized by inherited stories and significant ritual events. In a pluralistic world of multiple cultural orientations, confusion, and alienation, these values stand out as worthy of our deepest respect and appreciation. And this book, written with genuine devotion to exploring those values within an Odawa context, contributes significantly to a developing literature in which the narrative and ritual worlds of indigenous peoples are increasingly portrayed with a sensitivity for the preservation and importance of those values as they contribute to broader, more culturally interactive dialogues.

Acknowledgments

I will not try to list all the people who contributed to this work and my understanding of contemporary Odawa revitalization, both out of respect for people's privacy and fear of committing an oversight. Because of sensitivity associated with current political and religious activism, I have not used the names of the Odawa people with whom I work even when quoting directly. This is meant in no way to mask findings, but simply to respect their wishes and support their present efforts. Therefore, to the Odawa people, generally, I sincerely say *ki-megwetch* and limit formal acknowledgment to those who have made material contributions.

I thank the following people for generously taking their time to read parts or all of the manuscript: Åke Hultkrantz, Professor Emeritus, University of Stockholm; Dr. Lee Irwin of the Department of Religion and Philosophy, College of Charleston; Dr. Richard Hecht of the Department of Religious Studies, University of California at Santa Barbara; John D. Loftin, Esq.; and Dr. Elliott Wolfson of the History of Religions Department, New York University. The students in my American Indian Worldviews courses, especially J. P. Leary, Jon Weber, Rochelle Frounfelker, and Heidie Magritz deserve special acknowledgment. Thanks also to Dr. James Williams for his demographic data; Dr. David Brown, Dr. Jeremy Hein, and Dr. Robert McKeich of the Department of Sociology and Anthropology; Dean Ronald Satz; and Professors James Oberly and Richard St. Germaine of the History Department—all of the University of Wisconsin at Eau Claire. Special thanks to the late Dr. Arnold Pilling, formerly of the Department of Anthropology, Wayne State University, and to the other members of my graduate committee at WSU: Professors Bernice Kaplan, Bernard Ortiz de Montellano, Gordon Groscup, and Philip Mason. I am very grateful to John Drayton, Colleen Waggoner, Sarah Iselin, and other staff members at the University of Oklahoma Press for their interest and support, and especially to Larry Hamberlin for his excellent—and patient—copyediting. Most of all, my gratitude goes out to Professors Kenneth M. Morrison of the Department of Religious Studies at the Arizona State University and Fritz Detwiler of the Department of Philosophy and Religion at Adrian College, who listened to many ideas and forced their rethinking. Without their continual inspiration and guidance, this work never would have been finished.

...

Three chapters herein have previously appeared in somewhat different versions: chapter 7 is based on *"Pimadaziwin*: Contemporary Rituals of Odawa Community," *American Indian Quarterly* 20 (1996), no. 4; chapter 8 is based on "'Breaking Bread': Metaphor and Ritual in Odawa Religious Practice," *Religion* 22 (1992): 247–58; and chapter 9 draws on the same sources as "American Indian Justice Systems and Tribal Courts in Rural 'Indian Country,'" in *Rural Criminal Justice: Conditions, Constraints, and Challenges*, edited by Thomas D. McDonald, Robert A. Wood, and Melissa A. Pflüg (Salem, Wisc.: Sheffield Press, 1996), 191–215.

Ritual and Myth
in Odawa Revitalization

Introduction

This work explores ways in which people engage religious actions and ethics to support cultural cohesion, traditional identity, and sociopolitical purpose. For many contemporary American Indian peoples, whose struggle is to overcome a long-term process of marginalization, these functions of religious expression are primarily rooted in a practice of ethical gift exchange between sensitive and caring people.[1]

My aim is to address a broad audience: both academic specialists and general readers interested in American Indian issues and their religious implications. Because that audience constitutes a very diverse group, it would be impossible to "speak everyone's language" and to satisfy every reader's specific concerns. I simply intend to examine some basic aspects of religious behavior rooted in the indigenous system of ethics and actions among the Algonkian-speaking Odawa (Ottawa) Indians of the Great Lakes region.

I do not strive for a complete, comprehensive, and global treatment either of Odawa "religion" and its historical transformation or of all its meanings and significance for the Odawa themselves. Nor is my primary focus on epistemology and phenomenology (however that may disappoint some of my colleagues in religious studies). Instead, my emphasis draws on social-anthropological theory to present the dynamic role of religious actions and ethics in the Odawa's revitalization, which can be understood as a reclamation of *place*. I emphasize "place," which the Odawa comprehend to include relational, geographical, and ideological aspects; these definitional components are bound to issues of land, language, and a sovereign social identity that they once possessed, although some no longer do particularly because of Euro-American intrusion. The Odawa's efforts to reclaim a sovereign place, therefore, becomes an expression of social praxis—practicing the ethical religious actions that were once vital but are seriously in jeopardy.

During my ongoing relationship with the Odawa, I have come to know well many "traditionalists"—elders, medicine people, and community leaders who are the keepers of traditional Odawa cultural ways—especially in Michigan and Manitoulin Island, Ontario. We have spent much time discussing their strategies for maintaining traditional ways while facing the pressures of culture change.

I follow the preference of most communities in using the name *Odawa* instead of the French transliteration *Ottawa*. The one community I know of that has retained *Ottawa* is a group geographically and politically combined with members who call themselves by the French *Chippewa* instead of the Algonkian *Ojibwe*. One elder told me that the pronunciation *Odawa* belongs to the upper Michigan dialect of the Algonkian language family. The Great Lakes Indian historian Christian Feest notes that the appellation *Odawa* is Canadian and that its preference in Michigan is a recent manifestation of efforts to promote a unique sociocultural identity that is determined by an Odawa collective, instead of a social status and identity that has been imposed on them by outsiders (personal communication). Whatever the case, those who insist on *Odawa* reflect and reinforce current efforts to empower traditions and communities, and they voice sentiments about sociocultural unity and identity.

I also use the term *Indian* instead of the appellation *Native American* (which some of my academic colleagues prefer), as this is the term used most often by the people with whom I have interacted when not referring specifically to their clan, band, and tribal affiliations. The proper terminology remains a controversial issue, however. For example, as one elder expressed, "I don't want anybody to call me 'Native American.' I'm not an American and I've never been treated like I was" while another quipped, "Well, 'Indian' is OK, but it's a darn lucky thing Columbus wasn't looking for Turkey, or we'd all be called 'Turkeys.'" I also use the term *collective determination* instead of *self-determination*

because the Odawa do not restrict the process of identity formation to the individual but expand its purpose to an ethnically
related social network.

Additionally, the names of counties and all names of Odawa
people are pseudonyms. This choice, which I have made to protect
people's identities and to avoid any impediment of their activities,
is necessary because of the current political activism and reaction-
ism within the broad Odawa community based on sentiments
about Bureau of Indian Affairs (BIA) recognition, and because of
racial conflict between some Odawa and non-Indian residents.
The names I have used are traditional Odawan, often indicating
one's *dodem* (or power being), who defines clan affiliation. These
names I have translated into English, and although they typically
are accompanied by a Euro-American surname, I have deleted
surnames.

Because written sources devoted to the Odawa are limited, my
approach blends my own anthropologically based fieldwork with
a critical examination of both broad theories of religion and
existing ethnographic material from neighboring Algonkian
groups with whom some Odawa have had long-standing sociocultural contact and kinship relations, especially the Great Lakes
Ojibwe. We can draw this ethnographic parallel for two reasons.
First, the numerous studies of the Ojibwe that exist suggest a
worldview very close to the Odawa's. Second, such an approach
invites future studies of the overlaps, similarities, and any diver-
gences between the two. Information on the Odawa primarily
derives from many conversations, both formal and informal, with
elders, medicine people, and key community leaders who are
members of various bands throughout Michigan and Ontario, as
well as with tribal court officials and members of the Michigan
Commission on Indian Affairs (MCIA).

My interpretive method strives to explicate what is implicit in
these Odawa's religious expression and purpose—to achieve an
"ethnohermeneutics," as Armin Geertz (1994b:10–13) puts it. Although a difficult undertaking, I try to straddle two cultures to
peer into one, the better to appreciate its own terms. The integrity
of the traditionalists' purpose, I suggest, can be "translated" for a
non-Odawa audience by examining how these Odawa look to

religious actions and ethics as resources that inform and adjust their existence. Any attempt of one people to better its understanding of another seems crucial in this time of cultural plurality and coexistence. We will see that these traditionalists—those who mold a unique identity by asserting Odawa religious actions and ethics—are major agents for directing their own culture change.

Today, some Odawa elders, medicine people, and community leaders constructively promote their unique band and tribal identity. They hear the call to adjust to shifts in social circumstances and answer by affirming their claim of traditional cultural ways. This answer depends on a continual return to the ethics enacted through rituals and articulated in myths, thereby confirming their identity and sociocultural integrity, an identity that they equate with sovereignty in the fullest connotative sense of that word. These people's activities provide an opportunity to understand ethnicity and its importance, a history of change and continuity, and the creativity of "religiousness," which includes both ethics and actions as they dictate properly constructive behavior. These Odawa suggest new ways to conceptualize rituals and myths, especially those religious behaviors that non-Indians would associate with anthropological theories related to rites of passage and revitalization movements.

I must acknowledge the controversy that exists about the theoretical conceptualizations of ritual and myth; but I also must stress that the Odawa case illustrates the need to appreciate ritual and myth in indigenous terms. In this work, the term *myth* refers to narratives that traditionalists view as authoritative communications of reality assumptions; these narratives contain powerful messages that outline proper behavior for strengthening interpersonal relations. Myths "map" the traditionalists' ethos; that is, they outline the central ethics that inform behavior. Traditionalists contend that ethical persons give compassionately to others, and that gratitude expressed as gift giving is empowering. These ethical actions can be framed as three categories, which are intersecting in their purpose: "personing," "gifting," and "empowering." The purpose of such ethical action is to create, maintain, and extend proper relationships, which generate what the Odawa call *pimadaziwin*—the good, healthy, and moral collective life.

For Odawa traditionalists, mythic narratives provide maps that illustrate how the actions of ethical Great Persons powerfully direct events through these Great Persons' knowledge of place, way, and sociocosmic detail. As a map of purposeful behavior, myth can be "read" in a certain way to get at ritual action; therefore, myth is an interpretive device.

The term *ritual* refers to what these Odawa regard as their own purposeful behaviors and actions that articulate the time-honored cultural ethics mapped in myths. Rituals express the worldview that the sociocosmos is in constant motion; they are an expressive exercise in the strategy of choice outside the confines of the every-day social structure of secular American society, which allows the importance and immediacy of the issues at hand to be perceived. Thus, in the expression of their "religiousness," for these Odawa, rituals and myths go hand in hand (Kluckhohn 1962; Torrance 1994). Together, they fuse ethos and worldview (C. Geertz 1973).

We will see that myths among the traditionalist Odawa, unlike their role in many Western religious traditions, are not interior to rituals; that is, a given myth does not necessarily map one ritual exclusively, as may be the case, for example, with the Christian narrative of the Last Supper and the ritual of communion. The issue thus is not one of privileging the explanatory power of myth. Among the Odawa, rituals and myths make it possible to examine how they construe things and frame ethical responses at any given moment; they constitute a way of understanding the tradition-alists' approach to the world. Additionally, rituals and myths provide hints about how the Odawa examine and construe other people's behavior, as well as their own, in order to perpetually and constructively generate socioreligious reality. One can "read" mythic accounts for the existential postulates—personing, gifting, and empowering—that provide a "catalogue," to use Jonathan Z. Smith's concept(1982), for actual responses; rituals provide choices about reality assumptions while providing access to mythic Great Persons for empowering people through what these Odawa call "gifting." Ritual performances, together with myths, are articula-tions of these existential postulates for proper behavior and cata-logues for empowering responses that counter improper actions. Mutually reinforcing, they both serve to reaffirm basic Odawa ethics of caring, especially through humans' responsibility for their own actions and gifting.

The ways in which Odawa traditionalists apply rituals and myths to new social situations raises an important theoretical question: How do rituals and myths function in their everyday lives? Before we can examine this theoretical issue, however, I must note that Odawa traditionalists view cultural continuity and integrity as a collective experience based on "seeing," "knowing," and constructively acting with powerfully benevolent purposes. For them, cultural history is concrete and immediate, not abstract, and to them the term *religious tradition* equates with an active and vital cultural heritage. Cultural continuity and integrity are intertwined: on a continuum, they derive from the ethical Great Persons of mythology, from their ancestors, and from their own contemporary actions. Because each individual can speak ritually with the Great Persons of mythology, a bond is created among all sociocosmic powers. Equally important to these Odawa is the ritual recounting of accumulated experience, which contributes to mediating disagreements about status that threaten cultural integrity. Odawa traditionalists continually interact with Great Persons of mythology and with their dead, and these interactions perpetuate a cumulative experience that is immediately personal and collective. To elders, medicine people, and community leaders, the constructive interpersonal relationships mapped by the actions of the mythological Great Persons are made concrete and receive immediacy through ritual. For these traditionalists, to be Odawa is to structure proper relationships, and because myths portray these relationships, the ethics that they contain map social unity and are intertwined within ritual activity.

Prominent themes in myths emphasize the empowerment contained in ritual acts of sharing, gift giving, and various forms of reciprocity. The ritual recounting and enactment of these formative behaviors produce a significant result: social organization and personal behavior are structured, and in a sense, each person is "judged" by the degree to which he or she reproduces and applies themes of ethical duty to changing sociocultural circumstances. Therefore, we must consider the status of both myths and rituals in the contemporary lives of Odawa traditionalists.

Elders have told me repeatedly that rituals and myths are their tools to discuss and respond to new social situations. For them, both rituals and myths are discursive actions that express an ideal model of identity and collective determination. As undeniably authoritative communications, myths powerfully inform behavior; they reaffirm constructive ritual action. Rituals are practical methods of changing identity. Mastering ways to interpret myths and apply rituals forges a collectively defined identity. Engaging rituals and myths thus leads to social activism directed to collective determination. Traditionalists retain and recount the ethics that structure Odawa life through purposeful ritual actions, which are portrayed in mythic messages. The models for ethically living that are articulated in myths have a behavioral effect on daily life: their ritual enactment becomes as much ethical as economic, as much religious as political, and effectively manages interpersonal problems, disagreements, adversity, and hostility—sources of social disruption. Therefore, although their religious "theory" has not changed, they adjust their religious *practice*—the performed and verbal expressions of time-honored ethics—to changing interpersonal relationships, especially those caused by encounters with the U.S. government (which are discussed in depth as the story unfolds).

For Odawa traditionalists, religious actions and ethics promote proper relations because they demonstrate how one should approach the world morally and how one can overcome adversity. As part of everyday life, these religious actions and ethics are one significant avenue to the restoration of right relationships by lessening the tension caused by interpersonal distance and disagreements. Linking the time-honored ethics that rituals demonstrate with myths, especially the ethic of interpersonal caring, traditionalists mediate differences in social relations and maintain harmonious relationships.

Odawa traditionalists are committed to a prime religious ethic: the ethical person engages in powerful acts of benevolence to enhance the community, and the ethical community conducts itself benevolently to sanction its members. Empowerment between the community and the individual is thus reciprocal. These Odawa also contend that a person can change his or her state of being; powerful demonstrations of benevolence cause a transformation in nature, form, or status. That powerful acts of benevolence contribute to transmutation underlies these Odawa's revitalization efforts and is the hallmark of community strength: if a person can change his or her state of being, then a group can as well. Such transformation underlies their rituals while supplying a means of generating a powerful collective image that has been threatened but is now central to their revitalized identity. The Odawa's religious expressions voice the real lessons of a past punctuated by social threats caused by the disruptive actions of others. Some contemporary Odawa aim to purge their past of the misinterpretations and labels of non-Indians and other Indians who oppose them, a purgation they consider essential to an empowered future.

Many Odawa people have discussed with me one contemporary narrative as mapping a "new world," a transformed status, and the ways things should be (i.e., a "revitalization" in the Western scholarly sense). This is the narrative of the Seventh Fire, which blends leitmotifs from the corpus of Odawa mythology and oral tradition with real experiences of disagreeable encounters with Euro-Americans and other Indians. The Seventh Fire narrative, which traditionalists understand as articulating historical and contemporary social needs, is a critical and fundamentally creative enterprise. The Seventh Fire, because it expresses a nationalistic impulse, outlines the ways persons have and can rally an empowered Odawa identity. Today elders, medicine people, and community leaders call for cultural patriotism: they explicitly link nationalism to indigenous cultural traditions that others have tried to take from them. Myths such as the Seventh Fire and rituals together help these Odawa act out, concretize, and maintain their Odawa unity. In this way, the action of language produces powerful results.

Language—whether enacted orally, in writing, or in performance—ultimately results from the imaginative structuring and orienting of the world.[2] Through powerful religious discourse, Odawa traditionalists closely connect the so-called real world with the world of the Great Persons of mythology and with their ancestors. They make this connection because their religious discourse shifts images of a conventional past to a positive future through constructive actions in the present. For these Odawa, religiousness focuses on the power of the dreamed—the imagined, the envisioned—to triumph over immediate threats to identity and cultural existence. They use religious expressions, in which the real past and the imagined future inform the present, to change perceptions of reality. In this way, traditionalists shift their world and their imagined becomes real. "Act wisely, for imagine the consequences," counseled an Odawa medicine person. To equate wise acts with ethical acts means that we must understand the religious aspects, both ritual and mythical, of the Odawa traditionalists' current activism and revitalization.

Part 1 of this book examines the factors involved in desired social transformation. Chapter 1 defines the "traditionalists" and identifies different Odawa strategies for responding constructively to contemporary threats of social disruption. Chapter 2 discusses the legacy of previous social actors and their socioreligious movements as they inform contemporary Odawa revitalization efforts. Chapter 3 outlines the central ethics that the ancestral leaders called for people to uphold and that continue to orient and guide the lives of Odawa traditionalists.

Part 2 explores some reasons why people want the social transformation that they do and traces the ways in which mythic models map this change. In chapter 4, a review of predominant themes in myths, I suggest that because the cooperative actions of the Great Persons of mythology present the ethical model for creating proper relations, Odawa traditionalists have applied these lessons to recent experiences. Chapter 5 examines in detail the Odawa's culture hero and culture bringer Nanabozho as a role model for transformation. Chapter 6 describes how powerful messages contained in the myth of the Seventh Fire map both social and world transformation and articulate historical and social events.

Part 3 examines religious action as a source of collective determination. Chapter 7 highlights contemporary personal and collective rituals, emphasizing how both forms move from religious theory to practice. Chapter 8 focuses on how Odawa traditionalists have reinterpreted and reapplied one ritual, the *gi-be wiikonge*, as a fundamental example of the transformative nature of ritual. Chapter 9 examines the means by which Odawa traditionalists can retain, apply, and expand central religious ethics, especially as they are articulated as a concept of justice, to counter U.S. law and to maintain a unique and discrete cultural identity. Lastly, based on the Odawa's story, chapter 10 identifies two issues: the need to distinguish between "religiousness" and "religion," and the need to examine critically current anthropological theories of revitalization and ritual theory. I propose that the Odawa traditionalists' revitalization efforts are fundamentally a rite of passage rooted in past socioreligious movements that have manifested themselves in the Great Lakes region during periods of perceived social crisis. And finally, derived from these reevaluations, I show how a model of revitalization movements as rites of passage can serve as a heuristic device for understanding both the Odawa's activities and those of others.

The actions of Odawa traditionalists not only attest to their constructive response to new sociocultural situations but also invite cross-cultural comparisons and interpretations of socialization, ethos expression, and worldview. My many conversations with Odawa people suggest profound processes of collectively determined transformations. They also point to ways by which people periodically use aspects of their religiousness as integral means of retaining and modifying their tradition and identity. I have found that identity and tradition are simultaneously transformed and maintained by a select group that uncovers a concealed message and then reinterprets and reapplies this message to new social situations. I argue that contemporary Odawa traditionalists engage in a process of reinterpreting and reapplying the allegorical and metaphorical content of myths and rituals to current circumstances as a powerful means of revitalizing their unique and autonomous cultural identity. This process provides a vital collective rite of passage. The Odawa and their activities present one example of a select group of people who see assimilation as destructive, and who reaffirm and reassert cultural traditions as a constructive way to reclaim their sovereign place.

Part One

Seeking Social Transformation

What People Want

Charles Meyers

Chapter 1

Maintaining an Odawa Identity

On the one hand we are forgotten, abandoned; on the other hand
we are solicited and at times threatened . . . in such a situation
what can we do, what ought we do?

Leader of Great Lakes Indians to emissary Godfrey de Linctot (1780)

I want to tell about a story, a story told to me, a story of community and place. As with many people's stories, the Odawa
traditionalists' has no definite beginning and it anticipates a
conclusion instead of offering a succinct ending: we enter their
story in the middle. Like all stories retold, the challenge becomes
translation, being faithful to the integrity of the story while
making it significant to others. This is true especially when the
translator and audience really are not those the story is about or
those who crafted—or helped craft—the original. One of my
American Indian students in a seminar on American Indian
worldviews offered the following understanding: "We found a way
to handle this. We realize and acknowledge that in translating
from [our] oral [language] to oral English something is held back,
and then from oral English to written English still more is held
back. So at that point, you are not *telling* the story but simply
telling *about* it"—a subtle but important difference.[1]

In telling stories one has learned from others but of which one
inadvertently becomes something of a part, it is always a challenge
to avoid interjecting oneself and one's own perspective. To tell the
story on its own terms and from the perspective of those who
crafted the original is a goal we should strive for but may not be
able to achieve fully. Thus this story has two levels; it is about both
an Indian people's experience and my understanding of it.

The Power of Place

The place is important to the Odawa's story, important to its geographical, ecological, sociological, and demographic character and to the relational character of the indigenous population. The northern tip of the Lower Peninsula of Michigan typically is a patchwork of deciduous trees, the secondary growth that has followed the massive lumbering efforts of the nineteenth century, interspersed with vast fields cleared for agriculture. The growing season is short, with cool, wet summers. Winters are long and cold, the Great Lakes usually freezing over by February. Geographically, the area is narrow east to west, with many streams and rivers—formerly great trout, salmon, and grayling habitats, which were essential to the Odawa's precontact subsistence strategy—and one is never far from Lakes Huron and Michigan. Whereas Lake Huron offers a coastline inhospitable for fishing and boating, Lake Michigan has two large bays that offer sanctuary from storms, which arise quickly. The Lake Michigan shoreline has proved so desirable—especially to real estate developers—that it is now called "the Gold Coast," attracting many summer tourists and winter ski enthusiasts. Land not privately owned is controlled by the state.

Several distinct communities live on this land, especially around the large bays of Lake Michigan. One county, "Sturgeon," comprises 295,040 acres subdivided into eighteen townships. According to census data, the total population of Sturgeon County in 1990 was 25,040. The cultural composition of this county is similar to contiguous counties, and the general area can be understood with a brief outline.

The concentrations of people in tourist towns and those living in outlying areas include subgroups of non-Indians. One subgroup is composed of extremely wealthy "summer people," many from Detroit, Chicago, and Saint Louis suburbs who have established enclaves of Victorian residences often marked by private signs and association memberships. Most of these people have large homes with spectacular views of the lake. Cocktail parties abound and revolve from one veranda to another; equally popular are afternoons on the links of local private golf courses. Between their annual Labor Day exodus and Memorial Day return, populations of the towns drop about half. This group makes claims of "our place" based on the power of material wealth and ownership.

Another subgroup consists of year-round residents who identify themselves as the descendants of the first pioneer families. Some live in old farmhouses outside the towns and raise cattle and corn; others reside in the more modest houses in the towns, usually located away from the lake. Their claims of "our place" are made by the power of genealogy.

A third subgroup consists of merchants, many of whom, disgusted with big-city life downstate, have moved north to ply the tourist trade. Increasingly, these "downstaters" are buying the little remaining property and building neo-Victorian houses with attached garages to store their boats and four-wheel-drive vehicles. They make claims to "our place" based on a conviction that power derives from investments made and services rendered.

The sociocultural context of this place also includes a fourth subgroup: distinct communities of Odawa, who by far compose the minority of the overall population. For example, according to 1990 census data, the Odawa numbered 683 of the total population of 25,040 in Sturgeon County (2.7 percent of the total). This proportion also applies to the contiguous counties. Most but not all Odawa speak English as their first language and Odawa as their second. Many of these people live scattered throughout rural areas on their ancestral lands (generally gained during the federal government's nineteenth-century allotment policy) in the houses of their youth—often without running water, telephones, or electricity. Some engage in menial labor often associated with tourism (such as washing dishes at local restaurants or country clubs), which requires that they have a vehicle to drive to town and the money to operate it. Other Odawa live in the "Indian Town" sections of these communities, which generally are adjacent to Catholic mission churches established in the seventeenth and eighteenth centuries. Within this "Indian Town" subgroup of Odawa, a few work in stores, fewer are in local business, and many are either seasonally employed or altogether unemployed. Still other Odawa live in reservation communities and are therefore recognized and subsidized by the Bureau of Indian Affairs (BIA), the reservations having been established either by the federal government or by the people themselves (pooling allotment disbursements to buy land jointly, in the latter case). Other subgroups along politicoreligious lines also exist within this broad subgroup of Odawa. Some are devoted Catholics, mostly older people. Many claim to practice "native religion." Others simply "don't care." Whatever the specifics, these Odawa subgroups make claims of "our place" based on the power of cultural endurance and a claim of traditional "place."

What is my place in this story? I have spent almost every summer of my life in this area, mainly living in a log cabin built in 1906 by local Odawa for a physician from downstate who wanted a hunting lodge. It was built from virgin white pines cut across the road (then a dirt trial), and it sits on the bluff high above Lake Michigan in an area the Odawa traditionally occupied. The cabin passed from the physician to others, and through much of its existence it has been part of a summer resort. My mother has spent summers there, staying in this place, since she was a child. Her parents spent their honeymoon in the area (a trip taking two days to drive from Detroit in the 1920s). All in our family were thrilled when we discovered that the cabin was for sale. It became "our place," our claim simply being based on familial and sentimental attachment, a familial attachment that goes back to Oliver Williams (the nephew of Roger Williams, the founder of Rhode Island colony), who ran supplies from Detroit to Mackinac for the Americans in the War of 1812.

Although there is a community some two miles south of "our place" with a post office and general store, the nearest town of any size is about fifteen miles away. Most of the residents of this small community are retirees from downstate who leave in the winter for warmer climes. There are a few pioneer families, several Odawa families (one of which does not speak English), and for a long time one Ojibwe family. The summer population may reach two hundred, the winter about fifty. Another village about five miles north, which was founded by Père Jacques Marquette, consists primarily of Polish descendants and others who have mixed Polish and Odawa ancestry. Everyone knows each other well (and as is often the case with small towns, sometimes too well). It was to this place that I moved for three years, full-time, while doing fieldwork for my Ph.D. dissertation.

Originally I wanted to understand the sociocultural and particularly the political dynamics between the Odawa and non-Odawa. Largely because of the tutelage of an Odawa person, then a member of the Michigan Commission on Indian Affairs (MCIA), my interest quickly shifted to the relationship between politics and religion. I was invited to many MCIA meetings, which supplied a network to the wider community of Indian peoples in the state. Making contacts and establishing trust among the Odawa people "at home" was more difficult, however.

Initially I made these connections in three ways. First, through my associations with MCIA members, I enrolled in courses taught by Odawa people on Michigan Indian cultural history and contemporary social problems. Second, I made a point of making myself known in local stores that specialize in Odawa artworks. Third, I spent countless hours at the nearby general store, chewing the fat with the local non-Indians. This third set of conversations highlighted other non-Indian people's stories about Odawa encounters. One discussion led to lunch with the oldest Odawa person living in the area at the time, another led to a Kiwanis luncheon where I met an Odawa community leader prominent in non-Indian eyes. By the middle of my first winter I had compiled a lengthy list of Odawa names and issues.

One day I received a telephone call from a man who introduced himself by saying: "This is Lone Wolf. I heard from [a mutual acquaintance] that you're interested in Odawa history." We talked for over an hour. During this conversation Lone Wolf (Nazhikewizi Ma'iingan) revealed that he is a recovering alcoholic, a former substance abuse counselor for Odawa youths, a former council member of an Odawa band not federally recognized at the time, and currently a teacher of "traditional spiritual ways" especially for young men in trouble with the law. We talked about elders' councils and spiritual gatherings. Lone Wolf wanted to know my intentions in studying his people, as he put it. He invited me to talk some more after that, and I saw Lone Wolf almost every week at either his family's trailer home or the place where he works. During these many conversations, as his trust in me began to build, it became clear that Lone Wolf, a middle-aged pipe carrier (a specialist in healing, part of the category of "medicine people") who looks much older, was purposely telling his story—and his version of the Odawa's story—instead of merely answering questions. He sees himself as an educator. "I guess I'm something of a guide," as he put it. His explanation of what he sees his gift to his community to be and why he does what he does speaks for itself.

> I want to open the door to people who are sympathetic but perhaps unknowing and even misguided to begin to understand us and our traditions and history. This keeps our traditions alive and maybe will help a little to get things back in balance. They're sure out of whack now. It's a gamble, though, because too many people are too separated from others and too wrapped up in themselves. A lot of my people don't think that I should be so open in talking, especially to non-Indians. But I figure that if people are sincerely interested, why be secret? Trying to be invisible from the rest of the world doesn't work anymore—if it ever really did.

The summer following my introduction to Lone Wolf, another Odawa introduced himself to me as Soaring Eagle (Bimise Migizi) and said that he also was a pipe carrier and on the council of a non-federally recognized Odawa band. Soaring Eagle said that he supports his two children in the rural farmhouse that originally was his grandparents by washing dishes at local restaurants, by mowing lawns and doing other odd jobs, and by maple sugaring, hunting deer, and fishing on state land and waters—activities for which he has been issued many legal citations because of his non-federally recognized status.

Word of my presence and interests began to spread rapidly, and my relationships with the Odawa evolved and continued to expand. Since those early meetings I have come to know well many Odawa people. First meetings often have been cautious and sometimes seemingly superficial, and always participants have tested me. An example of the initial caution toward me is illustrated in the following exchange that I had with Lone Wolf.

> *Lone Wolf:* Tell me again what it is that you do.
> *Me: (wondering how to respond without alienating him by reiterating "anthropologist")* I'm a student.

Lone Wolf: Oh, I thought you were a teacher.

Me: I was teaching while going to school, but now I'm doing some writing and studying things that I want to know about that one can't necessarily learn in a classroom.

Lone Wolf: I thought you were an anthropologist.

Me: I'm working to be one.

Lone Wolf: I remember Brown Otter [a fellow elder] saying you were one of those 'ologists. You know, I was really uneasy about talking to you. You know what Russell Means says about 'ologists. And a lot of people around here warned me about talking to any more 'ologists. But I'm really glad to have met you and talk with you. I'm happy I didn't listen to them.

Soon I was asked to attend various band and tribal council meetings and such activities as feasts, powwows, elders' councils, and spiritual gatherings, and to help with proposal writing and issues related to land/property claims.

What People Want

The focus of this work unfolded during an annual gathering of elders. (*Elder* is a title of honor and acknowledgment by the community for a person's special deeds, especially in teaching traditional ways; note that pipe carriers—a particular form of "medicine person"—are always elders, but not all elders are medicine people.) I spoke with Great Elk (Ki-je Omashkooz), another elder from a non-federally recognized group, about his band's sovereignty project: its goals, the resistance to it by others, the responsibility of the elders. Although Great Elk is also a council member, he lives a considerable distance from the rural area where most of the members of his band live. One of the few members who has a college degree, he is active throughout the state in reconstituting museum displays to have greater sensitivity to native concerns and viewpoints, in promoting his band's cultural history, and in gaining the acknowledgment of Congress.[2] Such acknowledgment would mean that the government concedes that it once recognized the band as a legitimate tribal organization but has "since overlooked our sovereign status for the advantage of others," as Great Elk put it. Being a prominent spokesman for his band's sovereignty project, he has testified before both the U.S.

Senate and House. Great Elk said: "It's our goal to be politically and culturally sovereign. The only way we can do this is for our elders to lead the revitalization of Odawa traditions."

The term *sovereignty*, as Great Elk and others use it, has several complex levels of meaning. For example, as developed in U.S. law, "the concept of sovereignty consists of two main components: the recognition of a government's proper zones of authority free from intrusion by other sovereigns within the society, and the understanding that within these zones the sovereign may enact substantive rules that are potentially divergent or 'different' from that of the other—even dominant—sovereigns within the system" (Pommersheim 1992:421). As we hear Great Elk and other traditionalists in the pages that follow, we might identify two broad levels of meaning to be "ideological sovereignty" and "political sovereignty," within which there are legal, bureaucratic, and emotional ramifications. For example, Great Elk stressed that because the United States does not consider sovereignty to apply to Indian nations, federal Indian policy never has been framed by the above legal concept.

Great Elk pointed out a real issue:

> Lots of people use the word "sovereignty," but neither they themselves nor the people listening to them really have a clear understanding of precisely what is meant. For example, to the BIA and the U.S. government, generally, there are certain legal parameters to what "sovereignty" means that conform to constitutional law. Many federally recognized groups, and especially their tribal attorneys, largely because they're under the supervision of the BIA, know this and operate within these confines. But parallel to this kind of federal-level meaning, there's a more local level of meaning. This local-level meaning is "solidarity." And "sovereignty" as "local solidarity" is something based on exercising our traditions, especially to gain our own collective determination, not the U.S. government's legalistic dictates.

Although he did not use the word, it became clear to me that Great Elk sees his band's goal of having the U.S. Congress acknowledge their collectively determined sovereign status as being religiously motivated. When I asked him if this interpretation was accurate, he replied:

Sure. That's exactly what I mean by "revitalization." Over time, our traditions have been jeopardized—both by other people and our own digressions—and we've lost sight of who we are as a community. It's our moral responsibility to correct this. We once were a very vital and cohesive community, but for a time we weren't. For many reasons, we didn't practice our traditional ways, either because the government denied us the right or simply because we ourselves either forgot them or didn't care. But we have a lot more confidence now and are basically much stronger. We've been part of this place for a long, long time and neither we nor others should forget or ignore that.

By living in this place daily and taking part in community activities, I saw how each of the social subgroups makes unique place claims. Non-Indian claims run the extreme from being highly visible and based on wealth, prestige, and landownership to being relatively invisible and based on assertion of historical precedent. Odawa claims also are based on either visibility or invisibility, but both expressions claim sanction by cultural tradition. With these conflicting claims to place, each group identifies its own characteristic label of the others.

Among the sentiments toward pioneer folk by summer people and vice versa—each speaking derogatorily against the other—are the following:

I'll hire him to do maintenance work, cut wood, roof the house, that sort of thing. Have him and his family for dinner? Why, that's out of the question. They're just not our kind. But they're good people, though.

...

Those summer people. Always meddling. Why don't they keep out of our business? They think they run the place because they've got money, doing what's right for us, creating fire departments and all sorts of highfalutin city stuff. Why, one of them asked me what I'd do if my barn caught on fire. What'd he think I'd do? Neighbors would help, and if we couldn't put it out, it'd burn down and we'd build another. We take care of ourselves.

The sentiments toward the Odawa by summer people and pioneer folks range from expressed ignorance of their presence to tolerance to blatant prejudice. "What? You mean there are Indians here?" "I know some Indians. I give them food and stuff when they need it." Some call young men and even children "long-haired gill-netters." Others say, "They're drunken and dirty and all cause trouble, and we'll have nothing to do with them. We'll keep them out. Well, maybe they can do our yards." This latter is an attitude to which Soaring Eagle said: "I've cut a lady's grass for years and she's never let me in her house, even to use the bathroom."

The Odawa hold their own sentiments toward the others. Some Odawa look to wealthy summer people and the tourist trade generally for their economic survival, and they strive to ally them-selves at all costs. Thus they are highly visible in the general area, making and trading black ash baskets and quill and beadwork. Black Porcupine (Makad Ga'ag), who lives in a reservation com-munity in a house built with federal subsidies, explained her position: "We have to keep our relationship going. If they want baskets, then I'll sell them baskets. I've got six kids that have to be fed." A few direct their attention to young non-Indians and assert "things Indian" by leading weekend retreats, personal seminars, and spiritual meetings. Daniel, whom others regard as something of a self-styled "neo-shaman," said of his non-Indian clients: "They're young and don't know anything about Indians, and they're searching for something. Besides, I charge a hundred and fifty dollars for a weekend." A few engage in social activities on a more personal level, belonging to Kiwanis Clubs and local historical societies and giving Thanksgiving invocations and the like at pioneer family homes. "We need to keep our presence known. Some people understand that we're part of the history here," said Old Man (Akiwenzii), who in fact had gained some notoriety in the general community for being the oldest Odawa person in the area at the time. Out of economic necessity, other Odawa may do menial jobs for wealthy summer folk, but there is little mutual respect. Red Cedar (Miskwaawaak), Soaring Eagle's wife, said of her experience: "I'll clean their houses for them because I need the money to fix my car. But they don't respect me for who I am. They just want the labor." Some Odawa may have friends who are members of pioneer families, but as Laughing Gull (Baapi Gayaashk)—who considers herself a traditionalist, a council member of a non-federally recognized band, and a

prominent organizer of local annual feasts and elders' councils—
explained, those friends "don't always understand and they really
don't want to. That's OK. We get along on the surface, but they
think that because my grandfather sold them some land and
helped them build their house that we should be friends."

Odawa people's sentiments toward each other is a different
matter. The Odawa see themselves as divided into two subgroups,
which echo distinct and factionalized strategies among Michigan
Indians generally for maintaining cultural identity and asserting
collective determination. The members of one subgroup call
themselves traditionalist; I call the other subgroup *accommodationist*.[3] The following analysis of these different philosophies
derives from my interaction with individuals who are either
accommodationists or traditionalists (members of groups who
regard themselves as upholding a traditional Odawa identity), and
from personally attending meetings of organizations that represent either traditionalist or accommodationist constituencies.

Odawa traditionalists refer to themselves as "traditionals,"
keepers of their cultural heritage. "Traditional" does not refer to
static, unchanged behaviors, although many non-Indians may
infer this from the term. Instead it connotes the contemporary,
often changing expression of time-honored ethics considered
Odawa. It will become clear throughout the rest of this story that
ethics are something very different from abstract beliefs in the
Odawa traditionalists' thinking. Their ethical system is fundamentally action oriented and generates constructive interpersonal
relations: ethical persons give compassionately to others, and
gratitude expressed as gift giving is empowering. Such interactions
contribute to what traditionalists refer to as *pimadaziwin*: the
good, healthy, and moral collective life. Although the relative
numbers of traditionalists among the Odawa in the northern
Great Lakes area are not easily retrievable, people who are called
or who call themselves traditionals are the elders, and pipe carriers
and other medicine people, who interpret and apply these time-
honored ethics to new social situations as a strategy to revitalize
and assert their unique culture and to reconstitute an empowered
identity. Traditionalists do not have a word of their own for
the alternative "accommodationist strategy." Nonetheless, they

recognize it as opposing their own and as representing the participation of people who far outnumber them.

Although our story focuses on the traditionalists, it is crucial—
although not always easy—to understand the differences between
the traditionalist and accommodationist strategies and to recognize who is involved in each. Often, one community will identify
itself with one strategy and label other groups as using the
opposite. One community, for example, which has not been
federally recognized for most of the time of my association, generally regards itself as being traditionalist when the members
compare themselves with other communities, especially groups
recognized and subsidized by the BIA, such as the reservation communities. Brown Otter (Ozaawizi Nigig), a merchant, expressed
this opposition clearly: "Those people [with an established land
base to the south] have completely ignored our heritage—even to
the point of now calling themselves the Bands of Chippewa and
Ottawa. They have had lots of BIA funding and now make money
hand over fist with their casino and fishing business." Brown
Otter, this statement suggests, views pan-Indianism as a threat to
the integrity of a localized Odawa identity.

Conversely, accommodationist members of the recognized
groups view the activities and goals of traditionalists in nonrecognized groups—especially their goal of sovereignty—as being
wholly unrealistic. Matthew, an accommodationist attorney and
tribal court member in a recognized group (and only federally
recognized groups can legally establish tribal courts), expressed
this sentiment clearly: "What are they thinking? This whole
sovereignty bit is naive. Listen, in the world today no one can
entertain the idea of being sovereign. Who's more sovereign, the
U.S. or Japan? No one's sovereign. How do they think they're going
to survive as an independent band, let alone a politically acknowledged nation?" Recalling Great Elk's discussion of the levels of
complexity regarding the meaning of "sovereignty," Matthew's
statement sounds naive: he, like many others, seems to confuse the
political meaning of sovereignty in the United States' constitutional sense and its ideological burden as local solidarity and
socioreligious revitalization.

The confusion in understanding and using the concept of sovereignty, and the opposing strategies for maintaining cultural identity, are not so clear-cut as simply to run between distinct communities. It also exists within communities themselves. Next-door neighbors may reflect these alternative views. For example, Black Porcupine, who considers herself a traditionalist and is a member of a federally recognized group, said about a tribal court attorney from her community: "Oh, him. He's not traditional. He's given up his heritage." John, who lives off the reservation, claims membership in the federally recognized community and proudly shows his card asserting such association. Black Bear (Makad Makwa), a pipe carrier in a recognized group who lives off the reservation in the rural outskirts of one of the towns, said of John: "He's sold himself down the river. I'll never do that. I'm Odawa—not just an Indian, which is what the feds want us to be." The differences between the strategies for promoting cultural identity are perhaps more easily discernible than the participants themselves. Although embattled, these strategies must be viewed, each in its own way, as action taken to counter a series of historical and social events that have produced pressure for culture change and have threatened a collectively determined identity.

Before extensive non-Indian settlement, the Odawa practiced seasonal rounds along the eastern shores of Lake Huron, where they hunted, gathered, and fished. They exchanged resources with their Algonkian-speaking Ojibwe neighbors to the north and Potawatomi neighbors to the west, and they traded fish, furs, and wild rice for corn and other agricultural products with their Iroquoian-speaking Huron/Wyandot neighbors to the south. During the summer, many Odawa lived on Manitoulin Island, Ontario, and at L'Arbre Croche and the Straits of Mackinac in Michigan. Here they maintained social and political autonomy and a distinct cultural identity (see Kinietz 1940; Quimby 1967; Dobson 1978; McClurken 1988).

Subsistence changed in the seventeenth century. The Odawa initially became involved in the developing fur trade market economy but ultimately succumbed to the territorial expansion of the Six Nations of Iroquois. Many Odawa voluntarily moved or were forcibly displaced to other areas around the northern Great Lakes that traditionally were occupied by Ojibwe and Potawatomi peoples. The shifts in location, associated disruptions of clan and band organization and intertribal relations, changes in economic pursuits, and disease (both physical and spiritual) threatened and continue to threaten the Odawa traditionalists' autonomy and their distinct identity.

These shifts in cultural context also contributed to their social liminality, by which I mean more than marginalization in the colonialist sense: "made to be insignificant; pushed from the center to the periphery by a dominant culture or group."[4] Traditionalists themselves have rejected such a Eurocentric definition of the cultural center. Although the Odawa in the eighteenth and nineteenth centuries joined other Indian peoples in rebelling against an imposed center, the political and moral claim of that external center has been a real and enduring fact. Hence Odawa traditionalists should be understood as a liminal people, caught between their own traditional modes of consensual authority and the mode of authority of the institutionalized American political order.

The Odawa traditionalists' experience of social liminality results partly from two treaties that continue to define Odawa relations with the state of Michigan and the federal government: the 1836 Treaty of Washington and the 1855 Treaty of Detroit. As we will see in detail, events leading to the 1836 treaty are especially telling about the establishment of and enduring relations between some Odawa and the state, and about factors leading to their current revitalization and sovereignty efforts. These events are important to consider, as many Odawa still speak of these treaties and related encounters in the present tense.

For example, traditionalists speak of how, to avoid forced removal west of the Mississippi River, their Odawa ancestors signed the 1836 Treaty of Washington. This treaty resulted in the transfer of half of the Michigan Territory from Indian custodianship to American ownership so the area could be established as a state in 1837. The terms *custodianship* and *ownership* have great technical significance in Indian-Indian and Indian-white relations, and each has important religious meanings as well, which will receive extended discussion throughout the remainder of this story. Once established as a state, the land was developed for non-Indian settlement and agricultural and lumbering pursuits. Throughout the nineteenth and early twentieth centuries, federal and state policies of rural reservationism and urban assimilation isolated clans, bands, and kin networks, disrupted hunting-and-gathering subsistence practices, and threatened traditional patterns generally. During this time many Odawa considered it necessary to conform or accommodate to governmental dictates, especially by adopting agricultural pursuits on individually owned land, thus appearing "civilized" to non-Indians. Traditional religious practices were conducted out of the sight of non-Indians. Invisibility, especially to non-Indians, became the Odawa's strategy to retain their cultural integrity. Today the social situation has changed again, requiring new adaptive approaches.

Typically, many members of tribal organizations that have federal recognition through the BIA, as well as those seeking that status, adopt a cultural survival strategy characterized by accommodating governmental dictates and expressing, through centralized political organizations, an identity that is far more interethnic and less band oriented than that of most traditionalists. The accommodationist strategy for identity aims to satisfy all the BIA's criteria for legal recognition, including the status of "domestic dependents" as defined by federal jurisprudence. This strategy promotes the Michigan Commission on Indian Affairs (MCIA) as the arbitrating agency between the recognized groups and the state government. The MCIA leaders stress BIA recognition as essential to group success. Accepting the BIA's stipulations for federal recognition and acknowledging the MCIA as arbitrating agency offer visibility to these Indian groups. Accommodationists regard this visibility as the primary means of receiving federal subsidies for social services and programs. They view access to subsidies as essential to the survival of an Indian culture.

Conversely, some rural bands that have received neither federal nor state recognition rely on a traditionalist strategy for survival. Their members refuse to submit to the BIA. They shun "domestic dependent" status and everything associated with it in favor of their own collectively determined sovereignty, in the fullest connotative sense. Traditionalists partly regard this cultural status as a matter of not only having collective custodianship of land and educational determination but also retaining collective governance by decentralized band councils and community consensus. Striving for both political and ideological sovereignty creates a uniformity of views within those bands, including their negative attitudes toward accommodationist Indian groups.

Traditionalist members of nonrecognized groups recoil from federal bureaucratic recognition because they suspect the BIA would impose political control. Regarding federal recognition, BIA control, and sovereignty, Lone Wolf said:

> I am and will always be just Odawa. I don't recognize territories. The government says that my band of Odawa aren't recognized because we're not reservationed. So there's no subsidy now, although there used to be. They've "politely" forgotten what they've said before. Once we had subsidies for health and education, but no more. We want our sovereignty, to be a nation within a nation. But it's kind of hard to be a nation that's not recognized on one's own land. All this controversy and haggling is a continued means of control. The root of discrimination by whites against Indians is their wish to control us. The reservationed Indians are kowtowing to the government to get money, and their decisions are affecting us without our representation. Yet I refuse to be accountable either to other Indian groups with that kind of motive or to the government with its own motives.

Great Elk added:

> My band doesn't seek BIA recognition. You can't really be an independent community under bureaucratic control. But we are seeking congressional acknowledgment. We're making a claim to Congress that the U.S. once identified us as a distinct band but no longer does. They've closed the door to communicating with us as equals. Only a few groups can make and have made such a claim. But those who have been successful in gaining the acknowledgment of Congress enjoy great local solidarity. To me, they are much more independent than groups under BIA supervision that have confused this sovereignty with "domestic dependent" status. We're not looking so much for money from the government as we are attaining a redefined, sovereign status.

For Odawa such as Lone Wolf and Great Elk, the goal of sovereignty—asserting cultural and political autonomy and maintaining local solidarity and identity—reaffirms what they claim as
traditional ethics. While accommodationists partly agree with the
traditionalists' motive to assert political integrity, accommodationists strive to enact their own versions of Odawa ethics as a
powerful means of satisfying the BIA's recognition criteria.

Part of the BIA's requirement for recognition is that an expert,
most often a non-Indian, prove in a court of law that an Indian
community's claim as a traditional political entity is legitimate.
The petitioning procedures implemented in 1976 as part 82 of the
Federal Code of Regulations stipulate that a group must have "an
anthropologist, historian or other qualified scholar" prove its
political and cultural continuity. Few Odawa have the formal
education called for by the government to qualify as expert
witnesses. Many traditionalist members of nonrecognized bands
resent being seen as unable to substantiate their own cultural,
traditional, and political heritage. Many traditionalists view the
cost of federally recognized tribal status as losing the right to
define themselves as Odawa: They want to establish their own
standards for who is Odawa and not merely for who is Indian.

Like the definition of *Indian*, the concept of *land base* is an
equal source of controversy for traditionalists. Although they
recognize a tradition of territoriality, these Odawa reject the BIA's
concept of land base, which they understand to reflect Euro-
American attitudes about land use and ownership. They interpret
"land base" as a euphemism for "reservation." Brown Otter said:

> Having a land base is part of the process of recognition, but they're
> really reservations—plots of land controlled by the government.
> And we all know that what the government controls it thinks it
> owns. The government thinks it owns not only the land but every-
> thing—and everyone—on it. We seek independence through a
> policy of communal custodianship of land, not land dispensation
> under the control of the BIA.

Lone Wolf said:

> You know, I've been up to Sault Sainte Marie a hundred times in my
> life, and every time I go there I stand on that bridge, looking and

looking. And you know, even after all that looking around I'll be darned if I've ever been able to see this line they keep talking about. The government says I can cross this line and go over to Canada to visit my family and friends but can't stay there. And it says that my family and friends can cross the line to come over here for visits but can't stay. Who's the government, with its lines and rules, to keep me and my relatives apart? It's the same with the reservations. These lines and these words that the *sogonosh* [non-Indians] use, saying that there have never been any prison camps in the U.S.! "Reservation," "wards of the state"—well, they're prisons.

Land boundaries, geographic distribution of tribes, land base, one's own land, property ownership, physical presence, and territories all are distinct yet interlinked categories. As traditionalists voice conflict over land boundaries, they reveal a conceptual tension between federally recognized territories and "one's own land." They also show resentment of the BIA criterion that for a group to be recognized it must establish a "physical presence" by owning property.

Reluctance by Odawa traditionalists to comply with stringent legal requirements for federal recognition exceeds the issues of BIA control and immediate claims to land and identity. Gray Squirrel (Misajidamoo) gave her impression: "Efforts by the MCIA to create a pantribal community of Woodland Indians and especially a pan-Indian community—because Detroit has a lot of Indians living there who belong to tribes that aren't from Michigan—are just going to water down everything. This kind of loss of band and tribal tradition is bad." Brown Otter said: "Those people [the MCIA], they talk big talk but never get anything done. They sit there in the state capital haggling about what's best for the reservationed groups and the big lobbying groups in Detroit and Saginaw, but they never think about the rest of us." The traditionalists' greatest concern, these statements suggest, is both ideological and political: band and tribal identity are neglected by Indian accommodationists and denied by non-Indians.

Traditionalists today are convinced that nontraditionalists (both non-Indians and Indian accommodationists) fear an uprising and so regard traditionalists as dangerous and threatening. For example, one Odawa woman said, "Hey, we've got to get along with the feds. They protect us. It's silly to try to maintain—how many? fifty? a hundred?—separate little bands. They're only causing disruption and problems for us all. We'll never be able to communicate with Washington if each little group continues to cause trouble and threaten our subsidies. The government will never go for it—and shouldn't." Traditionalists contend the opposite, however: it is not they, but the Euro-Americans and accommodationists who try to subjugate them, who are dangerous and threatening. Misunderstanding and mistrust are three-way, leading to an absolute breakdown in communication and with it a social and political power struggle.

The politicizing of tradition informs, in different ways, both accommodationist and traditionalist social purposes. For accommodationists, because they have governmental legitimacy, the federal government does not threaten their existence, but the traditionalists threaten their subsidies, which they fear are limited. Conversely, for traditionalists, the accommodationists and the federal government are dangerous because they want to subsume the traditionalists under reservationed groups.

Traditionalists no longer seek cultural survival through invisibility either from non-Indians, as they have formerly, or from accommodationists. Instead, they consciously call for visibility to assert what they regard as their cultural rights.[5] The invisibility factor is waning largely because traditionalists recognize that their cultural integrity depends on collective initiative and assertiveness. Traditionalists exhibit an element of nationalism as they enact the ethics that they regard as Odawa; they do not tolerate threats to and departures from this central identity. They try to change non-Indian values and governmental policies and to resist the influence of non-Indian values and practices that they see as corrupting. Traditionalists particularly regard the federal and state governments as threats to their cultural integrity and local autonomy. As Soaring Eagle put it: "The government thinks it controls everything, and we all know that what it controls, it thinks it owns—land, people, right down to the bones of our ancestors. They've taken our lands and they've even tried to take our culture. And what have we ever been given in return?" Traditionalists view the government as failing to uphold its obligations—as *withholding*—

which, as chapter 3 describes, they consider the most profound display of unethical behavior.

Conclusion

The Odawa traditionalists' distrust of non-Indians is not surprising, especially given their suspicion of governmental authorities and policies as withholding and exclusionary, acts that traditionalists regard as ethically opposed to their tradition. We will see throughout the rest of this story that their goal is to reclaim a unique identity, language, land, shared ethics, and socioreligious solidarity; in other words, they aim to reconstitute a sense of place.

Traditionalists charge themselves with responsibility for their own success, which they consider fundamentally grounded in revitalizing traditional religious ethics and encouraging fellow Odawa to follow their model of the right way of living. For traditionalists, one part of the right way to live is to approach time as a sociocosmic reality located in a cycle of expanding social relations. They view this cyclical interconnection as radically disrupted and themselves as destined to set it right. In other words, they once shared a vital social cohesion, which was and continues to be undermined. From their perspective, the right way of living cannot be based in non-Indian values, which they associate with such behavior as private and state ownership of land, disrespect for natural resources (both land and water), Euro-American possession of cultural artifacts and ancestral skeletal remains, Christianity, and use of alcohol and drugs. Lone Wolf said:

> The political and religious affiliation of [my] group does not go along with pan-Indianism but is directly tied to the Manitoulin [Ontario] group of our relatives, where the Midéwiwin [a secret healing organization: see chapter 3] is still alive and led by Pontiac. With them, we're upholding our traditional commitment to helping people live a good and healthy life—*pimadaziwin*. In doing so, a key difference between this group and the groups that aren't involved is alcohol. This community is adamantly anti-alcohol. It's one reason—but only one—that we've moved away from Catholicism, which OKs alcohol in its ritual. Because of the corrupting influence of alcohol we can't take communion.

Traditionalists such as this elder organize and engage in activities, such as political activism and alternatives to Catholicism, as exemplary models for others.

Three other factors precipitate the traditionalists' revitalization. First, they experience conflict with the motives of accommodationists. Second, they experience conflict resulting from shifting federal Indian policy. And third, they are concerned that they lack the political status that federal and state policy and recognized tribal groups regard as being legitimate. Laughing Gull voiced her frustration over this situation: "Nobody is affected more than nonrecognized Odawa peoples by changes in federal and state policy, and by the activities of recognized groups that kowtow to those policies. Therefore political involvement is crucial. But it's tough to be politically involved and effective as anything more than individuals if our band councils aren't acknowledged as being legitimate by the feds." Although the resurgence of Odawa religious traditionalism may seem highly political, it is not exclusively so, because traditionalists do not compartmentalize these two ideas and so do not see them separately.

The traditionalists' revitalization is a collective enterprise in which all activities directed at cultural retention, renewal, reaffirmation, and autonomy necessarily enter both the religious and political arenas. Just as individual pipe carriers and other types of medicine people (the Odawa do not use the term *shaman*) classically function as social critics, traditionalists collectively charge themselves with the same role. Through their behavior, they constructively critique the ways in which some Indians, particularly accommodationists, and most non-Indians treat them on all cultural fronts, including kinship, land, language, economic, political, legal, and religious fronts.

Because the social sphere ultimately is the field of religious action, the traditionalists' revitalization efforts proclaim their conviction that the state no longer can displace and ignore their cultural identity. As later chapters show, what informs the traditionalists' claim to place and empowers an Odawa future are Odawa religious ethics, especially the quest for *pimadaziwin*, as a powerful source of cultural continuity and cohesion.

A key to an understanding of these Odawa's story is the legacy left by earlier social actors, a legacy described in the next chapter. These leaders called for religiously motivated and informed action to cause profound personal and collective transformation, which promised to be wholly revitalizing. It is methodologically central to view their revitalization process relationally, that is, as being collective, interpersonal, and interactive in its purpose. Doing so challenges us to examine two components of the traditionalists' past and present religious theory, especially as it is grounded in oral tradition: the next chapter asks whether the relevance of a relational view can be documented in terms of the visions and programs of historically earlier social activists in the Great Lakes region; chapter 3 asks whether the literature of historical revitalization movements has or has not seen them relationally, that is, each, in his own way, being framed by collective, interpersonal, and interactive purposes.

Chapter 2

Making Meaning and Making Sense
The Legacy of Shifting Identity and Tradition

A nation scattered in the boundless regions of America resembles
rays diverging from a focus. All the rays remain, but the heat is
gone. Their power consisted in their concentration: when they are
dispersed, they have no effect.

Samuel Johnson

The Odawa traditionalists' current revitalization movement
derives from a long tradition of intertribal discourse about the
meaning of Euro-American contact and enduring associations.
This chapter examines the actions of prophetic leaders who had
and continue to have a resounding influence throughout the
Northeast and Great Lakes, especially two Odawa: Pontiac and
The Trout (by "prophetic leader" I mean the spokesman of a movement or cause). These social critics recognized a crisis of traditional meaning caused by shifts in interpersonal relationships. I
argue that, like the contemporary Odawa traditionalists, these
prophets saw that traditional ways of doing things no longer
informed their people's behavior.

The purpose here is twofold. First, I want to present a
condensed, but surely not exhaustive, review of the religiously
informed movements that these prophets spawned in order to
apply the revitalistic theory they represent to the contemporary
Odawa traditionalists' setting. Second, I want to begin to show
processes of socioreligious transformation. Although much of the
body of work addressed in this chapter may be familiar to some
specialist readers, I address this synthesis particularly to the more
general audience. These historical prophets provide us with an
initial case study about how the examination of religious actions,

ethos, and worldview can help make sense of a particular instance of cultural change and continuity. We will see how prophecy, tradition, and identity combine to form a method for collective legitimation.

Armin Geertz, in his study of prophecy among the Hopi, is enlightening about how and why leaders draw on the powerful combination of prophecy, tradition, and identity: "Tradition and prophecy are a way of thinking, a way of speaking, and a way of acting. . . . [Prophecy is] a way of articulating and defining contemporary events within a context of a language of 'tradition,' so that it, therefore, is a cultural strategy for making meaning and making sense of the changing world and one's place in it" (1994b:6–7). Like the Hopi leader Simo, the eastern woodlands prophets constructively addressed changing social and political realities within a traditional framework. What called for their action was a disrupted world and the emergence of a renewed world (i.e., a renewed identity). Geertz shows how prophecy among the Hopi has been "a mechanism that incorporates contemporary affairs into the framework of traditional religious values [action-based ethics], evaluates those affairs in terms of conceived tradition, and interprets and judges those affairs on the authority of conceived tradition" (1994b:51). In this sense, prophecy informs and is part of a strategy to reconstitute a sense of the relationship between ethics and social structure.

During the eighteenth and nineteenth centuries each prophet's message addressed a specific, though broad, audience. The messages centered on ways to reconstitute an effective field of social-ritual action. Their call to action accounted for and responded to issues of territorial and economic displacement, the effect of disease, missionization, the disintegration of clan relations, and other sources of social disruption. They spoke in terms of revitalizing the well-being and vitality of either a local group or some larger collectivity. Although the circumstances and immediate concerns of such prophets as the Delaware leader Neolin, the Odawas Pontiac and The Trout, and the Shawnees Tenskwatawa and Tecumseh might have been vastly different, all were concerned with a meaningful future resting on a critical assessment of tradition and a realistic assessment of present conditions. In his own way, as a method of reconstituting tradition and therefore history, interpersonal relationships, and identity, each leader responded to Euro-American incursions by engaging traditional precedents for ethical action.

Power, as wisdom received in ritual visions from Great Persons of mythology, informed the prophets' actions. The actions that they called for in others were intended to confirm who "I" am to "you" and who "we" are to "them." In response to hostility from non-Indians and Indians converted to Christianity, the prophets' actions repeatedly announced an ethical responsibility to maintain identity on both a personal and collective level. The concern with Indian identity became widespread, and it "affected Indian actions in every conflict between the Seven Years' War and the War of 1812" (Dowd 1992:xiii). In articulating their message of the power of their own ethnic unity to counter Euro-American opposition, the prophets drew inspiration from the same source: a belief in bigenesis—a separate creation for Indian peoples than for Euro-Americans.[1] They showed other Indian peoples the power of recognizing themselves as a unique people, "separately created and required to perform special duties. [They also showed that] failure to fulfill these obligations had brought on a dispiriting loss of power" (Dowd 1992:xiii). These leaders of social movements articulated how power could be regained through rituals of resistance and revitalization.

As the following chapters show, the actions of contemporary Odawa traditionalists are very much informed by those of their predecessors. The prophets have left a legacy that calls for ritually informed action as the real means to perpetuate an important tradition and therefore collective identity. These leaders "experimented with 'new' ritual in 'traditional' ways . . . [and] introduced new cultural forms according to old processes . . . after having taken . . . heroic journeys in conscious imitation of ancient myths, after having embarked on traditional quests for power" (Dowd 1992:2). Often working with another leader, they sought to uphold *pimadaziwin*.

Gregory Evans Dowd (1992), Joel Martin (1991a, 1991b), and Richard White (1991) suggest that the actions of many American Indian prophets were informed by traditional ways of cooperative interactions. Dowd and Martin, especially, to one degree or another, suggest that traditional ritual was the rallying point for people's actions; neither, however, fully develops that proposition. Still, by synthesizing their works with White's and other ethnohistorical and anthropological studies, we can see that the actions of the prophets were well informed by ritual and traditional ways of doing things. Ontologically and phenomenologically, reality for these leaders was structured as a fluid and adaptive system to mediate interpersonal disagreements—the social distance between We and They—and to uphold ethically based relationships and identity.

Armin Geertz criticizes the conceptual duality We-Others as being a by-product of the Orientalist approach to the study of religion, in which "Orientalism is understood here both as the tendency to dichotomize humanity into we-they contrasts and to essentialize the resultant 'Other'" (1994a:2; see also Morrison 1994:11–12). It would seem to me, however, that instead of condemning the academy for condoning structures he identifies as "imperialistic," we should admit that many if not all people ritually approach social relationships by measuring both similarities and differences between oneself and others, whose intentions, at least initially, may be unclear. What Geertz does not acknowledge is the many systematic ways in which people act to define the relationship and to mediate social distance.

In different and varying ways, the leaders discussed in the remainder of this chapter all sought to revitalize the significance of their lives and changing relationships by acting for the benevolent purpose of reuniting "all relatives." In doing so, they sought to correct disrupted relations associated with historical encounters with others, both non-Indians and Indians of other tribal groups. Dowd's, Martin's and White's works, with less recent ethnohistorical material, begin to allow us to appreciate the profound legacy of revitalization left by these prophets, to whom contemporary Odawa still look.

The Legacy of Revitalization

Leaders such as Neolin, Pontiac, The Trout, Tenskwatawa, and Tecumseh had a resounding influence across the Great Lakes area.

We can explore their actions as exemplary ethical models, onto-logically grounded in what the anthropologist Grace Harris broadly identifies as "the continuity of self and [collective] identity" (1989:602). These prophets became the spokesmen for ways of reintegrating dissociated individuals and reorganizing social networks through methods of engaging or appealing to traditional concepts of power. Dowd stresses how for them, "most fundamentally, power meant the ability of an individual to influence other people and other beings. Power meant successful interaction" (1992:3). Because their worldview was informed by the question "Who causes?" instead of the impersonal "What causes?," the purpose around which they moved the collective to act was the redefinition and expansion of both identity and social relationships. Each actor worked within a traditional framework to invoke meaning and significance in a changed world.

It became increasingly clear to Indian peoples generally that two "roads" for living existed: The Red/Right road and the Wrong/Destructive road, "the red road evoked by conscious and critical resistance and informed by spiritual interpretation" (Martin 1991a: 688). Although in their conversion efforts missionary cate-chists used a two-road map to illustrate heaven and hell, these two distinct and opposing paths became understood by the prophets not as symbols of a vertical avenue between Satan below and God who judges and grants grace from on high but as a real and action-based way to regain power derived from right relationships.

To the external social disruptions outlined earlier "we should also call attention to the impact and power of new visions . . . amplified in communal discussions," which "innovated tradition and initiated new ways of life within the world created by contact," so that the "new world entered by Native Americans was also a new 'religious world' . . . a creative time when new systems of purity displaced old ones, and new myths and rites arose" (Martin 1991a:683, 684, 685). To counter threats to native identity, each leader acted as a personal model of a way to reconstitute tradition that was codified as ritual. Ritual, then, promised to resolve the crisis of meaning by reestablishing a proper under-standing of the relation between ethics and social structure. Shifts in traditional ethics were not signs of decline but creative adjustments to new sociocultural situations. A brief overview of these men's actions and teachings, placed within the context of their historical moment, can demonstrate how each sought to create a new order and establish proper relations within and between indigenous groups. First, we must glimpse what was recent in each man's cultural memory.

Several significant events in the seventeenth century resulted from the European presence throughout the Northeast and Great Lakes region. First, trade goods such as kettles, guns and ammunition, sword blades, and rum were introduced by Iroquoian-speaking groups before actual Algonkian contact with Europeans. Thus began a long process of integrating Algonkians into a new world-system mercantile economy. Second, French traders began to establish trading posts at strategic locations, especially areas traditionally used as seasonal fishing grounds such as the Straits of Mackinac. The trading-post economy fostered intertribal integration (initially Ojibwe and Odawa) through resettlement. Third, there was increased integration among tribes and with the French, who were anything but xenophobic. Multicultural integration was accomplished by expanding, especially through intermarriage, trade networks that traditionally were controlled by kin groups. The French engaged this practice because they knew that the Indians' cooperation and participation were indispensable to the economic success of their fur trade. In the process, however, a new generation of people was spawned, the métis, who by virtue of being ethnically mixed had a foot in two different worlds and therefore "paddled two canoes," to use Russell Means's expression.

During the French era, because of the Odawa's involvement in the fur trade at Mackinac and a good relationship with Antoine Laumet de La Mothe Sieur de Cadillac, Father Pierre de Charlevoix, and Father Jacques Marquette, some Odawa sought an intertribal and intercultural alliance with the Ojibwe, the Huron/Wyandot, and the French based on the empowerment resulting from reciprocal gift exchange. This particular process of reciprocity, especially in the case of the French, focused on the exchange of furs for guns and gunpowder. Other groups such as the Delaware were not so successful in generating alliance with the French; by the 1670s "the position of the Indian, who by now largely depended on white trade, was becoming less secure. This, coupled with the importation of the white man's rum and his diseases, seriously disturbed the Delaware's economic and social system" (Wallace 1949:2–6). The need to establish new alliances for trade, coupled with the demographic devastation caused by increasing alcohol abuse and disease, fostered dependence on French-made trade goods. To gain easier access to these goods, various Indian groups resettled together at forts, major trading posts, and missions, which further disrupted their traditional clan- and band-based social organization.

Resettlement at these French centers, which spawned further intermarriage and increased economic involvement in the fur trade, resulted in separate clan, band, and tribal disintegration and increased intertribal and intercultural integration. Indigenous language was undermined by the need to adopt French in trade negotiations and by the missionaries' "civilizing" efforts. The increased exposure to missionaries created a tension between old and new ways of doing things. A pan-Indian sentiment arose from a commitment to creating alliances intertribally and with the French.

Rituals intended to establish intertribal alliances were developed and expanded as a means of generating intertribal integration through the application of the traditional ethic of mutual obligations (*pimadaziwin*) and a desire and need to redistribute wealth accrued through trade with the French. The ethnohistorian Harold Hickerson (1960) shows how and why the economic disruption made manifest by the seventeenth century motivated new ways to approach such collective rituals as the Feast of the Dead, or *gi-be wiikonge*, discussed in greater detail in chapter 8. These collective rituals came to serve as a vehicle to create bonds with previously widely scattered individuals, even bands, now living in much larger village communities (R. J. Mason 1981:384–89; see also Pflüg 1992a, 1992b).

Hickerson explains that European goods introduced through the fur trade markedly changed the indigenous economic system and increased the demand to accumulate peltries. The Odawa became immersed in an economic system that required them to form political and military alliances with other Algonkians in the Great

Lakes area to expand markets for their furs. Intertribal relations changed with the shift away from a subsistence economy: the market economy established by the fur trade created new commercial relations that extended political perspectives, increasingly emphasized external relations, and highlighted the need for expanded alliances through planned diplomacy (Hickerson 1960:87). The Odawa's relations with other cultural groups were largely motivated by the need to accumulate huge numbers of furs for trade and assume the role of middlemen in the economic system (McClurken 1988). As we will see, a major function of such collective rituals as the Feast of the Dead was to establish and perpetuate alliances through communal aspects of ceremony (Hickerson 1960:91). Ritual became a social network mechanism, serving to position various communities in a large-scale socio-political process in a way that simultaneously expanded community relations and upheld the integrity of local communities.

Because prophetic leaders insisted that no compromise of identity was possible on this social scale, rituals such as the Feast of the Dead were used as collective techniques both to forge a new, collectively determined identity based on giving and to overcome socioeconomic disruption caused by non-Indian materialism. Eventual competition for goods and land fostered by this non-Indian materialism resulted in the Seven Years' War against British incursions and expansionism.

Between 1754 and 1760 the British blockaded all goods into the Great Lakes area, creating an economic crisis and accelerated economic dependency. This crisis partly resulted in a militaristic turn of the pan-Indian ideology and the fueling of various anti-British conspiracies. Again Gregory Dowd's work is informative: "No event intensif[ied] intertribal relations as [did] the Seven Years' War," which created great changes in diplomatic relations among, and social relations within, Indian groups and between them and the French and British. Intertribally, and interethnically with the French, leaders crafted new strategies to counter the British and to regain identity and power. For example, in 1755, "on the eve of British Major General Edward Braddock's spectacular defeat on the Monongahela River, the French officer Daniel de Beaujeu at Fort Duquesne, now Pittsburgh, employed traditional

Indian ceremony," in the form of wampum exchange and war songs, "when he sought to raise a fighting force among the Ottawas, Chippewas, Hurons, Mingos, Shawnees, and Potawatomis." Besides sharing wampum war belts, this intertribal group collectively sang a war song, which "suggests a growing identity of the people with one another" (Dowd 1992:25, 26). Previously scattered villages came together to exchange understandings of rituals, especially war rituals, and to form new versions of those rituals.

French posts such as Michilimackinac, which long had been established as centers for acquiring ammunition and organizing raids, drew diverse Indian peoples from many areas against the same enemy: the British. Conflict with the British was a common experience of Indians and French alike. New relations and polyglot communities led not only to reworked rituals focused on a similar cause, such as the Feast of the Dead, but also to reinterpreted mythological themes. Because myths traditionally echoed ethos, mythic themes came to identify the British with the destructive effects of alcohol and disease, and new mythic narratives focused on how individuals could receive powerful knowledge of how to counter these problems from the Master of Life (or "Great Spirit") instead of the traditional Master of Game (Dowd 1992:27, 29). In this way, drawing on the imagery of godlike language learned from the French Jesuits and incorporating it into original patterns, the Indians reconstituted traditional significance and identity. They reaffirmed the relationship between traditional meaning, identity, and collective social structure. "The Seven Years' War, terribly violent though it was, opened an opportunity for the elaboration of intertribal relations. The memory of the unions shaped by alliance with France [against the British] would persist long after France departed" (Dowd 1992:26). Ultimately, however, France and its Indian allies were defeated, and the French capitulation of Canada in 1760 propelled the British era.

A series of events in the British era threatened renewed crises. The defeat of the French increased Indian dependence on British goods. Between 1750 and 1760 the English advance in the Northeast forced indigenous groups to move north and west into the Great Lakes region and Ohio Valley. British control of the Northeast resulted in increased integration into the trading-post economy and colonial expansion into tribal territories. So began a long process of intercultural conflict and adjustments to territorial loss to settlers. The experience of the Delaware, as recorded in the literature, exemplifies that of many Indian peoples in the area at this time. For example, treaties in 1737 and 1754 completely uprooted the Delaware from their traditional lands. By 1755 English military expeditions had radically reduced the Delaware population. With this threat of depopulation, in 1758 the Delaware leaders called for negotiations during which they declared: "We have great reason to believe you intend to drive us away and settle the country, or else why do you come to fight in the Land that God has given us. . . . Why don't you and the French fight in the old Country, and on the Sea? Why do you come to fight on our Land? This makes every Body believe you want to take the Land from us, by force and settle it" (Dowd 1992:252). These were meant not as rhetorical questions but as questions of moral purpose. The Delaware leaders' declaration implies that they knew exactly what the English were up to and were seeking ways to confront it: perhaps questioning the moral purpose of the British would cause them to act differently.

During this time "Louis Antoine de Bougainville, after reporting the continued dependence of the Ottawas [Odawa] on their manitous [power persons], said that they had more recently added two Masters of Life to their cosmology. One was brown and beardless and had created the Indians. The other, who had created the French [and British], was white and bearded" (White 1991:283). Engaging this emerging conviction in bigenesis, Indian groups throughout the eastern woodlands and Great Lakes, including the Delaware and Odawa, attacked British forts when word of the threat of British usurpation of land spread to the Indians at Detroit (see Jacobs 1972). The belief in bigenesis morally legitimized militaristic actions against British incursions.

Economic hardships increased because the British refused to follow the former French pattern of engaging the alliance and cooperation of tribal groups, especially through cohabitation and intermarriage. Whereas the Indians had made the French allies through reciprocal gift exchange, the British did not engage this system. In fact, from the Indians' perspective, lack of reciprocity mirrored a British policy that Indian participation in the fur trade no longer was necessary: indeed, the British got them hooked on capital goods (such as guns) and consumer goods (such as ammunition, cloth, and blankets) and then left them high and dry:

> British policy [by] 1762 . . . dashed Algonquian hopes for accommodation. . . . Events had now put both their lives and their conceptions of the British at risk. . . . If the British did not act as fathers or brothers [as the French did], then they might very well plot the Algonquian's destruction. Men who refused to aid the victims of famine and pestilence could easily become identified as the source of famine and pestilence. [This lack of giving,] coupled with British trade policies, created an Algonquian image of the British not as misguided brothers, but as enemies, a malevolent people bound by neither kinship nor ritual obligations. The image of the British as merciless enemies gave renewed power to calls for revolt against them. (White 1991:275)

British-Indian relations became a battle of powers on several levels. From the Indians' perspective, the world was disrupted by the children of an alien deity, a people whose detachment from real or ritual kinship relations made them potential enemies.

The rapid depletion of beaver and other sources of fur caused tribal groups to migrate westward in search of expanded hunting territories.[2] These migrations consequently created hostile intertribal relations because of competition for hunting lands. Additionally, by 1762 crop failures, epidemics, and famine swept the area, and Indian groups had no choice but to seek British aid, which was not forthcoming. Also, Protestant ideology won increasing influence. Unlike the Catholic ideology and excluding the Quakers' focus on the power of community, Protestants stressed the individual and one's worth as weighed by the financial fruits promised by adopting the work ethic. Adding to these threats of a crisis of meaning and identity, by 1765 Indians in the entire eastern woodlands were faced with rampant smallpox, lack of ammunition, continual British attacks on villages, and internal factionalism over the proper response (Dowd 1992:36).

Neolin

The Delaware's experience during the British era—changes in land base and population size, technical and cultural influences, especially English and German—exemplifies that of many Indian groups during the period. Their experience called for a response that proved to have wide-ranging effect. Initially, the Delaware suffered intratribal factionalism. Among the eastern Delaware, one faction accepted Moravian Christianity while another group determined to maintain the "Old Ways" as a response to European intervention and the perceived betrayal of their people. This second group was led by Teedyuscung, who tried to stave off threats resulting from the colonists and the Indians who accommodated them, Iroquoian groups and the western Delaware (see Wallace 1949). Among the western Delaware, powerful tribal councils were retained and European culture was rejected by a ritual of resistance and revitalization articulated by Neolin, the "Delaware Prophet," who predicted that "there will be Two or Three Good Talks & then War" (quoted in White 1991:280).

In 1761 Neolin embarked on a ritual fast in which he received a vision "while he was alone by himself and musing & greatly concerned about the evil ways he saw prevailing among the Indians" (White 1991:280). He returned from his vision quest and told his people that he had journeyed along a path until he came to a fork where one branch led to unhappiness and destruction caused by non-Indian ways of doing things and the other to the traditional, good, healthy and moral collective life. Neolin told his people: "Hear what the Great Spirit has ordered me to tell you; Put off entirely the customs which you have adopted since the white man came upon us" (quoted in Mooney 1896:662). He particularly objected to such activities as alcohol use, which spawned fights, and overhunting, which caused ecological disruption. His message was that the people had become corrupt and greedy. He called for action within a traditional Delaware worldview, which would invigorate discussion with others.

Neolin gained a widespread following by explicating two messages. First, he drew upon the image of the Master of Life, "the Great Spirit," which was an extension of the Master of Animals or

Master of Game, the traditional Great Person of mythology. Second, he underscored that this Master was the source of the Indians' genesis and creative power. To articulate the wisdom he had gained from the Master, as a mnemonic device Neolin used a model of the path that he claimed the "forefathers use'd to ascend to Hapiness [sic]" that is, to a good, healthy, and moral life, but that was now blocked by the corrupting ways of "the White people." Neolin used this path image to illustrate "a cosmographic distinction between Anglo-Americans and Indians," thereby underscoring the powerful conviction in bigenesis (White 1991:280).

Although Neolin made alcohol a main focus of the Indians' problems, he recognized three additional threats: the disappearance of game, the loss of land to Euro-American settlement, and the British refusal to give gunpowder (Dowd 1992:33, 34). He reported that the Master of Life instructed him to show others that "Ye have only to become good again and do what I wish, and I will send back the animals for your food. . . . As for those [British] that come to trouble your lands, drive them out, make war upon them" (quoted in Quaife 1931:15). Neolin showed the need for Indians to reject dependence on the British by avoiding trade and elaborating ritual. The "Delaware Prophet" called for immediate action: each person was to purify himself or herself by purging corrupting non-Indian ways of living, which would achieve a return to the "Old Ways." A dedication to purification rituals, Neolin's vision promised, would ensure both the immediate return of traditional Indian life, including the game animals, and the abolition of all non-Indians, including the socially disruptive and morally corrosive values associated with them (LaBarre 1970).

In response to his own ritual visionary experience, Neolin preached that the Indians once had a direct threshold through which to arrive at a good, healthy, and moral collective life. By adopting non-Indian ways, however, the Indians themselves had blocked the doorway, forcing themselves along a different path to unhappiness and decrepitude. To regain the "Good Road," the right way of living, they had to relearn to do things "without any Trade or Connection with ye White people, Clothing & Supporting themselves as their forefathers did"; they must pray to "ye Son or Little God" who carried their requests and gifts to the

"Great Being who [is] too High and mighty to be spoken to"; and they must "direct prayer to a spirit of life [who] demanded a stricter respect for 'your brothers,' that is the game animals" (Journal of James Kenny, quoted in White 1991:270, 284). Translating the lesson of his vision into Christian-like terms while recognizing Euro-Americans as one source of the Indian's problems, Neolin emphasized that the Indians' problems lay within their own actions. In using Christian language, he turned "the supposed universality of Christianity on its head. [He] used it to emphasize Indian distinctiveness and a separate Indian path" (White 1991: 283)—bigenesis in its most connotative sense.

While Neolin saw both the British and the missionaries as sources of the Indians' plight, he also stressed the failure by Indians themselves to uphold ritual observance, a failure by which they had produced their loss of power and undermined a moral lifestyle. He saw that traditional ways no longer informed their actions, and perhaps was aware of ridicule by whites. Richard White summarizes Neolin's purpose: "Neolin might denounce white practices, but what he really preached was Indian guilt. Indians were guilty because they accepted from the whites things that were unsuitable for an Indian way. The great advantage of accepting guilt in this way is that it restores power to the guilty party. To take the blame is, in a sense, to take control" (1991:283).

By holding the Indians themselves responsible, Neolin articulated the problem as a crisis of meaning of their own making. Furthermore, he anticipated continued crises if the Indians did not first revolutionize from within themselves and then outwardly revolt. In this way, they could retake control of their lives. The paramount existential question that Neolin posed was, In this changed world, what now constitutes the right and moral way to live? He answered, in part, by resorting to the knowledge gained in his vision of the Master of Life: "If you suffer the English among you, you are dead men. Sickness, smallpox and their poison will destroy you entirely" (quoted in Kenny 1913:171). In his translation of the call for collective purification, Neolin advocated not only that people "quit all Commerce with ye White People" but that they also "practice sexual abstinence and a new diet that included the use of an emetic beverage imported from the Southeast"

(J. Martin 1991a:690; Kenny 1913:188). By 1763 Delaware councils seriously adopted Neolin's message and began to train boys in the traditional methods of warfare while they engaged in "a ritual diet that included the frequent consumption of an herbal emetic, after which they would be purified of the 'White peoples' ways & Nature'" (Dowd 1992:33). In effect, like Neolin himself, the boys would redeem themselves through encounters with powerful life forces in the ritual process.

During the 1760s Neolin's call for moral reform through the ritual reconstitution of tradition spread throughout the eastern woodlands and Great Lakes. The translation of his visionary experience into Christian terminology began to lessen, while a message of resistance intensified. John McCullough, who had been a captive of the Delaware, wrote of Neolin: "It was said that their prophet taught them, or made them believe, that he had his instructions immediately from *Keesh-she-la-mil-lang-up*, or a being that thought us into [existence], and that by following his instructions, they would, in a few years, be able to drive the white people out of the country" (quoted in Hunter 1971:43). Neolin called for resistance against English territorial expansion and cultural influence even if it meant warfare. Because of the conviction in bigenesis, Neolin could offer a solution to the Indians' problems that "came out of Indian traditions. Reform the world through ritual; recapture sacred power. The message took hold" (Dowd 1992:35).

Pontiac

Neolin's expectation of a return to ancestral ways was a call to reestablish proper relations and interpersonal unity. His intent was to carve an invigorated and revitalized identity and purpose. He stressed that by invoking traditional ethics, especially the moral gift of ritual relations, which extended to the dead, Indians "could regain their strength and identity, and drive out the whites" (Dowd 1992:46). It was a message that was taken most seriously by the Odawa leader Pontiac. By the 1760s Pontiac had called his people to take constructive action within an Algonkian worldview, which would—as did Neolin's call—invigorate discussions with others.

Pontiac relayed to an intertribal council a message that he purportedly received from the Master of Life in a personal vision quest. The message echoed the urgency of Neolin's call for Indians to overcome tribal differences and unite: "Do not fight among yourselves . . . but pray. . . . And when ye shall have need of anything address yourselves to me; and as to your brothers, I shall give to you as to them. . . . In short, become good and ye shall receive your needs. When ye meet one another exchange greeting and proffer the left hand which is nearest the heart" (quoted in Peckham 1947:115–16). To behave morally, especially through such ritual acts as prayer and shaking the left hand, would produce three results simultaneously: it would empower those Indians who sought to thwart foreign incursions, it would unify their purpose, and it would identify those Indians who did not share the same intentions.

Between 1762 and 1763 Pontiac, turning to Neolin's call for resistance, especially through ritual purgation, urged the Indians to coalesce and reduce the British strongholds. The threats that Pontiac addressed were the rise of English political power over the French and Indian subservience to British colonialism. In his rebellion against British incursions, often called "Pontiac's War," he spoke not only to fellow Indians but also to the remaining French, warning them not to speak of "Peace with the English" because to do so opposed "the orders of the Master of Life" (quoted in Dowd 1992:35). Pontiac rallied his neighboring bands and tribal nations, particularly the Odawa, Ojibwe, Potawatomi, and Huron/Wyandot, around Neolin's vision of constructive action, which served as a major impetus for Pontiac and his followers to attack the British fort at Detroit, and for the Ojibwe at the Straits of Mackinac to attack Fort Michilimackinac (both of which the British had captured from the French).

According to contemporary Odawa oral tradition, as expressed by an elder to me, Pontiac called together the leaders of several tribal groups at Apple Island (at Orchard Lake in Oakland County, Michigan). Regarding the English as disrupting their relations not only with the French but also with each other, they reached a consensus to overthrow the British at Detroit. The plan was to use ritual activities and gift exchange to gain entry for attack. The women and men went to the fort seemingly in peace, with furs to trade and food to prepare as a feast. On arrival, they were invited into the fort; while the women were cooking and milling about, the men put on a lacrosse match. During the match, the women threw off their robes, under which they were hiding guns, and the men attacked the British soldiers. After intense fighting Pontiac and his followers were defeated and, according to this account, the British retaliated by deliberately spreading smallpox.[3] But this tactic ultimately had little effect on Indian activism.

Richard White is informative about Pontiac's call to act: "Precisely because neither the world of the [area] nor the struggle against the British was exclusively tribal or local, his defeat at Detroit was not final. By 1764, Pontiac had clearly become more than an Ottawa war chief. [His] power was not tribally based [for he] claimed to speak for a larger common cause. . . . Pontiac recognized that his world was a shifting set of factional alliances that transcended villages and tribes" (1991:296). Pontiac came from a tradition replete with initiation rituals that were concerned with warfare and that established the identities and reputations of both individuals and groups. He unified the Indian peoples by claiming that "the Master of Life put Arms in our hands" (quoted in White 1991:285), thereby turning Neolin's ritual of resistance into a collective ritual of rebellion.

Pontiac intended his call for revolt to extend far beyond Detroit and create intertribal alliances that would overpower the British. Drawing on Neolin's message, Pontiac gave the Indians an explanation for their misfortunes "that squared well with their traditions: Indian abominations, including cooperation with the British, caused their loss of sacred power. Construed in this manner, the disturbance could be rectified by ritual and by steadfast united opposition to British expansion" (Dowd 1992:36). Confession of their wrongdoing was a starting point for Algonkian self-empowerment and rebellion against the British. "Confession . . . by making public the transgression committed permits the individual to recover. This is its ostensible purpose. But, confession has a wider social function. It makes others aware of disapproved types of conduct which act as a warning to them. At the same time, since patients who confess usually recover, the publicity given to such cases supports both the native theory of disease causation on which the sanction rests and the efficacy of confession itself" (Hallowell 1955:275). As chief, intertribal mediator, and highest in rank in the collective healing society, the Midéwiwin, Pontiac was unquestionably following an Algonkian path: he sought to reconstitute tradition by creating proper relationships through a ritual of rebellion.

The tradition of ritual resistance and rebellion established by Neolin and expanded by Pontiac was continued during and after the American Revolution. In the American era, the policy of expansionism and ownership of land through conquest (which was rooted in the doctrine of Manifest Destiny) provoked most Indian groups in the area to side with the British. From the Indians' perspective, the British were less favorable than the French because the British did not engage in gifting as a means of perpetuating alliances; but English colonists were preferable to American imperialists wielding marginalizing policies of removal and reservationism. "The new element [in the Revolutionary War years] was the widening support upon which militants seemed able to draw" (Dowd 1992:52). Between 1775 and 1777 there was a renewed emphasis on Indian unity through bigenesis and efforts to stave off Christianity. Because of American attempts to direct cultural change through Christian instruction, especially on reservations, where missionaries deliberately were chosen as government Indian agents, Indian leaders drew on traditional rituals aimed at engaging power. The focus of many rituals, such as the mortuary rite of the Feast of the Dead, was on empowerment gained through relationships with the ancestors and creative life force and through reconstituted collective meaning and identity. One example of power gained by expanding interpersonal relations occurred in 1776. Cut off from British supplies, a group of Odawa, Shawnee, and Mohawk traveled south to convince the Cherokee to enter into war against the Americans. They saw the urgent necessity of this intertribal alliance because of the decimation of tribal populations by war and disease, the decrease of traditional territories with the expansion of settlers, and the increased political control of the American government over tribal councils (Dowd 1992:47).

By 1783 and until 1816 the northern Odawa had to face continued American expansion and aggression, and they acted to resist and defend their land and political identity (Dowd 1992:91, 92, 93, 96). For example, in 1787 the northern bands of Odawa "lamented . . . that 'no more animals remain to call us out to the Woods,'" and in 1794, "at Michilimackinac, the [British] commander summoned and supplied Ottawas . . . and Ojibwes from near the straits of Mackinac to resist the Americans" (White 1991:488, 466). Alliances with the French and then the British, which ultimately were elusive, had been engaged in because of the need for guns and gunpowder, which proved a weak medium to bond relationships indeed.

Between 1792 and 1795 the Indians experienced continued defeat in warfare, largely because the French Republic was engaged in war with the English and Spanish in Europe, which resulted in decreased French supplies. At the same time, the British withdrew support, a policy officially confirmed in Jay's Treaty (1794) and the Treaty of Greenville (1795), both of which ceded huge tracts of land to the United States. The Indians viewed these actions as English betrayal. Increased land cessions to the Americans produced a crisis that threatened their autonomy and sovereignty. Ironically, the "American acquisition of Indian land perversely took on a philanthropic guise; taking became giving" (Dowd 1992:117): in exchange for the loss of land and decrease in hunting possibilities, the United States "gave" Indians farming. "The civilizing mission" of the United States to "improve" Indian economies through intensified farming endeavors, endorsed especially by Thomas Jefferson, was contradicted by "both increasing Indian indebtedness and decreasing Indian landholding" (ibid.).

The 1790s saw an increase in militant ceremonialism aimed at collective purification and transformation, particularly in the form of dances and feasts and a "new fire" imagery that was "symbolic of both the presence of the Great Spirit and of annual regeneration" (Dowd 1992:108)—an imagery particularly pertinent to our understanding the Odawa traditionalists' Seventh Fire myth in chapter 6. American imperialism, especially with the policies of removal and reservationism, resulted in an absolute loss of the long-established economy based on the fur trade. American policy also caused tribal disintegration through the further loss of traditional territorial land bases and resources. "American competition and declining numbers of furbearers were part of the problem, but particularly between 1789 and 1794 the fur trade suffered from war, which restricted the hunt, and from American expeditions and raids that hurt traders as well as Indians" (White 1991:481). The American system presented three options: move westward to avoid American expansionism, adapt to a market economy, or attempt to accommodate the newcomers. By the 1790s American governmental Indian policy became focused especially on reservationism, which forced tribal disintegration and intertribal integration.

The Trout

During the early nineteenth century the increase in domestic livestock and the decline of game became a focusing lens for Indians to identify additional threatening changes. For example, in 1805 white settlers increasingly pressured Indian groups, who endeavored to retain their hunting patterns and hold in the fur trade, to stop their practice of annually burning the forests to provide browse for deer. Algonkian hunters complained, saying that "if we are not permitted to set fire we cannot live . . . if we set fire to weeds or grass, it is to live on the game, we have no other means to subsist. All that the maker of Life placed on the Earth is to live upon and we endeavor to live as in the times of our first fathers. Why do you reproach us of setting fires?" (quoted in White 1991:490). They got an answer to this question almost immediately. The pressure to change their hunting techniques was evident especially in the Great Lakes area that had been newly settled by Euro-Americans, where in about 1807, a new Odawa prophet suddenly emerged: The Trout. Sometimes called Le Maigovis or Maya-Ga-Wy, The Trout is elusive as a historical figure, often discussed in the literature in relation to the Shawnee leader Tenskwatawa. The Trout seems to have originated in the Odawa community around Mackinac, then established a stronghold in the Odawa community of L'Arbre Croche (on the shores of Lake Michigan just south of the Straits of Mackinac) before finally moving to the area around Peoria, where he rather abruptly vanished.

The Trout received a visionary message from "the Great Spirit," which he relayed to the Odawa and Ojibwe living around the Straits of Mackinac: "You complain . . . that the animals of the Forest are few and scattered. How could it be otherwise? You destroy them yourselves for their Skins only and leave their bodies to rot or give the best pieces to the Whites. I am displeased when I see this, and take them back to the Earth that they may not come to you again. You must kill no more animals than are necessary to feed and cloathe you."[4] As with his predecessors, The Trout charged his own people with having created their current circumstances; essentially, he told them to quit complaining about conditions they had brought on themselves. He warned that "no Indian must ever sell rum to Indians. It makes him Rich, But when he dies, He becomes very wretched. You bury him with all his wealth, And he goes along the path of the Dead. They fall from him, He stops to take them up. And they become destroyed. He at last arrives almost at the place of rest. And then crumbles into dust himself" (quoted in Dowd 1992:127). Through the power of a war-club dance, The Trout showed the Odawa and Ojibwe the way to "destroy every white man in america [*sic*]" (quoted in Dowd 1992:128).

The Trout addressed concerns that he framed within traditional ethics. Recognizing that the environment had changed radically with the depletion of game, he called for ethical action to restore relations among human beings and between humans and animals, both of which the fur trade had disrupted. He framed the decrease of game as the Indians' fault because they neglected their ritual observance and gratitude to mythological Masters of Game (Dowd 1992:130). The Trout condemned the fur trade and those who fostered it for "altering ritual relations between humans and animals. Struggling to restore proper ritual relations between animals and humans, [he] spoke in terms of a Great Spirit who regulated the game in the same manner as keepers of the game had done earlier" (White 1991:491). He called on people to refuse to engage in trade and to recognize that the animals, too, were beings with whom it was one's ethical duty to maintain social relations.

The Trout purportedly gave a speech in May 1807 in which he claimed to be the "First Man." Holding eight strings of wampum, four white and four blue, The Trout told his followers:

These strings of wampum come from the great Spirit, do not despise them—For he knows everything—they are to go all round the earth till they are lost—They were sent to you by the first Man he created with these words.

Children I was asleep when the great Spirit addressed himself to another Spirit [and] said—I have closed my Book of Accounts, with Man; and [am] going to destroy the Earth. But first I will awaken from the sleep of the dead.—The first man I created he was wise. And let us hear if he has ought to say—He then awoke me and told me what he was about to do.

I looked round the world and saw my Red Children had greatly degenerated; that they had become scattered and miserable—When I saw this I was grieved on their account—And asked leave of the Great Spirit to come to see if I could reclaim them. I requested the great Spirit to grant in case they should listen to my voice. That the world might yet subsist for the period of three full lives, and my request was granted—

Now therefore My Children, listen to my voice. It is that of the Great Spirit . . . harken my Counsel, and follow my instructions. . . . The great Spirit bids me address you in his own words which are these—

My Children . . . the Whites . . . are not your Fathers, as you call them; but your brethren. . . . the Americans . . . are unjust—They have taken away your Lands which were not made for them.

My Children, you may salute the Whites when you meet them, but must not shake hands. . . . you must not drink one drop of Whiskey. It is the drink of the evil spirit. It was not made by me— but by the Americans. It is poison. Neither are you on any account to eat bread. It is the food of the Whites.

My Children. You are indebted to the White Traders—but you must pay them no more than half their credits because they have cheated you. . . . You must not dress like the Whites nor wear hats like them—But pluck out your hair as in ancient times, and wear the feather of the Eagle on your heads. . . .

My Children . . . you are to dance naked with your bodies painted and with the poigamangun [war club] in your hands—You must have this weapon and never leave it behind you—When you dance this I shall always look on with pleasure.[5]

The Trout's words reflect clearly the legacy of Neolin and Pontiac.

Tenskwatawa and Tecumseh

Like The Trout, and like Neolin and Pontiac before him, charging the Indians themselves with the responsibility for the decline of game was also the strategy adopted by Tenskwatawa, the famous Shawnee prophet and brother of the great leader Tecumseh. Tenskwatawa, who traveled widely throughout the Great Lakes region, claimed that the decline of game was the result of moral decrepitude and the unethical disregard of ritual to uphold proper interpersonal relations—which included the animals themselves. He announced that the game would return if the Indians followed proper ritual prescription. To Tenskwatawa, participating in trade activities was acceptable as long as it was done on just terms, and he proposed a new one-for-one exchange system, for example, one gun for one fur (Dowd 1992:130).

In 1805 Tecumseh's brother, then known as Lauliwasikaw, received a vision from the Master of Life. Like Neolin, in his vision Lauliwasikaw in "great distress . . . travel[ed] along a road, and came to where it forked—the right hand way he was informed led to happiness and the left to misery" (Dowd 1992:126). Lauliwasikaw claimed that he not only had communicated with the culture hero in his vision but also was now able to conquer death and therefore was the culture hero incarnate (similar to The Trout's claim to being the "First Man"). Thus he took a new name, Tenskwatawa, the Open Door, and began a conversion effort that rivaled the missionary efforts of the Christians. Taking the name the Open Door is not without its own ritual importance, as it offered the Indians a metaphor for the power to pass through their state of social marginalization or liminality (and here we might pause to appreciate that word's Latin root: *limen*, "doorway, gateway, threshold"). In effect, the Open Door embodied a way to empowerment.

Tenskwatawa adopted a strategy for reconstituting tradition and identity that was somewhat similar to that of his predecessors: perhaps having been ridiculed by non-Indians and converted Indians for the "strange" way he sounded when speaking in and of traditional ways, Tenskwatawa drew upon the language of Shaker and other Christian influences that non-Indians and converted Indians understood. Yet, again as with his predecessors, despite this seeming accommodation Tenskwatawa deliberately "cultivated otherness. He worked to disengage the white and Indian societies" by upholding the conviction in bigenesis. He showed the way to pass through their liminality by telling "stories of men isolated from, or abandoned by, their people who return triumphant, of people threatened and redeemed, of one-eyed monsters who serve as distorted reflections of the one-eyed teller of the tale himself" (White 1991:519, 521).

In telling stories by using himself as the image to overcome adversity, Tenskwatawa made himself a metaphor of—and rallying point for correcting—the consequences of immoral acts: "I told all the redskins that the way they were in was not good, and that they ought to abandon it" (Tenskwatawa, in Mooney 1896: 670). He grounded his anticipation of the "annihilation" of Euro-Americans in traditional mythology. He told how "he encountered a crab, a common 'earth-diver' in Native American creation stories, a being that brought up the muck from which the earth was made. The Great Spirit promised the Shawnee Prophet that if the Indians abided by his teachings, the crab would 'turn over the land so that the white people are covered'" (Dowd 1992: 128–29). Armin Geertz's study of Hopi prophecy is again informative to our purposes, as he highlights the "creative interaction between paradigm and agent" where the process is the "living into reality what is perceived about reality," a process that he calls "invention" (1994b:8).

Like many peoples before them, the Shawnee faced the loss of landholdings through treaties, with the same marginalized and culturally disrupted results, and the loss of traditional ethics through Christian conversion. Tenskwatawa's "greatest passion was not to vilify European Americans, but to identify and purge those natives who had betrayed tradition in order to pursue personal wealth" (J. Martin 1991a:687). In his efforts, Tenskwatawa engaged in ceremonies of public confession and cathartic weeping (Dowd 1992:128).

Working with Tenskwatawa, Tecumseh proposed that the land belonged to all Indians and no tribe could sell a part of it. He argued that all Indians should therefore be united and, through the power of numbers, uphold and assert a collective tradition. This could be accomplished even if it meant declaring war against the newly established U.S. government. Tecumseh purportedly told William Henry Harrison, then governor of Indiana Territory: "The President may sit in his town and drink his wine, while you and I will have to fight it out" (quoted in Mooney 1896:681). Tecumseh's call for collective empowerment was aided greatly by his brother, and in 1808 "Prophet's Town" (Tippecanoe Creek, Indiana) was built, where the dream of pan-Indian unification would materialize.

In 1811 several Great Lakes Algonkian advocates of Tenskwatawa and Tecumseh traveled from "Prophet's Town" to the Southeast to engage the military support of the Chickasaw, Choctaw, Cherokee, and Creek. In making their appeal for support they not only related Tenskwatawa's visions but also taught the Dance of the Indians of the Lakes or the War Club Dance (mentioned by The Trout in his speech of May 1807). "More than any other ceremonial act, belief, or practice, dancing the 'Dance of the Indians of the Lakes' distinguished those Southeastern Indians who joined the Shawnee intertribal movement from those who remained friendly with European Americans" (J. Martin 1991a: 693). Much like Pontiac's call to shake with the left hand, this dance became part of Tecumseh's and Tenskwatawa's ritual repertoire for identifying Indians who supported the purpose of Euro-American resistance.

Intertribal resistance to American efforts at economic and political control and territorial expansion eventually merged with the War of 1812, in which Tecumseh was killed while serving as a brigadier general in command of the Indian allies of the British.

Conflict Resolution: The Appeal to "All Relatives"

What these prophetic leaders have in common is that each claimed to have uncovered a concealed message. They interpreted and then applied this message to ritual as a way to reconstitute traditional meaning and identity. The initial ritual event was a vision quest that resulted in the formation of a new or renewed relationship with the Indians' creative force. These ritual visionary experiences served as the impetus for political leaders to engage resistance and get others to follow their lead. Each man's vision was a creative solution to real personal and social conflicts, and as Anthony F. C. Wallace suggests, each was "an effort at recovery by reinvesting the world . . . with . . . significance and meaning. The dialectic, the 'struggle' (to use an easy metaphor) between entropy and [re]organization, is what religion is all about. [The visions represent, each in its own way] attempts to reconstitute and reorganize self and cosmos" (1966:36, 38, 39). In other words, each leader sought to reevaluate tradition in a way that would reproduce group identity and therefore power.

They called on their people's moral obligations to each other and to animals and life forces—all one's relatives—by engaging the traditional ethic of cooperative action, which they used to reassess significance, meaning, and identity within changed cultural settings. They worked in cooperation through constructive interaction and thus exemplified and upheld the relations between and with Great Persons of mythology. To reconstitute tradition and identity in such a way, they achieved a new or renewed understanding of the relation between traditional ethics and shifting social structure. This is the legacy to which contemporary Odawa traditionalists look. The actions called for by these leaders, past and present, underscore the heuristic value of reconceptualizing Algonkian worldview, and especially Odawa, in terms of constructive and cooperative interaction instead of as abstract belief. Ritual action—especially as informed through visionary experiences—was and continues to be a method to reconstitute meaning and identity within traditional indigenous theory. I suggest that although each leader, to one degree or another, may have used terms such as "Great Spirit," "god," "angels," "heaven," and "hell" and may have espoused what seems to non-Indians as something of a transcendent perspective on life, these concepts do not accurately reflect how their lives were informed by the call for social transformation through religious action. To constrain their actions to being informed by abstract "belief" is to overlook the possibility that each, in his own way, purposefully spoke in terms identifiable to both non-Indians and the next generation of his people, whom he saw as being faced with a greater inculcation of Christianity, without sacrificing his own integrity and worldview.

Conceptualizing these early revitalizationists as exemplifying a way for people to constructively determine the course of their own social transformation allows us to grasp more fully the significance of the contemporary Odawa traditionalists' understanding of the moral gifts of ritual. The precursors to these Odawa's revitalization strategy have supplied traditionalists with a model. Their careers and works echo the centrality of the healing and regenerative power of enacting the interconnected ethics of generosity (personing), life giving (gifting), and wisdom (empowering)—together, *pimadaziwin*—all of which we will look at in depth in the next chapter. Thus we can appreciate that the lives of these revitalizationists—whether historical figures or contemporary—mirror two fundamental cultural aspects, the upholding of which each activist saw and continues to see as his ethical duty during a period of profound cultural transition. The first aspect of this worldview is the principle of empowerment contained in ritual; the second is the importance of ritual in the formation of ethical personhood and interpersonal relationships. This second principle raises the issue of the relational nature of identity.

Throughout their lives, each of these revitalizationists acted to empower himself and thereby strengthen his people, by calling on all persons to enact the ethic of generosity through acts of gift exchange. In understanding changed cultural landscapes, it remained the people's ethical duty to share their power both with literal kin and "all relatives." Thus the revitalizationists' claims of having been appointed or selected to lead after ritual communications with the "Great Spirit," "Creator," or "Master of Life" can be put in new light. Perhaps none of these leaders actually accepted a personal identity that was defined for him, in Christian terms, through grace from on high. Instead, each enacted his responsibility to perpetuate identity defined by ethical acts of giving as a means of constructively addressing the social disruption caused by others. Upholding the integrity of his traditional cultural ways, each viewed enacting the quality of generosity as a gift to cure his people. In other words, these leaders became exemplars of self- and collective empowerment through ethical behavior and action. They called for future generations to simultaneously retain an Indian cultural integrity and constructively adapt to a changed social sphere.

Conclusion

Between the seventeenth and nineteenth centuries, Indian peoples throughout the eastern woodlands and Great Lakes region no longer could focus their attention only on hostile tribal groups. Coupled with these threats, they now had to face a new source of tension in the system: Euro-Americans. These foreign "others," with their fur trade market economy, Christian missionaries, and policies of colonialism, expansionism, and imperialism, and who disrupted traditional relationships and forced experimenting with new ones, created sociocultural liminality. New trading systems and relationships, intermarriage, Christian conversion, decrease of game, geographical relocation, factionalism and disunity, alcohol, disease, and wars all contributed to a crisis of traditional meaning. The crisis was a threat to identity; the challenge was to reconstitute identity; the solution was to rework ritual and myth. The prophetic leaders worked to restore and establish right and ethical relationships by maintaining and reinforcing identity through ritual acts, to reconstitute tradition, and myths, to define "a people" and therefore a reintegrated group with renewed purpose. They engaged ritual to establish intertribal relations and alliances by first reshaping or metamorphosing an Indian identity, particularly one sanctioned by a creative source separate from the Christian god.

The prophetic leaders reinterpreted and reapplied rituals and mythic themes to reintegrate communities and overcome threats of divisiveness and liminality. In doing so, they not only reconstituted tradition but also carved a collective identity. They saw ritual, in these times of crisis, to be the essential way to expand and reaffirm one's own moral personhood. In particular, the ritual act of giving knowledge and the consequent transferal of power was seen to redefine identity and confirm collective unity and centrality by lessening interpersonal distance between Indians, thus allowing new concepts of identity to emerge and be reaffirmed. That they ultimately failed to achieve their immediate goal of unity to overpower the Euro-Americans does not matter—they have left a legacy still looked to.

Today, as we will see, Odawa traditionalists look to this legacy as the way to apply Algonkian, and especially Odawa, ethics to mediate the tension caused by others who are threatening. Efforts to mediate interpersonal distance in order to lessen a sense of danger through religiously charged activities, and the goal of total revitalization itself, engage many Odawa people. As did the earlier prophets, Odawa traditionalists approach these religious activities as their most significant means of establishing proper interpersonal relationships. As with the earlier prophets, contemporary traditionalists' current revitalistic activities attempt to restore just relationships and therefore contain a ritualistic aspect. As part of this purpose, these activities focus on rejuvenating an Odawa identity and thus recapturing power.

The next part of the traditionalists' story begins to illuminate how these Odawa simultaneously enhance social solidarity and reflect changing socioreligious experience through mythic and ritual discourse. We will see that the Great Persons of mythology act cooperatively and, as they did for the prophets, provide a map for unifying instead of divisive actions. Odawa traditionalists look to myth for guidance in responding to potentially threatening changes in social circumstances. For them, myths are powerful reaffirmations of constructive ways for generating social reorientation, maintaining tribal ways, building social cohesion, and transforming their identity. Myths reinforce the traditional religious structure, voice essential ethics, and echo periodic changes in social experience. Using questions presented in myths as a model, the Odawa subtly adapt their definitions of themselves and other people: With whom should proper relationships be established? How should interpersonal distance be mediated? And who should be regarded as dangerous? The actions of the Great Persons of mythology define people and proper behavior by mapping the ethics that guide Odawa life and revitalize a distinct Odawa culture and identity, especially the ethic of *pimadaziwin.*

Chapter 3

Pimadaziwin
The Quest for the Good Life

Human life is reduced to real suffering, to hell, only when two ages, two cultures and religions, overlap.

Albrecht von Haller

During a conversation about the current state of Odawa affairs, Great Elk angrily remarked, "Not only is the government trying to overtly destroy us by keeping us fragmented, it's sitting back and letting us—maybe hoping that we will—self-destruct by adopting non-Indian ways, such as alcohol abuse. It's up to us to get back on the Right Road." This comment echoes the purposes of the earlier prophets and especially harks back to their Two Road imagery. It also suggests that because they lack federal and state recognition and subsidies, Odawa traditionalists in nonrecognized groups suspect that governmental policy is structured deliberately to defeat them. They see this threat as emanating especially from the government's refusal to respond to critical health concerns such as rampant alcoholism and diabetes, which these Odawa equate with non-Indian ways of life. This statement further suggests that, as with the earlier prophets, the traditionalists' effort to carve their own collectively determined identity and survival must address both internal and external social pressures.

This chapter articulates the theme that one way Odawa traditionalists revitalize social relations, and thereby reconstitute their tradition and sociocultural status, is by enacting the ethic of empowerment contained in collective moral behavior and carefully considered acts of giving. This analysis is necessary before we can move on to understanding how Algonkian myths highlight the ethic of gifting as a model for constructive change.

Traditionalists such as Great Elk aim for *pimadaziwin,* which A. Irving Hallowell, in his extensive work on Salteaux Ojibwe worldview, identifies as the central ethic that organizes all Algonkians' lives and the core of their worldview. Hallowell defines *pimadaziwin* as "a long life and a life free from illness and other misfortune" (1955:104). It means a life of longevity and well-being. *Pimadaziwin* counters such socially disapproved and collectively disruptive acts as inhospitality, stinginess, greediness, and especially ridicule. Achieving this goal calls for constructive interaction by each person with "dream visitors," or *manidos* (power persons), who confer power on the individual to overcome personal adversity (1955:121). Hallowell also relates that "pimadaziwin [can] only be achieved by individuals who [seek] and obtain . . . the help of superhuman entities and who conduct . . . themselves in a socially approved manner . . . it is important to note that superhuman help [is] sought in solitude, that the 'blessing' or 'gift' [can]not be compelled, but [is] bestowed because the superhuman entities [take] 'pity' upon the suppliant who, in effect, ask[s] for Life (i.e., pimadaziwin)" (1955:360). Important as this insight is, Hallowell does not address the significance of "superhuman" and human agents interacting to mutually uphold the good life. A behavioralist, Hallowell locates the goal of *pimadaziwin* and its harmonious state of being within the self and identifies its achievement as an individually driven motivation (1955:174). By doing so, however, he overlooks or at least underplays how the ethic of *pimadaziwin* informs the interrelational nature of the Algonkian sociocosmos and worldview, which sees persons as being interactive and constructive agents in society.

Lone Wolf is informative about this relational nature of the sociocosmos and *pimadaziwin.* When I asked him about how he approaches the world and identifies his place in it, Lone Wolf replied while sketching on the ground a kind of interrelational cosmographic map:

> I see myself standing here in the center, and immediately encircling me is my family. Surrounding them are all our family members. Out from them are those who share my clan *dodem.* Next are all members of my band. In a wider circle are all Odawa. Encircling them are all Indian peoples, then all people. Around them are all

the ancestors. Out from them are the animals and plants. Then come A-ki [Earth], Mishomis [Sun/Sky], and Nokomis [Moon]. The next largest circle are the great powers, or *manidos*. In the widest circle is Ki-je Manido. It's everyone's job to keep these relationships held together, across all the circles, and from their own place as center. When all are connected, that's what we mean when we say *mino gwayako pima'adizi*, "he lives a good and honest life."

For Algonkians such as the Odawa, then, the central purpose of each person is to behave in ways that uphold *pimadaziwin* on an interpersonal or collective level within an ever-expanding spectrum of relationships. For Odawa traditionalists, *pimadaziwin* has much more to do with personal and social identity, interpersonal connection and interdependence, and moral integrity than Hallowell seems to realize from his Ojibwe study. Lone Wolf's statement implies that Odawa traditionalists understand *pimadaziwin* as a state of being that every person, human and otherwise (such as the *manidos*), is ethically charged with upholding. Each person doing so thus contributes to the goal of gaining a good, healthy, and interactive ethical life for the collective.

For these Odawa, collective social healing, harmony, and unity is achieved by redefining and enhancing a unique and discrete identity through actions that constructively address threats of social disruption. Traditionalists pinpoint two sources of threats to an Odawa identity: one derives from conflict between themselves and other Indians who oppose their goal of sovereignty; a second stems from conflict over culture change and social control by non-Indian outsiders. Traditionalists act to change governmental Indian policy, which they understand as an abstraction for various legal issues. For them, policy shifts partly have eliminated economic opportunities and most assuredly have contributed to their factionalism, social marginalization, and general state of liminality.

Because traditionalists recognize that survival depends on their own initiative, they structure their revitalization around the existential ethics that we may frame as personing, gifting, and empowering, which they regard as being time honored and therefore applicable to social changes. They understand that the most profound way their ancestors encountered Euro-Americans was to enact these traditional ethics, especially as they are associated fundamentally with the central goal of achieving *pimadaziwin*, which is precisely what the earlier prophets called for. Appreciating the features of these Odawa's revitalization requires understanding these traditional, time-honored ethics, especially as they continue to be their most significant means of countering social disruption and threats to their identity.

Personing, Gifting, Empowering: The Source of an Odawa Identity

We can begin to grasp how myths articulate both Odawa ethos and the ethics that traditionalists associate with their goal of *pimadaziwin* by "listening" to the following account of the Odawa's origin. This version of the Odawa's origin was told by Gray Squirrel, first in Odawa and then in English, during an elders' council.

> Our ancestors, the Anishinabeg, originally lived along the Atlantic coast, and they migrated westward in search of Turtle Island, populating the land along the way. The search for Turtle Island began with the stage of creation when Ki-je Makinaak helped form the gift of the earth. Ki-je Makinaak repeatedly dove into the Ki-je Gan searching for Form, and finally emerged with *mégis*. From these shells A-ki emerged, who Ki-je Makinaak then carried on his back, making a place for the Anishinabeg to live. The ancestors, searching for their sacred central island, or place, migrated westward, carrying Ki-je Makinaak's gift of *mégis* for guidance and safety.

Anishinabeg (singular *Anishinabe*) is a term used by the Odawa to refer to all the Algonkian Indians of the Great Lakes region and their ancestors. *Ki-je* is a prefix meaning "great," so that Ki-je Makinaak means "great snapping turtle" and Ki-je Gan, "great waters" (Kitchi- or Mitchi- gan in Ojibwe). A-ki is Earth, and *mégis* are shells with powerful attributes. It is unclear in local tradition whether "Turtle Island," the "sacred central island," refers to modern Mackinac Island, Michigan (named after Ki-je Makinaak), to Manitoulin Island, Ontario (named after the *manidos*, or *manitous* in Ojibwe, meaning "power persons"), or to an island that no one now remembers. It is clear from this version of the myth, however, that the ancestors were charged with peopling the world and with returning to the "cosmic center" (which upholds Lone Wolf's cosmographic map).

Gray Squirrel later told me that her point in telling this story was not so much to establish a chronology as to illustrate the formative importance of traditional Odawa ethics, which, as we will see in later chapters, are generic throughout the tradition. Two central ethics thematically highlighted here are *personing*, acting with continuing moral purpose, in which the category "person" is not restricted to people, and *gifting*, which is an ethical act of mutual empowerment. In much of their storytelling, Odawa traditionalists stress that ethical persons interact through what they call gifting, and they underscore the profound importance of the moral gift of ritual to maintain and extend relationships. With this understanding, a third central ethic is revealed: gift exchange is *empowering*; it makes for and extends from ethical persons. Acting ethically with benevolence thus becomes the primary way to respond constructively to others whose intentions are unknown or blatantly hostile. Framed relationally in Odawa ethical categories, through gift giving the Odawa intend to empower themselves and others in such a way that the personhood of all involved in the exchange is respected.

In Gray Squirrel's version of the origin myth, the meaning of personing, establishing ethical personhood, is suggested by her use of the term *Anishinabeg*, a reference to the continuity of community between the living and the ancestors. Acknowledging the ongoing relationship between the living community and ancestors, the Great Persons of this myth, although not human beings, behave with constructive intentionality by gifting: giving to each other with positive intent. Nonetheless, personal effort is part of the paradigm. For example, the animals—here Turtle—make tremendous efforts for others, thereby expressing their compassionate nature. They also express an inherent ability to act with benevolent intentionality. Displays of personal effort are thus important and interconnected with demonstrations of interpersonal effort.

That interconnection is revealed by Ki-je Makinaak, who acts ethically by helping to form the earth. A-ki is a gift to the people. Ki-je Makinaak perpetuates this gift by carrying A-ki on his back.

The Great Water, Ki-je Gan, also cooperates in forming the earth by giving *mégis*, another gift to the ancestors. *Mégis* are a powerful source of guidance to "find the island," the Anishnabeg's central place, to reach it safely, and to help endure unfamiliar threats and dangerous people who might be encountered along the journey. Because they act with powerful benevolence, especially by gifting, Ki-je Makinaak, A-ki, and the *mégis* all establish themselves as ethical persons.

Despite his narrow interpretation of *pimadaziwin,* Hallowell does suggest how personing (what he calls "personhood")—the category that determines persons to be ethical or not—is key to understanding the ethos of Algonkian groups in general.[1] Hallowell demonstrates that Algonkian social organization and kinship terminology reflect an orientation to a world structured by both the actions of persons and the expansion of interpersonal relations outward from the individual (1955:76–104). To further understand this relational nature of personing, we can turn to the anthropologist Grace Harris's insight about personal empowerment gained through just and ethical relationships. She identifies that the "individual," the "self," and the "person" can be understood as a continuum in which "the individual [is] a member of humankind, [the] self [is a] locus of experience, and [the] person [is an] agent-in-society" (1989:899). Using this framework, we can approach personing to mean acting ethically based on one's experience as part of a larger network of persons. We can appreciate Hallowell's insight that while Algonkian language distinguishes between animate and inanimate, it does not differentiate among nature, culture, and the supernatural (1967:211). Ontologically and phenomenologically, then, the sociocosmos is structured to include within personhood what Hallowell calls both "human persons" and "other-than-human persons" (such as the actors in the origin myth). A better description of the latter, however, is Lee Irwin's "more-than-human person" (1994:72–73). Since the Odawa, like other Algonkians, do not distinguish between the natural and supernatural, each person, as a constructive agent in society, can interact ethically with more-than-human persons in their daily and ritual life (as Lone Wolf's comments suggest).

In Algonkian mythology, Algonkian language dictates that ethical persons are mutually responsible for proper relations with all persons, human and otherwise. Algonkians view both daily life and history in terms of personal actions, inherently asking, Who causes? instead of What causes? Therefore the cause of events is always interpreted personalistically: events are caused by personal actions that reveal the actor's intentions. Because all agents in society, or persons, are motivated by good or ill purposes, all events need either an affirming or resisting response. (And as we saw with the prophets in the last chapter, some events are interpreted as being so personally insulting and disruptive that they call for outright rebellion.) To maintain sociocosmic harmony, the inter-personalistic nature of events calls for a way to reduce the distance between beings, particularly those who are antisocial. Acts that establish and maintain ethical relations result in a transformation of personal, social, and cosmic being: humans and more-than-humans may be discrete entities, but they are interconnected through the pervasive interrelational nature of their acts of person-ing (see Hallowell 1955). Again, Grace Harris is informative about the generative power of interpersonal relationships: "If human-persons can gain access to external power, that is an aspect of humanity's place in the cosmos to be considered in delineating the agentive capacity of human and non-human persons. . . . To focus on . . . persons as agents-in-society directs attention to systems of social relationships whose participants, performing actions and responding to each other's actions, live in a moral order" (1989:603) Again, framed relationally within Odawa ethical categories, gifting with ethical purpose is the primary means of simultaneously empowering oneself and others in a way that respects and acknowledges the personhood of all involved in the exchange. For Odawa traditionalists, this moral order is expressed by the contribution of ethical persons to the well-being of the group by enacting the ethic of gifting in their behavior—*pimadaziwin* in its full connotative sense. For example, the gift of *mégis* from some Great Persons of mythology formed the identity of the ancestors.

Odawa traditionalists contend that ethical acts of personing are a cardinal component of a living and acting world to whom each human must become oriented. Personing extends beyond human beings to include other beings such as the *manidos*, who are powerful life forces such as Ki-je Makinaak and A-ki, and *dodems*, who are guardian spirits such as *mégis*. Great Elk remarked:

> I simply don't understand why Anglos have such a hard time getting what we mean. After all, Christians speak of Jesus as human and as Christos—which is something different from a regular human being. But in both cases he's a person, isn't he? He just changed forms and in both is still the model of a good person.

Personing, for these traditionalist Odawa, entails fluidly expanding and transforming identity and communal membership. Black Bear, a pipe carrier, affirmed the quality of transformation:

> Unlike your society that demands scientific proof for anything to be true, we believe that all things are possible. All life is connected. We see that all things are always in motion; they can change forms in this life and the next. At one moment a person may take the form of a human but in the next moment may take the form of that tree over there. Everything is in motion and has power. We need to be always listening.

As with many Algonkians, for Odawa traditionalists the quality of personhood does not necessarily include anthropomorphic traits (see Hallowell 1955, 1960, 1967). Instead of morphology, the distinguishing feature that all ethical persons share is that they behave properly and powerfully act with constructive intentionality to establish and uphold *pimadaziwin*.

Odawa traditionalists consider power itself as neutral, its positive or negative character depending on the intentions of the other person. Mary Black, in her close examination of Hallowell's understanding of power as it operates in Ojibwe worldview, underscores the "many instances of uncertainty about the actual current power of a given person—and therefore about the outcomes of encounters" (1977:141). At one moment a person may act more powerfully than another, but in the next moment the reverse is possible. Because the entire system is interactional and dependent on everyone's intersecting purposes, traditionalists consider either benevolent or malevolent displays to define relationships with others.

Lone Wolf related how ethical persons are empowered by their enacting "the seven ways of being Odawa," which he identified as being "pure in heart, pure in mind, pure in body, humble, honest, loving, and respectful." He went on to explain that "when we are all seven of these things, we become strong. It's then our duty to acknowledge our power and act upon it wisely. These seven ways of being set the right way to behave as Odawa. This is what we mean by leading the good life." Clearly, these seven ways of being define proper ethical behavior (i.e., personing is their purpose), and they lend themselves to collective *pimadaziwin*.

The ultimate goal of ethical behavior, engaging power constructively, is to achieve personal control; the person's duty is to be in charge of self-determination and to extend this moral responsibility to the wider social sphere (Black 1977:145, 146). Black Bear confirmed this ethic: "It's wrong for people to make positive statements without being absolutely sure of what they're saying because the world always is an uncertain place from one's limited skill to see." Given one's limited "sight," which Black Bear understands as a precondition of knowledge as power, one may not be able to discern the particular ways in which the world is moving.

Being part of a dynamic physical and social world requires that each person "read" the course of action carefully. As we saw with the earlier prophets, "reading" events for signs of personal intentions is possible for these contemporary traditionalists because, for them, the powerfully benevolent actions of the Great Persons of mythology have mapped proper behavior. According to Lone Wolf, the Great Persons of mythology "gave our ancestors three things to guide and help us if we pay close attention to what they say: *dodem, manido,* and Midéwiwin."

Dodem, meaning "I have him for my family mark," is the more-than-human person from whom each Odawa clan and therefore each individual is descended, such as Turtle, Otter, Fish, and Bear. Ernestine Freidl, in her study of self-directed culture change among the Ojibwe (1950), shows how the *dodem* is a powerful life form that helps to maintain the unity and unique identity of the clan. Adding to this insight, Fred Eggan, in his sociocultural analysis of culture change among American Indians (1966), demonstrates how the *dodem* promotes social cohesion by determining kinship relations and marriage eligibility. This is still very much an organizing principle. For example, Lone Wolf told me that after having been married to an Ojibwe woman for many years, they had to divorce when they suddenly discovered that they shared the same *dodem.*

Paul Radin, in his classic study of American Indian religions (1914), suggests that instead of manifesting power that structures social groups, as with *dodems*, the *manido* is a type of more-than-human person with whom individuals seek contact during vision quests and other rituals and gain as a source of life-long aid. For example, when I once asked Soaring Eagle if he would chop up some trees that had fallen down over the winter, he replied that he would cut them all except a hemlock, which he could not cut because it was his personal *manido,* or "power guide."

The Midéwiwin, whose name literally means "health," is a secret organization of specially trained individuals who act together to engage the *manidos*, and who then bring that empowering experience of knowledge back to benefit the community.[2] Black Bear, a pipe carrier and Midéwiwin member, said that through special training, especially visionary experiences, and "soul flight" or "sky journeys," "we contact the *manidos* and gain their assistance. We help keep the group healthy by showing others the knowledge that we gain from these powers."

Traditionalists recognize that powerful acts, either malevolent or benevolent, differentiate people, and they also understand that powerful acts of gifting mediate that distance. Persons attend to others by gifting. The empowerment contained in gifting lies in the exchange itself, not in the functional or material value of the gift. Gifting structures Odawa social relationships and powerfully enhances social solidarity. Solidarity is reinforced by gifting because such acts have the power to mediate the distance between the individual and other individuals, and between the group and other groups.

Here are a few examples of gifting between myself and the Odawa. I always give silk cloth and tobacco when meeting elders, medicine people, and pipe carriers, especially for the first time. I have a canoe that I give to one group for their annual elders' council. I also have money and food (and a strong back for such chores as chopping firewood) to contribute to this event and others such as powwows. In exchange, Odawa elders have invited me to these events and have encouraged my active participation. At one powwow, for example, in gratitude for monetary support, I was given a small bag of tobacco tied with a ribbon and invited to dance with the head dancer. In exchange for help in writing grant applications and proposals related to land claims and the goal of sovereignty, I have been invited to attend and take an active part in tribal board meetings. Several times, after trips to the West, I have brought back sage, for which I have been given sweetgrass. Once, suspecting that I had "fallen ill" because I had offended someone, two pipe carriers showed me how to overcome "fear," which they identified as the source of my illness, and therefore to empower myself.[3] Another time, in exchange for loaning him my car so he could attend a Midéwiwin ceremony in Wisconsin, Lone Wolf took me to the annual powwow and spiritual gathering at Manitoulin Island, Ontario, to meet Pontiac, a pipe carrier who is descended from his eighteenth-century namesake. These are but a few examples of gifting between myself and the Odawa; generally, the gift I have received is measured information or knowledge. Here, then, gift *is* power.

Through carefully considered acts of gifting, traditionalists revitalize, reinforce, and cement social relations. As with the earlier prophets, they regard their revitalized social solidarity and therefore survival as a continuum of interacting persons who behave ethically both toward others (such as myself) who are socially and symbolically different and toward the living and ancestral communities (through such acts as decorating deceased relative's graves as part of the annual Ghost Supper ritual, as detailed in chapter 8). Traditionalists lessen interpersonal distance by serving others, by overcoming danger, by diminishing differences, and by unifying community, thus upholding collective *pimadaziwin.*

Odawa traditionalists, like their prophetic predecessors, focus on their responsibility to give—especially of themselves instead of some thing—as a religiously charged way of mediating conflict and transforming the hostility of others. Gifting provides them with a means of addressing interpersonal distance. Compassionate acts, such as explaining the seven ways of being Odawa and the means of living *pimadaziwin*, overcome social disruption and other threats to their sociocultural integrity by mediating the distance between disagreeing people. Therefore such acts are empowering. As we saw with the earlier prophets, the lesson that the ethical system teaches is this: if other people participate in the exchange, they are no longer dangerous; if they refuse or withhold, however, other persons define themselves as dangerous outsiders. To paraphrase Great Elk, distinctions derive from perceptions of who "they" are, how "we" behave toward them, how "we" expect them to behave toward us, and how "they" actually do behave. The ethic of gifting, along with the many related behaviors it calls for, ultimately structures Odawa life.

Conclusion

Traditionalists underscore the interrelational nature of socio-cosmic life. Black Bear explained:

> The gift has the spiritual power, *gi-be manidoowaadese*, that is in everything through Ki-je Manido, Grandfather, the great power person. It is in the burning tobacco that we offer Ki-je Manido and the many *manidos* or little grandfathers. It's in the prayers and the food eaten for me while I'm up on the hill [vision quest]. There's power in returning food to A-ki [Earth]. It's in my use of *mashkiki* ["medicine," or more accurately, "power of the earth"] in the pipe ceremony to heal. It's in the *wiikonges* [feasts] that we have for our families and members of other clans and bands. It's also in the councils we have between our many Anishinabeg groups [the Odawa, Ojibwe, and Potawatomi, plus the ancestors].

Showing compassion through acts of gifting empowers ethical persons and displays a generosity that diminishes differences. Through these actions, the power of life is shared with humanity; furthermore, when ethical people give back, they ensure the benefits of harmonious life: *pimadaziwin* in its most compre-hensive sense. Ethical beings who make up the world—including more-than-human persons and the ancestors (such as the Odawa prophets Pontiac and The Trout)—give to the human person and the community, and the ethical person and community give back to them: personing as a generative and interactive empowering process. This exchange makes a continual connection among all ethical persons, human and otherwise.

Renewed identity through expanded ethical relationships is possible for Odawa traditionalists because, as Brown Otter said, "All life is circular and continually changes. It has many phases. But everyone, in all their different phases, is related, and we must honor that relationship by giving to each other." He went on to say that individuals acting together create a "circle," so that the connection between all ethical persons is continually regenerated. Traditionalists contend that because life is in a constant state of motion, it is essential for the person, the community, even the cosmos, to ritually transform the present moment and emerge with a renewed identity.

The next chapter reviews how some central narratives, especially those that scholars would identify as cosmological myth "texts," articulate the fundamental Odawa ethics for living—personing, gifting, and empowering—thereby providing maps of change that model why people want what they do.

Part Two

A Map of Change
Mythic Models for Why
People Want What They Do

Charles Meyers

Chapter 4

Tales of Cooperation and Opposition

You tell us fine stories, and there is nothing in what you say that
may not be true; but that is good for you who come across the seas.
Do you not see that, as we inhabit a world so different from yours,
there must be another heaven for us, and another road to reach it?

Huron/Wyandot leader to the Jesuit Jean de Brébeuf (1635)

"Why can't people, especially Anglos, see that there's more to the
world than themselves? Everything's life-giving, and its power
deserves respect. Every living thing is tied to another. All life is
unified. So we must honor everything's place in life so life won't
become unraveled and its power lost. This is what our tradition
teaches us, and it's our duty to act to make sure it stays alive." This
remark, which I overheard Black Bear make to Lone Wolf at a
powwow, illustrates the Odawa traditionalists' dedication to the
vocation of social healing and empowerment by interacting with
a living universe. Such people have knowledge of and the skill to
work with a power that extends beyond the individual to include
the entire community, enabling them to correlate their revitalization movement to a variety of interactions.

The Odawa traditionalists' revitalization movement provides a
context for examining those cultural and historical processes
through which people create, maintain, and transform whole
worlds of meaning, particularly as those meanings are expressed
religiously, sociologically, and politically. In this chapter I discuss
how Odawa traditionalists perceive a universe inhabited by a
plethora of beings, human and otherwise, who perpetually either
generate or threaten existence for all through their actions. This
ethos is articulated in various myths. Conflict between interpersonal

intentions and purposes necessitates a response to other persons' behaviors. This construction of the sociocosmos and how things work spearheads these Odawa's view that causality must be understood and apprehended in interpersonalistic ways. Our purpose is to begin to understand "mediation" and "competition" in terms of an ethic of cooperation that is morally contrasted to opposition. This chapter and the next highlight how certain myths articulate real experiences and map ways of proper behavior to counter threats to identity.

To appreciate why some Odawa pursue their revitalization, or sociocultural reconstitution, requires understanding how the fluid character of Odawa tradition, which includes myths and rituals, guided responses to events that threatened social disruption in the past. We have already begun to see how this process works in our discussion of the prophets in chapter 2. A brief review here of the thematic trends in certain myths illustrates how to respond constructively to and transform socially disruptive events stemming from others' uncooperative and hostile actions. We can approach Odawa myths—those narratives that articulate ethos—as one medium for the Odawa to reconstruct the assumptions about reality that shape their assessment of others.

By first reviewing the myths themselves and then considering their historical context, we can see that the emphasis on the tension created by competition and acts of hostility mirrors threats created by the Odawa's historical encounters with Euro-Americans. Besides loss of land and socioeconomic disruption, the Odawa have faced many sources of social change, which have threatened their traditional meaning and identity—as we saw with the prophets, threats often necessarily located and articulated in internal relations among themselves. Power bases became centralized, as American institutional authority, and were no longer formed by consensus. Identity was threatened, and personhood became defined by outsiders. Conflict developed in relationships primarily because the new social system and moral order were not grounded in ethical gifting. These threats forced the Odawa to address three questions: With whom should proper relationships be established? How should interpersonal distance be mediated? And who should be regarded as dangerous? To answer these questions, some Odawa have looked and continue to look to models for behavior presented in myths. As part of a tradition that is adaptive and flexible, myths show that Odawa history derives from the stories of active participants.

Since some Odawa remember the crisis-threatening historical events already presented in the context of the prophets, we can approach some myths as mapping the ways to constructively meet, understand, and resist a history imposed on them from the outside: as Kenneth M. Morrison suggests with other Indian people's, for Odawa traditionalists "myth . . . provides the template [for] shaping ethnic identity" and transforming that identity when needed (n.d.:10). As Black Bear's comment that opens this chapter suggests, the prophets taught that myths express moral responsibility, frame experience, and inform the methods by which to define and engage "otherness," particularly the religious creation of social life. That is, they articulate the Odawa's ethos—the way the world should be. For Odawa traditionalists, certain myths outline ways to approach a social universe that includes ethical and unethical persons. Mythic themes highlight the ethical process of personing and the transformative power of ritual gifting, including the personal attributes of both compassion and gratitude, hostility and conflict.

A. Irving Hallowell identifies that Algonkian myths generally emphasize the following constructive behaviors: not being destructive or greedy; enduring hardships of all kinds; being self-reliant; never torturing any animal; and being an ethical contributor to the creative process (1955:361). The Odawa elder Simon Otto (1990) also stresses the themes in Odawa myths that define taboos, animal's characters and man's relation to them, the meaning of situations and how to approach and maybe change them, and specific ethics and patterns of social interaction for achieving collective *pimadaziwin*. Certain of the Odawa's myths also illustrate that the world changes and that the Odawa's place in it is not the product of one person's intentionality; instead, the ethical Great Persons of mythology pool their resources for empowerment. This mythic theme of cooperation has several levels of meaning: it articulates a theory of empowerment, it underscores the importance of maintaining ritual relations between the living and the dead, and it pinpoints processes for mediating differences that disrupt social unity and identity.

Myths illustrate an assumption that conflict continually threatens balance in the universe. To get a better grasp of these Odawa traditionalists' understanding, Mary Black's (1990) analysis of the Ojibwe is again suggestive. Examining the taxonomic structure implicit in Hallowell's reconstruction of Ojibwe worldview, she finds that the system itself shapes ethical and behavioral uncertainty. Applying Black's insights to Odawa myths, we can begin to see that within the Odawa traditionalists' ethos, the world continually is affected both by constructive and destructive actions. One example of this ever-present ambiguity of purpose is Nanabozho, who is both trickster and culture hero. Exemplifying the two extremes of potential behavior, Nanabozho presents a central dilemma of human affairs, namely, the hostility, competition, and resistance that others threaten. The agents in society include ethical Great Persons and "monsters," as well as those who, like Nanabozho, express the empowerment of transforming from negative to positive actions. Nanabozho learns by trial and error, which in itself is not evil but ultimately empowering, and he exemplifies the category personing.

Already from the last chapter we have begun to surmise that the Odawa use the term *manido*, meaning "power person," as a qualitative adjective for measuring ethical and unethical characteristics. All persons are powerful agents in society, but some act with malevolent instead of benevolent purposes. *Ki-je*, meaning "great" or "large," is a prefix added to the names of many persons and places in myth. For example, Ki-je Manido (literally, "great power person") is the center from which everything is comprehended ethically in both a quantitative and qualitative sense. Brown Otter explained his understanding of Ki-je Manido; looking at a stained glass window, he said:

> I suppose you look at this in Christian terms, with the red circle in the middle meaning your god. But I see it differently. The red center is the concentration of power; it gives us a focus. This is how we understand Ki-je Manido, "Grandfather." Radiating out from this center creates a circle that unites all things—A-ki [Earth], Mishomis [Sky/Sun], Nokomis [Moon], and all Odawa, including our ancestors.

This is what I mean when I say that I go out in the yard in the morning and lay down tobacco and pray. I'm not praying to Ki-je Manido like Christians say they pray to Jesus or their god. I'm really praying to know how to wisely use the knowledge of this powerful connection and my place in it.

Although an almost reversed cosmography from that described by Lone Wolf (in chapter 3), this description suggests that purposeful acts of benevolence powerfully create ever-expanding relationships. Therefore Brown Otter's interchanging Ki-je Manido with the kin term "grandfather" is an expression of the traditionalists' personalistic and relational worldview. Here we must appreciate that Ki-je Manido in the full connotative sense cannot be equated with "god" in the deistic/theistic sense of Judeo-Christian tradition.

Brown Otter's remarks imply that we can understand Ki-je Manido as pointing to the holistic possibilities and the powerful transformative potential of acting for benevolent purposes. In opposition to Ki-je Manido is Mo-je Manido, *Mo-je* being a prefix denoting *de*centering adversity, competition, and opposition. Mo-je Manido, often imaged as the great underwater power being who threatens existence by creating storms, refers to the holistic possibilities and potential of malevolent acts. To counter such unethical purposes, Ki-je Manido acts in consultation with Nanabozho and other ethical Great Persons. Together, they all map the goal of Odawa ritual action. Ritual cooperation, as mythically mapped, sets the precedent for such traditional social structures as councils, which as political institutions seek consensus and as social institutions seek collective unity and identity. This dual purpose of ritual cooperation is suggested in the following account taken from the Lake Superior Ojibwe (see Miller 1972).

In 1885, because the federal government had not upheld prior treaty agreements, a council meeting was held between the principal Algonkian leaders and U.S. government officials. The Ojibwe Indian agent William Warren, a métis (i.e., half Indian, half French), acted as interpreter. Translating a U.S. official's question, Warren asked who was the hereditary "chief." In answer, an old elder and Midéwiwin member, Tug-waug-aun-ay, relayed this story. His response was perhaps prompted by his thinking that the question was somewhat absurd because it

overlooked the reality of the ever-expanding spectrum of ancestors
and "relatives."

> Kitchi Manitou [Ki-je Manido] once made a bird, and he sent it
> from the skies to make its abode on earth. The bird came, and when
> it reached halfway down, among the clouds, it sent forth a loud and
> far cry, which was heard by all who resided on the earth, and even
> by the spirits who make their abode in its bosom. When the bird
> reached within sight of the earth, it circled slowly above the Great
> Fresh Waters, and again it uttered its echoing cry. Nearer and nearer
> it circled, looking for a resting place, till it lit on a hill overlooking
> Boweting (Sault Ste. Marie); here it chose its first resting place,
> pleased with the many white fish that glanced and swam in the
> clear waters and sparkling foam of the rapids. Satisfied with its
> chosen seat, again the bird sent forth its loud but solitary cry; and
> the No-kaig (Bear clan), A-waus-e-wug (Catfish clan), Ah-auh-
> wauh-ug (Loon clan), and Mous-o-neeg (Moose and Martin clan)
> gathered at his call. A large town was soon congregated, and the
> bird who [Ki-je Manido] sent presided over all. Again, it took its
> flight, and the bird flew slowly over the waters of Lake Superior.
> Pleased with the sand point of Shaug-ah-waum-ik-ong, it circled
> over it, and viewed the many fish as they swam in the clear depths
> of the Great Lake. It lit on Shaug-ah-waum-ik-ong, and from there
> again it uttered its solitary cry. A voice came from the calm bosom
> of the lake in answer; the bird, pleased with the musical sound of
> the voice, again sent forth its cry, and the answering bird made its
> appearance in the wampum-breasted Ah-auh-wauh (Loon). The
> bird spoke with it in a gentle tone, "Is it you that answers my cry?"
> The Loon answered, "It is." The bird then said to him, "Your voice
> is music—it is melody—it sounds sweet to my ear, from now on I
> appoint you to answer my voice in council." So, Loon became the
> first in council, but he who made him chief was Bus-in-aus-e (Echo
> Maker), or Crane. (quoted in Warren 1885:86–88)

This story stresses three purposes. First, cooperative interactions
create social relationships and identity. Second, there are constructive ways to address others whose actions are socially disruptive.
And third, social identity and power derive from consensus.

   By considering a set of myths in relation to an Odawa history
of socially disruptive events, we can see how mythically mapped
acts of consensual cooperation show how to address others whose

hostile and competitive purposes threaten social disunity, and how such constructive interactions transform the situation and maintain social solidarity and identity.

Addressing "Otherness"

Some of the following myths derive from neighboring Ojibwe people, with whom the Odawa long have had contact. These well-known narratives are often included in the oral storytelling repertoire of Odawa traditionalists today. Our purpose here is neither to establish a mythological compendium nor to analyze any transformations. Instead, the intent is to examine general thematic trends for what they articulate about the enduring yet adaptive character of Odawa religious theory, particularly as it informs the traditionalists' current revitalization movement. These select narratives show the value of mediating interpersonal distance and outline constructive methods for overcoming dangerous others. While they have many more functions, the important one I want to explore here is that of mediation as it lessons the conflict created by others whose behavior suggests questionable intentions.

From the earliest documented myths that I have isolated to the contemporary versions recounted to me, we can delineate five general themes that have parallels with the transformative events that have occurred throughout the Odawa's historical experience. The first is the general theme of *food and the threat of not having it*, which parallels the tension between their traditional subsistence pattern of seasonal rounds and the postcontact experience of socioeconomic disruption and loss of land. This theme is expressed through a duality of references to fish, animals/game, birds/fowl/ducks, and flowers/herbs/plants in contrast to starvation, famine, drought, and floods. The availability of food obviously is uncertain. The food supply and therefore human existence are periodically threatened not by abstract events but by persons, especially those who withhold. Anger and death, particularly resulting from lack of food and most poignantly imaged by Mo-je Manido, also threaten existence.

Second is the general theme of *time and change*, expressed as daily and seasonal cycles that parallel traditional shifts in social organization and the experience of cultural changes, with their concomitant threats to traditional meaning and identity. The theme of winter, for instance, is imaged by references to cold, ice, freezing, north, and old. Conversely, the theme of spring includes images of warmth, growth, south, and youth. The theme of night, including dark, contrasts sharply with images of day, including light. Winter submits to spring, however, just as night surrenders to day. These mythic themes acknowledge both the cycle of life and the changes within that cycle; more important, they articulate the possibility that change can be either positive or negative. These myths also clarify that although the cycle itself does not change, the condition of the stage in the cycle changes. They underscore, moreover, that the moment of change is not always a comfortable one.

Third is the theme of *transformation*, which parallels the experiences of threats to identity and ways to overcome them, especially as informed by the prophets. Transformation myths do not suggest that the characteristic of life itself can change. Rather, their intent is to show how the periodic changes in the cycle of life processes can be influenced for good or ill, for benevolence (by Ki-je Manido or Nanabozho, for example) or malevolence (by Mo-je Manido), by a person's response to events. A related theme, that of giving as the medium for transforming the direction of change, models a constructive response to the seeming obstacles created by another person's hostility.

The fourth general theme underscores the reality that a *duality exists between ethical and unethical persons*; this theme parallels the experience of relational conflicts with other Indians and especially with the British and the Americans. Ethical persons are distinguished by the attributes of sharing, generosity, and compassion. Others who do not possess these personal qualities are particularly dangerous, as they threaten to disrupt an orderly existence. The ethical models for behavior are displayed in two ways: first, in the behavior of the Great Persons of mythology, and second, in the ways in which the Great Persons are pitted against others who threaten danger. The human person may apply to his or her life the models for behavior mapped by the acts of the Great Persons of mythology by affirming the ethical principles associated with gifting.

Identifying the theme of constructive adjustment suggests how the ethical principle of gifting informs the fifth theme: *the moral responsibility to engage in and uphold interpersonal relationships on the social, environmental, and ancestral planes*; this theme parallels the experience of social disruption caused by lack of gift exchange, especially with the British, and even more so the U.S. government's withholding treaty stipulations. These ethically based interpersonal bonds are perpetuated through the moral empowerment contained in the ritual act of gifting. Certain Odawa myths highlight the interconnected ethics associated with *pimadaziwin*, the interconnected ethics that we have been calling personing, gifting, and empowering. These myths voice the theoretical means of promoting the cohesion of the total environment, especially the solidarity of the social sphere that derives from the animate, relational, and transformative nature of the Odawa world.

For Odawa traditionalists, myths articulate the distinction between those who do not behave properly and those who do. They also focus on ways to mediate threats to balanced interpersonal relationships. Consequently, myths link the ethics of moral personhood with the empowerment contained in the moral gift of ritual in order to address "otherness." Odawa traditionalists especially understand that certain myths highlight a personal and communal duty to uphold the integrity of a living and acting cosmos and one's place in it.

Place and Cosmos

We can begin to understand the ethical lessons that inform the traditionalists' understanding of the cosmos and their place in it by considering an account of the creative and transformative power of cooperative interactions, first documented by Nicholas Perrot, a French explorer to the Great Lakes region. Perrot's accounts are from the late seventeenth and early eighteenth centuries, a period that roughly parallels the transition between the French Jesuit and fur trade experience and British colonialism (quoted in Blair 1911:31–40). One account, which is somewhat different from Gray Squirrel's contemporary version of an origin myth, describes a stage before the existence of A-ki, the earth, when there was only water and in which creation is dependent on the earth diver's compassion and personal ability.

According to Perrot, on the "vast extent of water floated a great wooden raft [*cajeux*], upon which were all the animals, of various kinds, which exist on the earth; and the chief of these . . . was the Great Hare" (quoted in Blair 1911:31–32). Great Hare, who is the Master of Game (and generally regarded as one form that Nanabozho takes), searched far and wide for a solid place on which to land but could find none. Finally, disenchanted, he appealed to Beaver to dive to the bottom of the sea and bring up a piece of sand. Great Hare told Beaver that he could create land, and therefore food for all, from only one grain. Beaver first balked at this request, but with the entreaties of the other animals he finally conceded. Down went Beaver, but he was gone for so long that all on the raft were certain he had drowned. Finally, Beaver floated to the top of the water, motionless. All the others came forth to haul him back aboard and examine his paws: nothing. With Beaver's failed mission, Great Hare appealed to Otter. Otter readily agreed to the challenge. Gone longer than Beaver, Otter finally emerged in a similar condition and equally unsuccessful. The animals became desperate for a concrete place to live. Quite unexpectedly, Muskrat volunteered his service, but to the mocking of the others, as he was not much revered for either strength or bravery. Gallantly, he dived off the raft and was gone for a very long time. Suddenly he emerged, belly up, with his feet tightly clenched. Bringing him aboard, the animals examined his paws and found one grain of sand.

This earth diver theme, repeated frequently in various myths, illustrates the creative power of renewal. Working in ethical cooperation with other Great Persons of mythology, the earth diver is a transformer.

Perrot's account continues: "The Great Hare, who had promised to form a broad and spacious land, took the grain of sand, and let it fall upon the raft, when it began to increase" (quoted in Blair 1911:35). Great Hare began to scatter the growing land about, which made it increase more. Great Hare then asked Fox to go about the land and see if it was now large enough. Fox reported that it was—after assessing that it was sufficiently large to guarantee his own supply of food. But Great Hare took his own survey and found Fox had been selfish and greedy in his assessment. Because of Fox's improper behavior, Great Hare perpetually regenerates the earth to insure the livelihood of all beings.

After the creation of land and the animals, including fish, all beings found their proper niche. But as some were predators and others prey, soon the first animal beings began to die. Great Hare then intervened and transformed the corpses of the dead animals into various types of persons, human and animal. Different groups of Indian peoples, in their association with clan *dodems*, still look to these original animal persons as their first relatives.

Similar accounts confirm that the ethical Great Persons of mythology support proper behavior and illustrate the cosmic consequences of ethical transgressions. An Ojibwe elder and tribal historian, Basil Johnston, documented another earth diver account about two hundred years after Perrot's. In it, Johnston underscores that the world is not stagnant but has been transformed a number of times—created, destroyed, and recreated—as a result of personal actions. The world's genesis began when Ki-je Manido (Johnston uses the Ojibwe appellation Kitchi Manitou) had a visionary message not only of the beginning, growth, and end of all things but also of their perpetuation (much as the prophets did in their visions). "Amidst change there was constancy." Having to make his message realized, Ki-je Manido made rock, water, fire, wind, mountains, valleys, plains, islands, lakes, bays, and rivers, and breathed into them "the breath of life." Then he made the plant beings and after them the animals. Lastly, he made people and gave them "the greatest gift—the power to dream." But suddenly all went awry and disaster hit. A great flood made by Mo-je Manido followed until the mountains were covered with water. "All that was left was one vast sea. All men died," as did all plant and animal beings except for the birds and fishes, and "the world remained a sea for many generations" (Johnston 1976:12, 13). Finally, the rain stopped and Mishomis (Sun) emerged.

"High in the heavens there lived alone a woman, a spirit. Without a companion she grew despondent. In her solitude she asked Kitchi Manitou [Ki-je Manido] for some means to dispel her loneliness. Taking compassion on the sky-woman, Kitchi Manitou sent a spirit to become her consort." Sky Woman and her consort were happy, and soon she conceived; but before she gave birth, her consort left her. She gave birth to two children alone, "one pure spirit, and the other pure physical being," two siblings of "opposite natures and substances [who] hated one another" (which suggests a thematic tradition of the Good versus Bad Twin symbology; Johnston 1976:13). They engaged in a great battle that ended with each destroying the other. Again, feeling compassion for her loneliness, Ki-je Manido sent another companion, and Sky Woman soon conceived once more, only to have this partner leave her.

The benevolent water beings saw all that had happened and felt compassion for Sky Woman. "In their compassion . . . they persuaded a giant turtle to rise to the surface of the waters and offer his back as a haven." Sky Woman came down from the heavens and then asked the water beings to bring up ground from the bottom of the sea. Beaver volunteered first, dived deep, but came up exhausted and empty handed. Then Marten tried, but to the same avail. Loon, too, tried, but without results. Finally, Muskrat stepped forward. All the animal beings laughed because in comparison to the others they thought him so weak. Yet he set upon his mission with great perseverance despite their scorn. Long, long he was gone, and there was no sign of him. Finally, he floated to the surface "more dead than alive." His paws were clenched tightly, and in one he had a small bit of ground. The animal beings then realized the impropriety of their low estimation of Muskrat and restored him to health (*midéwiwin*). While they were reviving him, Sky Woman edged Turtle's back with the soil Muskrat had brought and "breathed upon it and into it the breath of life" (Johnston 1976:14). The soil grew to be a great island called Ki-je Makinaak, "great turtle island" (which harks back to Gray Squirrel's version of the myth of origins that opened chapter 3).

The day came for Sky Woman again to give birth. Once more she produced twins, but this time a boy and a girl. "The new beings were unlike her first children who had destroyed one another. They were composite in nature . . . at the same time they encompassed vast differences. Although they were different, they tended toward union." Together they had purpose and meaning and thus the "cycle was complete; creation, destruction, and recreation." They became the Anishinabeg. Their first winter was very harsh, however, so Great Medicine Bear (Ki-je Midéwiwi Makwa), fearing their death, sacrificed himself to them. From then on, the animal beings gave themselves for the survival of the Anishinabeg. "Men and women survive and live because of the death of their elder brothers" (Johnston 1976:15, 16).

One day, when Sky Woman was sure of her offsprings' survival, she called them to her and told them that she was going back to her original place. "She also told them that when they had lived out their term of life and had done sufficient good in life, they too would leave their bodies in the Land of the Living and go to the Land of Peace as soul-spirits, and live there in another way." She left them but is recalled by the people as Nokomis ("Grandmother" Moon). The Anishinabeg flourished, but their success did not last—disease suddenly threatened to wipe them out. Nokomis could not help. "For their disease there was no medicine; from this affliction, no escape or relief was possible. Many died. Fear and sadness prevailed" (Johnston 1976:16, 17). Their only chance for survival was to have a teacher come to them who would show the Anishinabeg the proper way to live. This teacher finally appeared among the people as Nanabozho (Nanabush, in Ojibwe), the great culture hero.

A nineteenth-century account of the origin of First Man and First Woman by the German ethnographer Johann Kohl, who lived in the Great Lakes area among the Ojibwe, suggests a thematic shift despite Johnston's seeming retention. It is no longer earth divers acting cooperatively with Great Hare, Nokomis, or Ki-je Manido who are the creative force. Ki-je Manido, here called "The Good Spirit," acts alone to make the land by scattering little roots (Kohl 1860:195–204). The animals, birds, and fish are already existent, and they move to this new land, to which Ki-je Manido adds something every day. Although this account has no explanation for the creation of either more-than-human persons or First Man, it does give us insight into the events happening at the time Kohl was living among the Ojibwe. Most importantly, it implies the tension created by the Algonkians' attempts to appear "civilized" in the eyes of the white world to avoid forced removal and reservationism, especially by adopting agriculture as the primary subsistence mode (which reflects on The Trout's purpose in claiming to be the "First Man"; see chapter 2).

According to Kohl's account, Ki-je Manido encountered First Man one day while walking the beach; a lone being who could not speak, he was covered with shiny fishlike scales for protection but otherwise looked like a human person. "The sight moved Kitchi Manitou [Ki-je Manido] with compassion to the highest degree," and he set out to create a woman to be the man's wife. It was the woman, Mani (a name Kohl equates with Mary [1860:196]), whom Ki-je Manido created. When the two people met, both suddenly could speak, and Ki-je Manido took them off to live on his island in a "house with glass windows" and a fine garden (Kohl 1860: 197). However, Ki-je Manido warned them of a tree in the garden that would bear tempting fruit but that they must not eat, because "Matchi-Manitou," [Mo-je Manido], the Evil Spirit, had planted it. Nevertheless, first Mani and then her husband succumbed to temptation. Suddenly, all but twenty of the protective scales—ten on the hands and ten on the feet—fell off, and they found themselves totally vulnerable. Ki-je Manido announced that because they behaved improperly it was now necessary for people to die.

Despite the apparent Christian influence, especially the story of Adam and Eve, this narrative provides clear evidence of the "personalizing" of evil (see Dowd 1992). The story carries on the traditional themes of sociocosmic disruption caused by interpersonal opposition and the consequences of improper behavior. It suggests that for the Odawa to have adopted agriculture for the "wrong" reason, to appear "civilized" to whites, their identity changed and their culture was disrupted.

Henry Schoolcraft, an Indian agent at Mackinac, collected a nineteenth-century account of the "birth" of place, Mackinac (Turtle) Island, that illustrates the consequences of social disruption (retold in Gringhuis 1970). Ki-je Manido made the Great Turtle Island and lived there alone. "Here . . . also were buried the dead chiefs and their families that they might be forever under his protection. Most believed the island was created for this very purpose." Ki-je Manido gave the people bountiful supplies of fish and game, the council leaders the power of speech, and the warriors strength. "But one day the white man came. Then, seeing the harm wrought upon his people," the disease, corruption and social disruption, Ki-je Manido "fled in anger and sorrow to the frozen north as the caribou had done before him, to live forever in the flickering flames of the Northern Lights" (Gringhuis 1970:1, 2). Ki-je Manido left because the people had succumbed to doing things in a new and different way, and the world was forever changed.

Two other myths documented by Schoolcraft in a period that roughly parallels the 1836 and 1855 treaty experiences suggest how the conflict between compassionate giving and withholding is a map for guiding behavior. Schoolcraft's account "Peboan and Sheegwun: An Allegory of Winter and Spring" focuses on the tension created by powerfully benevolent versus powerfully malevolent acts (Schoolcraft 1856:86–87). In this account, a wintry old man opposes a youth of spring, and they compete to test their powers, especially through acts of breathing. Peboan, an old man who thrives in winter with no fire and makes winter storms, threatens the food supply. He makes rivers freeze and forces the animals and birds to migrate. Countering Peboan's destructive intent, the youth, Sheegwun, ensures the food supply with the coming of spring when he makes the streams thaw, the plants grow, and the game return. The winter/spring dualism in this myth reflects a central awareness that persons with opposing intentions are part of the world.

Schoolcraft's narrative "Shingebiss: An Allegory of Self-Reliance" speaks to the potential consequences of people's opposing purposes (Schoolcraft 1856:98–100; also in Bemister 1912:26–28 with few differences). It also highlights the individual's obligation to act with ingenuity and persistence for survival. The myth focuses on a duck who resourcefully overcomes the threat of winter starvation. Kabebonicca, the Northwest, was envious of Shingebiss's hardiness and fearlessness. Kabebonicca threatened: "I will try whether he cannot be mastered" and whether his fire—power—could be put out. He made the severest cold and wind, but Shingebiss was undaunted and his fire continued to burn brightly. Miffed, Kabebonicca decided to go to Shingebiss's lodge and snuff him out. Shingebiss, the ethical hunter because he took only as many fish as he needed to survive, was aware of his visitor but paid him no attention. He cooked and ate his fish, then lay on his side by the fire singing the power song he had gained in a vision. In Schoolcraft's rather romanticized rendition, this song goes:

> Windy god, I know your plan,
> you are but my fellow man;
> blow may you your coldest breeze,
> Shingebiss you cannot freeze.
> Sweep the strongest wind you can,
> Shingebiss is still your man;
> heigh! for life—and ho! for bliss,
> who so free as Shingebiss?

With his power song, Shingebis underscored his personal sovereignty, and his resiliency and persistence in living a good life—*pimadaziwin*. Finally, Shingebis rose to poke his fire, which made it burn more intensely. Soon tears flowed so profusely down Kabebonicca's cheeks that he cried, "'I cannot stand this—I must go out.' At last, Kabebonicca was compelled to give up the contest [saying] 'He must be aided by some Monedo [*manido*]. . . . I can neither freeze him nor starve him; he is a very singular being—I will let him alone'" (Schoolcraft 1856:98, 99, 100). This myth highlights how personal effort is part of the paradigm for proper ethical behavior.

The ethnographer Frances Densmore's more recent account describes the First Earth, called Ca'ca, in which it is also the case that people already were in existence, but were ignorant and lazy. "Then the spirit of the creator sent a man to teach them." Ockabe'wis, the Messenger, went to the northern land, where the people suffered, naked and homeless. When the Messenger asked them why they sat naked doing nothing, they replied that it was because they did not know what else to do. So Ockabe'wis began to teach them the right way to live. He first showed them how to make and use fire. Then he taught them how to build wisdom and empowerment by fasting and through visions. The people were instructed to "regulate their lives by dreams . . . [and to] live moral lives . . . they were especially taught that their minds would not be clear if they ate and drank too much" (Densmore 1929:98).

Living a moral life, *pimadaziwin*, meant overcoming obstacles and temptations, especially those associated with Euro-Americans, with constructive persistence.

Myths I have heard at communal gatherings add new material to this ethnographic literature and address ways to counter the threat caused by persons whose actions oppose one's own, and one's group's, moral intentions. One myth, called "The Medicine Tree," identifies the problem of interpersonal disagreement and presents the means of countering it. This version of the myth, which I heard at an Odawa elders' council, highlights sociocosmic interdependence.

> Now, you must keep in mind that the world is very complex. It's made up of four layers: the vault of the heavens; the sky, which is a combination of Mishomis (Sun) and Nokomis (Moon); A-ki (Earth); and the underworld. But Ki-je Manido couldn't watch over four separate worlds—that would be too much. It would be bad if they all didn't get along. For example, once Mishomis decided not to come down to A-ki. It was a very bad situation because if Mishomis stayed away too long, everything would stop growing. So Ki-je Manido made a giant cedar tree and planted it in the center of the world. Its roots grew deep into the ground, but the tips of the branches grew so high that they pierced the sky so that Mishomis had to reach down to A-ki. Ki-je Manido named this tree Ki-je Gishik, which means both "great red cedar" and "great day." He then told the people that if they guarded this *manido*, Ki-je Gishik, it would be a powerful guide to keep them together.

Great Elk explained that this story really is about the creative potential of confrontations between those who behave cooperatively and others who do not, especially those who withhold or compete. He also implied that such disagreements can be resolved by the reciprocal giving of both parties when he remarked: "If Mishomis withheld his power forever, A-ki would die. So Ki-je Manido had to step in and give Ki-je Gishik, who made everyone and everything work together." Here we see clearly the conviction of Odawa traditionalists such as Great Elk that giving has the power to foster constructive interdependence and produce *pimadaziwin*.

Life-Sustaining *Pimadaziwin*: The Road of Life

Two elders and Midéwiwin members, Gagewin and Main'gans, explained to Frances Densmore how they understood their specific responsibility to contribute to collective *pimadaziwin* (Densmore 1929:86–95). They stressed their personal duty to uphold these interconnected ethics: that acts of ethical compassion oppose the hostility that others threaten, and that passing on their knowledge empowers others. Paraphrasing, Gagewin said that his moral responsibility was to preserve the knowledge of right living and herbal medicine used to prolong life. This life-giving wisdom originally was distributed to the elders through the *manido* Great Medicine Bear, who wandered around the earth for a very long time spreading the message of the path to *pimadaziwin*.

Main'gans described not only the moral actions that one must make to walk the Path of Life carved by Medicine Bear but also the great difficulty of doing so. He said that on the Path of Life from youth to old age there were seven side roads that were tests of one's character. The first test or side road lures youths, and if they divert from the Right Path, they soon die. The second test soon appears, which threatens the same result if people stray. The third test, if surpassed, establishes "religious responsibility." The fourth test happens in midlife, in which one is charged with upholding life-giving and life-sustaining *pimadaziwin*. The fifth test calls for each to assess his life and the integrity of his behavior. The sixth test is whether "all religious obligations have been fulfilled." With the seventh and greatest test "an evil spirit" confronts the person "and if he has even so much as smiled during a [healing] ceremony, he must reckon with it then" (Densmore 1929:89).

Other accounts provide further evidence of the life-giving actions needed to achieve *pimadaziwin*. These also report how Medicine Bear traveled over the earth with the Pack [or Bundle] of Life, which he was enjoined to carry by the many benevolent *manidos* along the Path of Life (see, e.g., Landes 1968:95–108). Medicine Bear was charged with the ethical duty to spread the gift of healing and empowerment throughout the world because the people complained of a problem: they appealed for guidance in

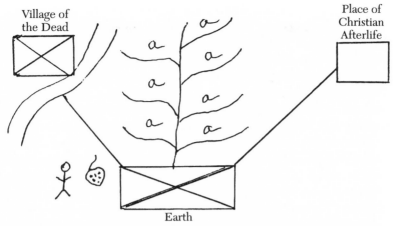

Figure 4.1. The Path of Souls to the Village of the Dead

addressing illness and death, in confronting the disruptive cultural incursion associated with following Euro-American ways, and in regaining *pimadaziwin.*

One version of the tradition of the Path of Souls, a path leading to the Village of the Dead, stresses interpersonal obligation and survival, especially the obligations of the living toward the dead (Kohl 1860:214–17). The myth illustrates that the deceased paradoxically are "alive" and call for a constructive interdependence with the living. When Johann Kohl asked how the Ojibwe understood the Path of Souls, an elder answered by using a map as a mnemonic device (illustrated in figure 4.1). In the center of this map, at the bottom, is the earth: a rectangle crossed with an X. From the center top of this rectangle leads a long straight road, the Right Path (the Path of Life), but with many side paths branching off. From the right upper corner of the rectangle a diagonal road leads to another rectangle: the Christian paradise, where no Indians can go. From the upper left corner of the rectangle runs another diagonal road, the Path of Souls, alongside which lies a giant strawberry guarded by a man who tempts people to eat it. If they do so, their souls are lost. Suddenly, the

Path of Souls stops at a large river. Partway across the river, from the opposite bank, lies a log, but it does not reach all the way to the near side. People must jump across, and if they fail they turn into toads or fishes. This leap is hard especially for children and old people, so the living must help them by not binding them in any way, and by honoring them during their four-day journey. Across this river and connected to the log is another rectangle crossed with an X: the Village of the Dead.

Another account by Kohl records that Wakwi, the Village of the Dead, was made by Nanabozho, who had aided Ki-je Manido in creating the world (1860:216). Neither Nanabozho nor Ki-je Manido had thought of the need for any other place where persons might go. "Men, such was their decree, should be happy on this earth, and find a satisfaction in this life" (Kohl 1860:216). But Mo-je Manido intervened and caused evil, disease, and death. When Ki-je Manido saw this devastation and the dead wandering hopelessly, he had compassion for them. So he enjoined Nanabozho to make for them a paradise in the west, and to teach people to help their relatives make the journey successfully. Thus *pimadaziwin* extends to the ancestors through ritual obligations first shown by Nanabozho.

Two other examples of the life-sustaining intent of *pimadaziwin* are documented; the first by the Michigan historian John Wright (1917:18–19), and the second by the Ojibwe historian William Warren (1885). The first myth highlights the life-perpetuating purpose of *pimadaziwin*. Once, Earth and Sky were connected by a great vine down which "spiritual beings could descend." Humans, however, were forbidden to ascend. One day a youth, delirious from illness, climbed the vine, and his mother started after him to bring him back. Together their weight was too much, and the vine crashed down. Then Ki-je Manido was angry with the Anishinabeg and told them: "Now . . . sickness and disease will prevail amongst you, and instead of living forever you will die when you grow old. There is only one thing left for you to do. Remember that everything that grows has some value—nothing was made in vain. Therefore you will gather roots and herbs and compound medicines and these will help you when in distress" (Wright 1917:18). This version suggests not only that existence for the living is more difficult than for the dead but also that rules for behavior exist for both classes of beings.

The second myth is an account by an elder, who explained that "our forefathers, many strings of lives ago, lived on the shores of the Great Salt Water in the East. Here . . . while they were suffering the ravages of sickness and death, the Great Spirit, at the intercession of Nanabush [Nanabozho], the great common uncle of the An-ish-in-aub-ag, granted them [a] rite wherewith life is restored and prolonged" (Warren 1885:79). The intent to restore and prolong life (*midéwiwin*) is to uphold *pimadaziwin*; thus its life-sustaining ethic was established by Nanabozho.

Still other accounts focus on the powerful gifts of healing and life, given by the ethical Great Persons of mythology, that elders are charged with ritually upholding to benefit the community. These myths illustrate how "considerate social relations could begin the process of healing" (Dewdney 1975:22): the acts that empower the collective. As the next chapter shows, it is Nana-bozho, as the Great Transformer, who sets the stage for acts of constructive interdependence to create social solidarity and over-come "illness;" that is, to achieve *pimadaziwin* on a collective level.

Conclusion

The myths we have reviewed here concerning the cosmos and one's role in it suggest that the Odawa, like other Algonkians in the Great Lakes area, are less concerned with the creation than with their place in it, and that they focus on their role in upholding an orderly existence, especially *pimadaziwin*. This issue of place in religious theory and practice allows each individual to be ethically person-alized (i.e., the process of personing). Although Euro-Americans, especially with the introduction of Christianity, created a tension between tradition and a new way to do things, some narratives concerned with Great Persons of mythology and their narrative transformation into godlike language (especially Ki-je Manido) show that some Odawa entertained the possibility of Christian truth claims. Instead of replacing their old system, however, they simply added another layer to it: the purpose of some myths to map how cooperative actions overcome tensions in human relations. At least certain myth "texts," like those concerning

Ki-je Manido, suggest that some Odawa approached the sociocosmos in innovative ways "to account for the great persons of Christianity" (Morrison n.d.:23). *Pimadaziwin* still could be achieved even in a changed social world. Echoing the moral challenge of responding constructively to historical changes resulting from a causal "who," these myths articulate the Odawa traditionalists' conviction that the Great Persons of mythology gave them a religious system that works: the proper course of action—upholding *pimadaziwin*—is life giving and life sustaining. The Great Persons show them how to transform themselves and others—as we will see in the myths of Nanabozho in the next chapter and especially the myth of the Seventh Fire in Chapter Six.

Chapter 5

Nanabozho
The Great Transformer

The times are exceedingly altered, yea the times are turned upside down; or rather we have changed the good times, chiefly by the help of the White people.

Mohegan leader to the Connecticut Assembly (1789)

By trial and error Nanabozho learns that benevolent actions effectively counter the disruptions caused by others. Through this learning process he transforms from trickster into culture hero, so establishing himself as an ethical Great Person—the exemplar of personing. Becoming a culture hero and ethical Great Person, Nanabozho is the Great Transformer—the model of humane responsibility and of each individual's potential to engage the ethic of personing successfully. The intent of this chapter is not to examine his trickster aspect but to show the lesson of Nanabozho's life that one can outgrow or overcome childish behavior and learn to act wisely and with maturity. That is, through his own personal transformation Nanabozho illustrates not only that persons do not always behave with constructive purposes but also that powerful personal and social metamorphosis is possible if each person acts to contribute to *pimadaziwin*—the good, healthy, and moral collective life.

The theme of potential disruption caused by antisocial and selfish behavior is portrayed in several accounts of Nanabozho that were told to me. Old Woman, for example, tells us something about Nanabozho's unethical character as a youth, when, having an insatiable appetite, he steals the Indians' dinner for himself but ultimately suffers for it.

The people had gone to a great deal of trouble and effort to catch ducks to eat. They made a big pit fire and put the ducks in to cook, covering them over with sand so that only their legs stuck out. While the ducks were cooking, the people went out to gather berries. Along came Nanabozho, who thought "Yum—ducks for dinner, and they're already cooked." After eating all of the ducks, Nanabozho felt very tired and fell asleep beside the fire. Suddenly he woke up with a start, realizing that his backside was on fire. Getting up, he ran through the sumac bushes to put the fire out, but he was so burned that his bloody skin turned the bushes red.

The consequences of selfish and greedy misbehavior also are addressed in the accounts of how the young Nanabozho gave Chipmunk his stripes and why maple sap has to be cooked to make sugar or syrup, which I heard at elders' councils.

Chipmunk would tease and tease Nanabozho endlessly. So one day, having tired of this continual taunting, Nanabozho decided to teach him a lesson. Reaching out to grab Chipmunk with his long fingernails, Nanabozho scratched him all the way down his back so that Chipmunk would always have a stripe to remember.

...

In the Old Days, the ancestors only had to go up to a sugar tree and make a hole in it and out would come maple syrup. Nanabozho watched this for a long time and one day decided that the people had it too easy. "They should have to work harder for their food than that," he thought. So Nanabozho climbed up into the Great Maple and pissed into it. Ever since, we've had to boil the sap to make sugar.

The elders who told these stories stressed several ethical principles. People should not be greedy and steal from others. They must always give something in return for a gift given. Chipmunk was punished by Nanabozho for misbehaving, but in his own way, Nanabozho was cruel, which is a behavioral transgression. And Nanabozho enacted the reality of life's tribulations and the continual threat of change.

Despite Nanabozho's ethical shortcomings early in life, the elders underscored that his most significant act after his personal transformation from immoral immaturity to ethical maturity was to teach living persons the moral gift of ritual. It is worth repeating two myths from the last chapter concerning Nanabozho as the Great Transformer who, through his own actions and initiative, makes himself a virtuous agent in society. The first is Johann Kohl's nineteenth-century account of the formation of the Village of the Dead. Paraphrasing:

> Nanabozho helped Ki-je Manido create the world, but neither anticipated a need for any other place for people to go, as all were supposed to be happy and satisfied with life on earth. But Mo-je Manido intervened, producing disease, misery, and death. Witnessing the destruction and the dead wandering helplessly, Ki-je Manido and Nanabozho felt compassion. Nanabozho made a place in the west for them to go and taught the living that they had a responsibility to aid their deceased relatives in getting there.

Nanabozho thus extends *pimadaziwin* to the ancestors through ritual obligations of the living toward the dead. The second myth is John Wright's documentation of an elder's account. Again paraphrasing:

> Our ancestors lived on the shores of the Great Salt Water in the east. Here they succumbed to the ravages of sickness and death. Nanabozho, the great common uncle of the Anishinabeg, intervened and gave them a ritual through which life is restored and prolonged.

The purpose of restoring and prolonging life (*midéwiwin*)—to uphold *pimadaziwin*—was established by Nanabozho. Odawa elders emphasize that the balance of the world and cultural order were a gift from Nanabozho that calls for respectful giving. They also stress how Nanabozho, as the Great Transformer acting in consultation with other mythological Great Persons, overcame such disruptive threats as misbehavior and established the precedent for ritual action to achieve collective *pimadaziwin*.

The theme of how Nanabozho constructively counters and transforms the opposing intentions of others is portrayed in an account of his being Ki-je Manido's "emissary" (Johnston 1976:17–21). In this narrative, the Ojibwe elder Basil Johnston relates that Nanabozho had a human mother and a more-than-human father: the West. When Nanabozho was born, his brothers had already left home, so he only knew their names. Soon after Nanabozho's birth, his mother died, "although some said she had been destroyed" by the West Wind. Not knowing his parents, Nanabozho was raised by his grandmother, Nokomis (Moon). While a child, he kept quizzing Nokomis about his father and mother. Finally, she told him about his mother's demise and that his father lived in the west. On learning of his father's possible betrayal of his mother, Nanabozho "decided to test his own powers and those of his father." During his journey to the west, Nanabozho heard a voice that gave him the message to beware of his father, who had great power and knew he was coming. Knowing that Father West was out to destroy Nanabozho, the voice offered counsel: "Go to the place of flint. Gather the pieces. Collect them and put them in a bag. Sharpen them; give them another force. They, in turn, will give you another power. They have within them the element of fire. It is the only substance your father fears" (Johnston 1976:17, 18).

After gathering the flint, Nanabozho at long last encountered his father and challenged the West's personal integrity on his mother's behalf. The West took offense, and soon they engaged in a great battle. The fight was not going well for Nanabozho, but he then drew out a piece of flint that he had wrapped in a pouch around his neck. With it Nanabozho slashed his father severely until the West conceded defeat. The West then said to Nanabozho: "Let us make peace. I shall remain in my place. Return to the land of the Anishinabeg. Teach them until they are strong. In this way you and your purpose will be fulfilled and you will know love. As a remembrance of our contest and peace, take this pipe; carry it with you always. It is the emblem of peace and goodwill. Give it to the Anishinabeg" (Johnston 1976:19).

They smoked the pipe together "as a symbol of reconciliation," and the West, having been transformed into an ethical person, explained the significant purpose of the ritual: "The Anishinabeg are to remember as they smoke their special relationship to and dependence upon the sun, earth, moon, and stars. Like the animal beings they depend ultimately upon the earth and sun" (Johnston 1976:21). Nanabozho departed to return to the Anishinabeg.

But Nanabozho did not know yet the extent of his powers. Soon he would learn that he could change his form and being at will: at one moment he could transform into the Great Hare, the next a man, the next a stone or plant. However, Nanabozho also learned that whatever form he took, he had to accept the limits of that being. Certain that Nanabozho understood this powerful ability to transmute but also its limits, Ki-je Manido made Nanabozho the Master of Animals, able to communicate with and transform into any one of them. He also became the teacher of the Anishinabeg, showing them how to live properly and how to use *mashkiki* ("medicine," "the power of the earth") to heal and keep people on the Right Road. So ritual relations, especially through councils and smoking the pipe, became the precedent for proper relations.

Another account, by the Michigan historian John Wright (1917: 34–35, 80–82), illustrates Nanabozho's character as the "Ottawa Wonder Worker" and highlights the benefits of his attempts to take constructive actions to transform the effects of unethical behavior, if not the miscreant. This is especially true when he asks Muskrat to dive to the bottom of the Ki-je Gan, or Great Waters, to help him form an island for people to live on. As an adult, Nanabozho becomes a great chief with much power: a wise leader "and a sage who benefitted mankind and overcame the power of evil" (Wright 1917:34). It was Nanabozho who learned that the great flood, which once destroyed the world, had been created by Mo-je Manido, who had been born a human person of some familial prestige and trained to be a great leader but who had since become a being who delighted "in torturing people." After engaging Muskrat's help in recreating the earth and all beings, Nanabozho took on Mo-je Manido as an enemy in order to protect the animal, plant, and human beings. Nanabozho called together the first great council, "and it was decided that all the warriors should turn out en masse, to get him [Mo-je Manido], dead or alive" (Wright 1917:80, 82). But Mo-je Manido escaped to the depths of the Ki-je Gan, where he still lives, and where he creates great and threatening storms.

Although "evil," or persons who act unethically, still exists in the world, Black Bear suggested at an elders' council how Nanabozho, as culture hero, acting with other Great Persons of mythology, establishes proper ritual action to maintain and govern relationships between the living and the dead:

One day, Nanabozho sought out Ki-je Manido and said, "I've been thinking. The people have a good life, but it's so good that A-ki is being overrun. Something has to be done. We must make another place for them to go after they have lived long and prospered." So Nanabozho made the Village of the Dead. Nanabozho taught the people how to help those who were to depart to the Village of the Dead follow the Path of Souls. But he also warned that along the way everyone would meet a giant strawberry that is very tempting after their long journey. It's bad, though, because Mo-je Manido stands right next to it and tries to get everyone to eat. Anyone who does immediately loses their identity and wanders around forever. For those who pass this test, there is one more challenge before they reach the Village of the Dead. They come to a large river that blocks the way except for a shaking log that looks like Mo-je Manido as a great snake and threatens to drown them because it doesn't quite reach all the way across the river. They have to jump. Those who manage successfully go to the Village of the Dead with the other ancestors, but those who fall in the river wander forever and continually remind people of their unhappiness.

This account, which is very similar to the "map" drawn for Johann Kohl in the nineteenth century and reproduced in figure 4.1, suggests the feeling of Odawa traditionalists that if people fail in their ethical duty to assist the deceased ritually, then the wandering dead can threaten the living.

Ancestors are more-than-human persons in the sense that their relationship with the living and their physical status has transformed. They are not always benevolent or even passive, and they are not always received openly. In fact, they are treated with as much fear as respect. For example, in one situation where skeletal remains of an unknown age were inadvertently disinterred from an area next to a local Odawa cemetery, Soaring Eagle was unwilling not only to touch the bones but also to have them either in his home or mine. He wanted them to stay outdoors until they could be purified and properly reburied.

It is Nanabozho who taught elders such as Soaring Eagle that living persons must help the deceased travel to the Village of the Dead and periodically reaffirm kinship bonds with them. This ethical responsibility rests on a telling fear: "If we don't take care of them, they won't take care of us," expressed Soaring Eagle.

The dangers of the Path of Souls can be overcome only through constructive aid by the living toward the dead.

During the conversations at the elders' council that followed Black Bear's story, I became aware of these traditionalists' views of Nanabozho. These narratives show how actions express personal intentions and how some beings act in threatening ways, such as Mo-je Manido (whose threats roughly parallel those posed by Euro-Americans in general). The elders especially emphasized two things: first, that the sociocosmos results from *manido* figures acting together, and second, that these cooperative efforts set the stage for Nanabozho to establish constructive interdependence as the goal of Odawa life. I began to see how Nanabozho, as a culture bringer who counters a series of dangerous and threatening beings, enjoins the Odawa with the ethical responsibility to work for the balanced life that contemporary traditionalists understand as social solidarity, including maintaining relations with the dead. It is when the benevolent dead watch over and protect the living, and vice versa, that efforts of cooperative gifting are realized. This is particularly the case in such events of remembrance as powwows and Ghost Suppers (see chapters 7 and 8).

Nanabozho's transformation into an ethical Great Person through compassionate concern for others parallels a profound world transformation. Nanabozho, like other Algonkian culture heroes (and those who claim such status, as did The Trout and Tenskwatawa), "left a religious heritage of ritual acts empowering people with the responsibility for the ongoing job of maintaining and transforming the world" (Morrison n.d.:20). As the ethic of gifting dictates, by engaging and interacting with the ethical cooperation of others, Nanabozho successfully addressed problems of personal alienation, social conflict, and antisocial behavior. His personal growth and transformation stresses how moral integrity radiates outward from the actions of each ethical person (as Lone Wolf suggested in chapter 3).

Nanabozho exemplifies the ethical ways in which the Odawa face the challenge of history by offering "human beings [a] model . . . of cooperation, symbolizing as [he does] the ethics of political behavior."[1] A revealing lesson emerges from his gradual transformation from ignorance to wisdom: to act with powerful benevolence that creates solidarity is the goal of both kinship relations and relationships with foreign others. We can understand more clearly the emphasis on the ritual responsibility to act ethically as it is powerfully transformative—to apply Nanabozho's lessons, especially the power of cooperation in council—if we consider the historical context that parallels these myth "texts."

"Texts" and Contexts: Applying Nanabozho's Lessons

Odawa traditionalist leaders, drawing on the legacy of the prophets and applying the ethics inherent to Nanabozho's lessons, have approached and continue to approach new cultural forms and processes in traditional ways. Their actions reaffirm Nanabozho's lessons that power is amplified in communal discussions, and that persons and groups can work collectively to transform their status. In their history of encounters with Euro-Americans, these Odawa have reworked and applied traditional themes of ways to oppose unethical and hostile acts through powerful acts of sharing, compassion, and interpersonal cooperation—much of which harks back to Nanabozho's battle with his father, the West.

Jonathan Z. Smith (1982:36–52, 66–89) identifies the importance of establishing the cultural and historical context of a "text" in order to understand its reinterpretation as part of a modern-day strategy for revitalization. Because such reinterpretation is an adaptive strategy by which Odawa traditionalists respond to extrinsic pressures of culture change, we can better appreciate Nanabozho's role as a model for activism by looking at relatively recent events in Odawa cultural experience and memory that help establish a context for his lessons.

In the 1830s, at the height of the federal government's removal policy, Michigan Territory experienced the fastest growing population in the United States, largely from immigration of Euro-Americans. The northern bands of Odawa felt the pressures of American governmental Indian policy, both federal and local. Although some members of Odawa bands traditionally wintered within the southern part of the Michigan Territory, the impetus for the Odawa to cede land resulted from competition for subsistence resources. "Starvation and destitution were widespread [because] by 1830 the Indians were deeply in debt to the American Fur

Company and their agents. . . . The [northern bands of] Ottawa [Odawa] . . . were living in even worse poverty than their southern neighbors" (P. Mason 1978:1–2). By 1833 the economic situation was so desperate that a few Odawa bands appealed to Henry Schoolcraft, the federal Indian agent at Mackinac, to contact Washington and arrange to negotiate the sale of land. (Some of the myths that he documented during this time were discussed in the previous chapter.)

Schoolcraft's documents suggest that the initial meeting in 1833, which led to the 1836 Treaty, was based on two unrelated factors. First, the Euro-American settlement pattern in southern Michigan was so expansive that settlers were moving westward and turning north, pressuring governmental acquisition of more land traditionally occupied by the Odawa. Second, Odawa bands were taking their own initiative to sell land to the United States. In 1835 leaders of the southern bands of Odawa "approached Schoolcraft . . . regarding the sale of Indian land north of Grand River [Michigan]," the Grand River being a loose geographic demarcation between the northern and southern bands (P. Mason 1978:4). Schoolcraft hedged in acting because the leaders of the northern and southern bands of Odawa did not agree about ceding, especially because the area in question was claimed by northern Odawa bands. Although the northern bands first opposed land cessions, by November 1835 some leaders had conceded; they went to Washington "without the permission of Henry Schoolcraft" to act on their own behalf (P. Mason 1978:5, 6). Schoolcraft followed and, with other federal Indian agents, chose a "representative" delegation of Indian leaders to engage in a future meeting.

The delegation chosen was made up of both Odawa and Ojibwe leaders. This should not imply a peaceful coalition, as "it is necessary to know that there was a cleavage between the Ottawa [Odawa] and the Chippewa [Ojibwe] tribes" (P. Mason 1978:10). Conflict between these two tribes largely resulted from competition in the fur trade economy (McClurken 1988). Maybe even more divisive than conflict between the two tribes was factionalism within each of the tribes. In December 1835 "a delegation of Ottawa from the Straits [of Mackinac] area went to Washington . . . [to discuss with] the President and Secretary of War the sale of the Manito Islands [in northern Lake Michigan] and lands on the north side of the Straits" (P. Mason 1978:10). Intertribal controversy erupted again, as the Ojibwe traditionally claimed the lands at issue north of the Straits of Mackinac but allowed the Odawa to use these lands for hunting and fishing and gave them right of way on trade routes (McClurken 1988). Besides acting without intertribal agreement, the Odawa leaders acted without intratribal consensus: unanimous approval for this land cession did not exist within the northern Odawa bands.

Because of the U.S. federal policy to treat the Odawa and the Ojibwe as two distinct groups, Henry Schoolcraft told the delegation in March 1836 that "a separate proposition [will be] made to the Chippewa living north of the Straits . . . to purchase their land. In the meantime, [if] the Ottawas . . . agree to come into the Treaty and sell their lands, they would have the opportunity of communicating the same on Tuesday next previous to the proposition being made to the Chippewas. Otherwise the Government has nothing more to say on the subject of their lands" (quoted in P. Mason 1978:11–12). Schoolcraft's pronouncement was provoked by federal disagreement over how to define ownership of lands north of the Straits of Mackinac. It ignited conflict between individual Indian leaders who, like Nanabozho as a youth, acted independently and therefore improperly because they lacked intertribal, or even intratribal, council consensus.

President Andrew Jackson and the Senate received the first draft of the Treaty of Washington in March 1836. The federal legislature made several changes in the document. Article 3 was amended to state that tracts of land would be set aside for the Indians for only five years. Article 4 was amended to state that permanent reservations would not be established: instead, fourteen tracts of land would be held under U.S. federal supervision for a limit of five years. The government would hold two hundred thousand dollars in trust and pay out the interest annually for the five-year period after which the trust would be disbursed. Article 5 was amended to abolish the federal practice of treating the Odawa and Ojibwe as one nation, and to state that three hundred thousand dollars would be set aside to be administered by the federal Indian agents for the Indians to pay their debts. Article 8, which originally stated that a permanent area would be set aside for the Odawa and Ojibwe members living outside Michigan Territory, changed from "west of the Mississippi and the country between Lake Superior and the Mississippi" to "southwest of the Missouri River . . . for final settlement . . . which the United States will forever guarantee and secure said Indians" (P. Mason 1978:36). Additional amendments to clauses related to disbursements: "The payment of annuities under Articles IV, VI, and IX; the payment of claims against the Indians in Article V; and the provision for blacksmiths, interpreters, and teachers in Article VII were [also] controversial and sources of discontent among the Ottawa and Chippewa. . . . There was no question that the wish for more secure titles to land was a matter of concern and motive for the Indians . . . but equally important were financial considerations" (P. Mason 1978:3–4).

When the final treaty went before the Senate, it stated that the Odawa held tenure to the reserved lands for a period of only five years, after which either they could stay on the lands as private citizens and therefore pay taxes or move to the western reservations—both situations that threatened severely to hamper Odawa economic development. After the five-year period, Odawa leaders formally requested that George Manypenny, the federal commissioner on Indian affairs, supply information about the financial stipulations in articles 4, 6, 7, and 9 of the 1836 Treaty. Their request concluded, "We further desire a statement of our rights, and of the amount of money due us under the old Treaties made with our ancestors" (P. Mason 1978:8, 9).

The Odawa leaders had three reasons, for themselves and future generations, to negotiate the Treaty of Washington in 1836. First, they sought to reserve lands in the territory for increased agricultural production. Second, they sought to preserve hunting and fishing rights on lands in the public domain. Third, they sought to establish cash reserves for developing a commercial fishing industry in the Great Lakes in order to become competitive in the U.S. market economy. Despite negotiations, the Odawa did not receive what they asked for: instead, it turned out to be a one-sided deal. The 1836 treaty resulted in half of the land mass in the Michigan Territory—including the entire northwest quadrant of the current state, comprising the Lower and Upper Peninsulas—being transferred from Indian custodianship to the U.S. government.

Odawa claims that the U.S. government had not upheld financial agreements in the 1836 Treaty of Washington led to their negotiating the 1855 Treaty of Detroit. The need for further negotiations also stemmed from a shift in federal Indian policy resulting from the failure of the removal policy. Instead of the costly process of removal to and support of reservations, the federal government adopted a policy of allotting land parcels to individuals. The most crucial section of the 1855 treaty is the release clause in article 3:

> The Ottawa and Chippewa Indians hereby release and discharge the United States from all liability on account of former treaty stipulations, it being distinctly understood and agreed that the grants and payments hereinbefore provided for are in lieu and satisfaction of all claims, legal and equitable on the part of said Indians jointly and severally against the United States, for land, money or other things guaranteed to said tribes or either of them by the stipulations of any former treaty or treaties. (P. Mason 1978:1)

The 1855 treaty stripped the northern Odawa bands of any further collective dealings with the United States (an act consistent with a developing shift in federal policy that culminated in the Dawes or General Allotment Act of 1887, by which many contemporary Odawa received the ancestral lands on which they presently reside).

The 1855 Treaty of Detroit established the right of the Odawa to stay on individually owned and therefore taxable land. This treaty stipulated that the lands set aside by the 1836 treaty were to be divided into eighty-acre parcels, each of which would be deeded first to a head of family under restricted title. Then, after the federal government received proof that the head of family could pay the taxes, an unrestricted title was to be granted in fee simple (an inherited estate, unlimited).

The allotment of private property was a crucial event for the Odawa. It opposed the traditional land use pattern based on the ethic of collective custodianship, an ethic amplified by Nanabozho. Between the 1850s and the end of the nineteenth century the state of Michigan sold unallotted, traditionally used Indian hunting and fishing territories to non-Indians. Most of the lands set aside by the treaties passed to non-Indian ownership, and the northern Odawa lost not only their trust relationship with the federal government but their traditional land base as well.

By the late nineteenth and early twentieth centuries the policy of the state of Michigan—unlike that on the federal level—was to treat the Odawa and Ojibwe as one political unit: "The Ottawa and Chippewa Nation." Although this policy officially was dissolved in article 5 of the 1855 treaty, some Odawa and Ojibwe bands adopted this nontraditional joint tribal organization to gain recognition by the federal Bureau of Indian Affairs (BIA) for political and economic advantages.

Similar to the shift from the reservation policy to the allotment policy, another policy shift happened in the 1930s following the Meriam Report (1928), which affected state procedure. John Collier, director of the BIA, implemented the Indian Reorganization Act (IRA). That act allowed the creation of tribal organizations through which trust relationships with the federal government could be reestablished with the BIA as arbitrating agency. Collier found the northern Odawa's request for tribal reestablishment, and their claim of continual tribal government, valid. The federal government deferred both the Odawa's request and claim, letting the matter fall to the state, arguing that Michigan had economic aid programs for which Indians qualified. During the Great Depression of the 1930s, however, Michigan circumvented the IRA and used article 5 of the 1855 treaty as the basis for denying the Odawa hunting and fishing rights. The state argued that if Indians were citizens, then they were assimilated and treaty rights thus were obsolete.

In the 1940s some northern bands of Odawa began to coalesce, upholding Nanabozho's lesson of the empowerment contained in councils and interpersonal consensus. These Odawa established the Michigan Indian Foundation, the Native American Foundation, and the Northern Michigan Ottawa Association (NMOA). The organizers of the NMOA formed it as a nonprofit corporation with membership open to all Odawa in Michigan. Originally, the NMOA was established as a business council of band units and not as a centralized political body. The NMOA was to act as a mediating agency for bands pursuing land claims and fishing rights under the U.S. Indian Claims Commission (Osoinach 1976:270). In its early years the NMOA won some land claims and successfully renewed health and education benefits for a few bands. The NMOA developed a file of potential claims recipients, in the form of an official roster based on proved descent from persons listed in the 1908 Durant Roll. Although the Claims Commission acknowledged the NMOA for litigation purposes, the BIA did not (Osoinach 1976:272).

Following the Civil Rights Act of 1964, Lyndon Johnson's administration earmarked federal funding for Indian "populations" but generally directed this money to Indians living in urban centers. By this time the localized and apolitical organizations established by the Odawa were becoming less effective. The state of Michigan assumed responsibility for organizing tribal units and established the Michigan Commission on Indian Affairs (MCIA), with a governing board and director appointed by the state governor.

The original composition of the MCIA included Indians and non-Indians. It was formed as a cultural organization representing and working to retain the traditions of all Indian groups within Michigan. Although its purpose was not to foster political development, circumstances in the NMOA encouraged the MCIA to gain centralized political power. Although the NMOA had been the official mediating agency between the Odawa and the state and federal governments, conflict developed within the organization. This conflict mainly resulted from personal power struggles, disenchantment by some members over what they interpreted as the "politicalization" of the organization, and frustration by other members over its seeming ineffectiveness. The MCIA took advantage of the factionalism weakening the NMOA, increasing its own political power.

In 1986, on the 150th anniversary of the 1836 Treaty of Washington, the MCIA called together an intertribal council. According to Richard, a former director of the MCIA, every elected tribal official was present, from both federally recognized and urban populations. When I asked him, however, Richard was unclear whether the council included representatives from rural communities and nonrecognized band organizations. He explained that the discussion had gone as follows: since most Indians in Michigan lived in the most populated area in the southeastern part of the state, they effectively could control voting power. Because of this, they argued, it would behoove others to ally with them and have this group be centrally organized. The representatives of some groups, however, saw this strategy as "selling out" because it abandoned the tradition of political decentralization and undermined the authority of individual band councils, the power of which was originally established by Nanabozho.

In effect, this MCIA-chosen intertribal council created a new "treaty" to establish a relationship with the state. Since treaties create a political and legal relationship with the U.S. government, the intertribal council and the MCIA sought to establish a political and legal relationship both among tribes and between tribes and the state government. Despite its success in establishing an organizational liaison between the state and recognized Indian groups, from the perspective of nonrecognized bands, the MCIA has been ineffective. As Brown Otter put it:

> Those people [are] all talk and no action. Their interests used to be with both urban and rural communities. Now their interests are just with the federally recognized groups and the urban communities: organizations that have BIA supervision and are easily targeted for state funding programs. You know, the commission is an organization supported by the government, especially the BIA.

Because of the actions by the MCIA and the decline of the NMOA, many bands of northern Michigan Odawa reorganized and sought federal BIA recognition. Brown Otter said that one of the recognized groups

> organized themselves, acquired their land base, and are operating without ever having a consensus of all the northern Odawa leaders. They've centralized their governmental organization rather than following our traditional ways. They split off from the other local bands, voluntarily fragmenting themselves for their own self-interest, mainly controlling the 1836 treaty–stipulated waters for fishing. The leaders from the different bands were never consulted.

They even combined with Ojibwe groups to increase their power. They're just down there setting themselves up at our expense, without the approval of the elders.

Several separate—and competing—bands are organized independently. Only a few have attained their goals, most often at the expense of other bands. In jockeying for recognition and visibility, several bands have been squeezed out of the arena.

Some recognized groups have moved to take over some non-recognized bands, largely because of the former's conviction that the system provides state and federal funding for larger tribal membership. Brown Otter remarked about a recognized organization: "They're afraid of our organizing ourselves independently because they think that the available sources of funding are limited, and they're threatened by the thought that there'll be less to go around." Lone Wolf complained that "the reserved Indians who are recognized are kowtowing to the government to get money and things they don't really need. I refuse to be accountable just to get money. Nanabozho has shown us the trouble caused by being greedy." The success of newly organized but non-federally recognized bands threatens groups already recognized: recognized groups believe that the eventual recognition of these other bands means decreased disbursements available to them.

The peculiar structure of the Michigan state government has had and continues to have a profound effect on tribal and band organization and success. For example, the state's government structure comprises nineteen separate departments. Michigan continues to lack a coherent governmental policy for the Indians in the state; instead, each of the state's departments has a separate policy. Without a consolidated, formal state policy, each of these separate departments still is asking, Who is "Indian" in Michigan?

Definitions of the term "Indian" create conflict within and between Indian groups in Michigan. Totally contrary to Nanabozho's example of establishing identity through council consensus and ritual, some state departments define Indians as people with a certain blood quantum who live in a federally recognized community or who carry a card certifying their membership in one. This definition does not include members of nonrecognized communities. Members of nonrecognized bands understand there is no funding without either congressional acknowledgment or recognition by the BIA and various state departments. But as Laughing Gull asked: "Without funding, where is the money supposed to come from to conduct the genealogical and ethnohistorical documentation required to prove an individual's membership and to use to establish the band's roll for group acknowledgment purposes?"

Today, besides seven federally (BIA) recognized tribal organizations in Michigan, and along with four bands that recently received their acknowledgment, several band organizations have consolidated as the Confederation of State Historic Tribes (CSHT). The CSHT is upheld by the Michigan Commission on Indian Affairs and is recognized by the state.[2] Other bands exist that are not recognized by either federal or state agencies, including many Odawa scattered throughout pocket rural communities. These nonrecognized and nonrepresented bands feel pressure to act. Based largely on Nanabozho's lessons, they identify a need to assert Odawa culture and collective identity in relation to federal affirmation of their real existence and political legitimacy.

Although the events we have just reviewed seem political in nature, for many participants who are Odawa traditionalists, their actions were and continue to be informed by the traditional ethics promoted by such prophets as Pontiac and The Trout and articulated by some of the Great Persons of mythology, especially Nanabozho as the Great Transformer. Religiously driven action—in this case, to address problems resulting from encounters with "culturally other" people—continues to be the Odawa traditionalists' most significant means to apply Nanabozho's lessons of constructive ways to transform status and identity, and to promote collectively directed change.

It is clear from the above historical overview that those encounters and events have profoundly affected the present Odawa cultural context, including their population size and distribution. Today the Odawa represent the smallest percentage of the roughly sixty thousand American Indians of various tribal affiliations living in Michigan.[3] Of this total Indian population, most live either on rural reservations or in industrial urban areas, such as

Detroit and Saginaw. Only about 20 percent belong to organizations recognized and supported by the BIA. Recall that few Odawa belong to federally recognized groups, one of which is a community of combined Odawa and Ojibwe peoples. Treaty rights do not apply to many Odawa because they are not members of organizations regarded as legitimate political entities by either the federal or state governments. Therefore these nonrecognized Odawa have no reserved rights to engage in traditional economic and cultural activities, such as birch bark harvesting, maple sugaring, and fishing and hunting. Much like Nanabozho's Father West in the myth of their battle for ultimate supremacy, the covert intent of federal and state policies consistently has been directed toward marginalizing Indians from mainstream society and from separate tribal groups. And for many Odawa this policy has been successful.

Additionally, these Odawa people do not receive state, and most importantly federal, subsidies for housing, education, and health care. Diabetes is endemic, and everyone has been directly or indirectly affected by alcoholism. Traditionalists view combating these problems as a process dependent on their own initiative and modeled after Nanabozho's lesson of powerful transformation, especially the establishment of social harmony through the pipe ceremony (gained after his battle with his father, the West). When I asked Great Elk how he saw overcoming these problems, he said: "Nanabozho shows us how to overpower adversity. He had is own personal problems when he was young, but he overcame them. That's our model. We can all beat our problems at the moment and become ethically responsible. It's a challenge, but it's possible, especially with the help of others who care." As Great Elk suggests, Odawa traditionalists regard it as their ethical responsibility to overcome alcohol and other substance abuse, activities that they associate with corrupting non-Indian values, and to help others do so, thereby maintaining the moral integrity of interpersonal relationships on at least the local level.

Also, lacking funds to assist in developing tribally run education programs, which exist mainly in the reservation context, most Odawa youth must attend public schools that do not include courses in the Odawa language, history, and tradition. Significantly, much of their parents' generation attended Catholic boarding schools, where they were separated from their families and kin networks, much as Nanabozho was from his mother and father, and they were taught Christian doctrine by Catholic priests and nuns who denied them the right to speak Odawa. Language and cultural traditions thus are threatened, and the process of transmitting tradition from one generation to the next has been interrupted. Many rely on a handful of elders who, as members of an older generation, have retained the language and tradition, particularly Nanabozho's lesson of powerful transformation. Through old age and death, however, this generation of traditional elders is suffering rapid attrition, and another source of cultural retention is being lost. Given this context, it is not surprising that the Great Persons of mythology are sometimes spoken of in a way that non-Indians might consider as godlike, that Ki-je Manido especially seems to take on a rather transcendent quality, and that the relationship between Ki-je Manido and Nanabozho is not always clear (for example, sometimes Nanabozho seems to be Ki-je Manido's helper, sometimes his son). Despite these ambiguities, however, the main thematic thrust of these "texts" echo their historical contexts. Additionally, they retain the tradition that the actors, as agents in society, present the model of cooperative action as the most significant way to simultaneously address and counter the opposing intentions of others, and to transform one's status, identity, and integrity.

Conclusion

"Nanabozho started out his life as an ignorant person. He made every mistake one could possibly imagine, and he thumbed his nose at all the principles for good behavior until he finally learned what it is to be Odawa: behaving according to traditional ways. He then passed this knowledge on to the Odawa people." Thus spoke the pipe carrier Lone Wolf when I asked him how he maintains his identity as an Odawa traditionalist and elder in a changing world. Certain terms in his statement exemplify the traditionalists' understanding of several things: Nanabozho as a model of transformation; *pimadaziwin*—the good, healthy, and moral collective life; the clash between Odawa and American cultures; and the mythic articulation of ritual processes, especially those established by Nanabozho. Terms such as "ignorant," "mistake," "thumbed his nose," "principles for good behavior," "traditional ways" and "passed on" echo the cultural, political, and ethical issues raised by Nanabozho with which the Odawa still grapple. Lone Wolf's words suggest much about the nature and importance of ethnicity, and about the relationship between narrative and identity.

Living out traditional ethics, especially that of *pimadaziwin*, is inseparable from establishing and maintaining social bonds as they radiate outward from each person. Odawa traditionalists approach ordered life as it is mapped by a series of mythological events. This map illustrates the existence of a union of Earth (A-ki and her lunar corollary, Nokomis) and Sky (and his solar aspect, Mishomis). It shows that this union results from the cooperative interactions of power persons (*manidos*), the great power person being Ki-je Manido, and continually is regenerated through Nanabozho. As culture hero, culture bringer, and Great Transformer, Nanabozho is a model for ethical behavior and mediation of interpersonal conflict. The map also indicates that union between all life forms is reinforced by the quiet persistence of the ethical person. The ethical person recognizes the essential need to establish unity between people and the whole environment (for example, this concept drives the traditionalists' insistence that land cannot be owned). Odawa traditionalists take most seriously Nanabozho's lesson that life is organized and maintained through ethical acts of gifting that establish a connection between persons. The map's focus on gifting to establish and maintain this interpersonal connection outlines one way for the Odawa to mediate personal, social, and cultural differences.

Considering the social activism of Odawa traditionalists, we also must appreciate that the primary condition of their contemporary cultural experience has been social marginalization and liminality, which has occurred on two planes: they have been separated by the surrounding non-Odawa social worlds, especially as a result of shifting governmental policies, and they have formerly secluded themselves by adopting a strategy of invisibility for cultural survival. As we have begun to see, liminality is a crucial factor in the Odawa's story, as it prompts premeditated reinterpretations and reapplications of mythic themes that are rooted in the traditionalists' constructive use of conflict, especially as it is established by Nanabozho's actions: conflict with Euro-Americans and with Indians who accommodate them leads to group identity and cohesion and a profound transformation from a formerly invisible (liminal) status. Traditionalists do not tolerate departures from a central Odawa identity, departures that they associate with Indians who accommodate Euro-American values and ideals. And they have adopted an element of radicalism as they fight for their own group ideals. Modeled in part on Nanabozho's great personal transformation, their activism aims for a metamorphosed and empowered sociocultural status by eliminating non-Odawa values. They seek to retain an autonomous, sovereign identity defined by shared language, land, and traditional ways of doing things. The entire process of these Odawa's revitalization includes several steps: the initial event of social liminality; the reinterpretation and reapplication of myth and ritual; the purposeful production of positive change; and ultimately group solidarity and cultural sovereignty. This process aims to reconstitute Odawa meaning and significance within traditional theory and to mediate problems stemming from non-Indian culture and Indian accommodationists.

From the perspective of traditionalists, the history of Odawa relations with non-Indians displays an institutional racism that threatens the successful mediation of cultural differences. The traditionalists' social liminality/marginalization and need for revitalization is witnessed clearly in Odawa and Euro-American language differences, in the sense that indigenous understandings are profoundly significant. These Odawa feel that non-Indian language once stressed separation through removal, which then moved to integration through forced multitribal reservationism, which in turn quickly transformed to assimilation (i.e., tribal termination) through urbanization. As non-Indians practice these policies, the Odawa do not understand them as voicing cultural pluralism or secular humanism. They understand the goal, as framed in Euro-American language and practice, not as mediation but as obliteration. "They think that if they force us to either live on reservations that they control, or they force us to be like them, then they'll have no more problem," as Brown Otter put it. Traditionalists do, however, draw a correlation between Euro-American proposed processes of cultural separation, transition, and reincorporation, and their own classical rites of passage, particularly that exemplified by Nanabozho's transformation; they simply have a different goal for what the passage of transformation is to achieve—solidarity and sovereignty. One of the factors precipitating the traditionalists' revitalization is that they interpret the Euro-American notions of solidarity and sovereignty as conflicting with their own: a lesson learned from Nanabozho, real experiences and the legacy of their prophets. As we have seen, their revitalization is also connected with other concerns about shifting federal and state Indian policies, political and cultural autonomy and sovereignty, recognition, definitions of "Indian," and landownership—threats that emanate from dangerous outsiders.

For Odawa traditionalists, myths—especially those involving Nanabozho—contain the models of how to transfer, transform, or change people from being threatening, which we might frame as Not-Like-Us, to being neutral, Like-Us. Myths show both groups how to become ethically person-alized. Focusing on the contemporary myth of the Seventh Fire, I discuss in the next chapter how this narrative particularly picks up and carries forward Nanabozho's lessons by outlining a theory of transformation and supplying a map for constructive ritual action.

The Seventh Fire myth illustrates how, in their revitalization process, Odawa traditionalists draw on behaviors thematically revealed by the actions of the Great Persons of mythology, especially Nanabozho. Mythology is one way to articulate the essential ethics structuring the lives of Odawa traditionalists: personing, gifting, and empowering as they interact to produce *pimadaziwin*. For example, in his role as culture hero, Nanabozho images the possibility of mediating conflicts between disagreeing people and conflicting worldviews. The interaction of all the Great Persons of mythology voices the ideal for ethical behavior. Throughout myths, including the myth of the Seventh Fire, the interconnection of both the past and the future defines the present, establishing a sense of "everywhen." The ritual act of repeating myths makes their message immediately uncoverable and subject to reinterpretation and reapplication. The Seventh Fire testifies that although the Odawa traditionalists have juxtaposed old and new cosmologies and sociologies, traditional meanings, themes, and forms have been retained.

The Seventh Fire
Mapping Metamorphosis

The condition of truth is to let suffering speak.

Cornel West

As we have begun to see in the last few chapters, the Odawa
traditionalists' view of the sociocosmos and their place in it highlights ethical acts of cooperation. For traditionalists, the maps of
ethical cooperation laid out in certain myths illustrate how people
can act together purposefully to strengthen their ethnic identity
and power. In accomplishing their goal of solidarity, this chapter
suggests, some Odawa do modify tradition as social circumstances
change. What is happening among Odawa traditionalists today, as
expressed in their own language, is similar to transformations in
other people's traditions (such as the earlier prophets and their
revitalization movements). One aspect of these transformations is
the reinterpretation and application of the allegorical content of
certain myths (as, for example, we saw The Trout and Tenskwatawa do). The purpose here is to use allegory, as it shapes human
perception, cognition, and behavior, as a heuristic device to understand how Odawa traditionalists engage those mythic "texts" in
their revitalization process. Such an analysis makes it possible to
identify how traditionalists use the ethics outlined in certain myths
to generate identity and solidarity, thus reinforcing the close
correlation between narrative and ethnicity. Allegorical analysis
shows how mythic models for behavior structure the traditionalists' sense of identity and their social construction of reality.

One mythic theme we have already encountered is the ritual
tension between the actions of ethical and unethical persons.
Ethical persons are distinguished from others by their compassion,

especially through acts of gifting; others who do not share the quality of compassion are particularly dangerous, as they threaten to disrupt orderly existence. A second theme is personal and collective transformation. Such metamorphosis is needed to counter others whose malevolent acts threaten danger and therefore social crisis. By cooperative actions, persons may be influenced to act benevolently, and once they become benevolent, persons become ethical through the process we have labeled personing. In myths, especially those of Nanabozho as the Great Transformer, the theme of metamorphosis is often signaled by references to health and healing, the heart, compassion, power, and fire, which denote the process of gifting, by which persons constructively respond to the unethical and opposing behaviors and intentions of others.

Certain narratives are not unchanging but are added to, like layers of an onion, so as to both articulate and inform the Odawa traditionalists' transformative identity, cultural integrity, and revitalization. In particular, the myth called the Seventh Fire echoes how the development of U.S. and Michigan policies toward Indians, which we reviewed in the last chapter, has made it difficult to practice a social life that some agents in society, especially Nanabozho and the earlier prophets, call for. This myth also suggests that the issues raised by the prophets endure in specific goals and practices now, especially the issue of how the ritual establishment of right relationships can sustain in a culture struggling with imposed cultural forms.

Traditionalists counter threats to Odawa cultural integrity and identity by acting as the progenitors of their unique cultural history. They seek to retain traditional cultural ways, however remembered, by charging themselves as the authorities of reinterpreting and reapplying the underlying religious themes and messages presented in some myths to changing social contexts. Focusing on the traditionalists and their revitalization, we must read the "text" of the Seventh Fire in light of the contextual social shifts outlined in the last chapter. Incorporated into the traditionalists' strategy for collectively directed social change is the narrative's message of the importance of and methods for mediating interpersonal distance. Furthermore, this myth has come to articulate the impact on the traditionalists' social sphere of the changes resulting from encounters with persons who oppose their intentions.

Mediating "Otherness"

We have begun to see how Odawa traditionalists not only distinguish between malfeasance and proper ethical behavior but also focus on ways to mediate threats to ethical interpersonal relationships. The following myth of the Seventh Fire images a world affected by many persons, some of whose actions do not suggest constructive intentionality. In addition to outlining some events in Odawa history, the myth provides a map of how one should act as an ethical person and how people so acting generate ethnic identity, solidarity, and a revitalized social sphere.

During a private conversation with Lone Wolf about what he thought his community needed most, he told me the story of the Seventh Fire. In the last few chapters we have already heard significant parts of this myth related by other elders, suggesting that the myth, although an expansion of others, is pervasive in the Odawa's contemporary setting and supplying evidence of an Odawa exegesis in relation to the narrative. In this telling we can hear clearly the emergence of the traditionalists' vision of collectively directed social transformation.

Let me tell you about our vision of the Seventh Fire. Our prophets said that the world was created with seven ways of being, each with its own fire that lights up and contributes to the specific lifestyle of that level, giving it power. Each fire represents a world and a people.

Ki-je Manido made the First World in the East and the First Couple, and he gave them everything they needed to exist. We were all related back then. But as the First People multiplied, they began to be tempted by Mo-je Manido, the Great Snake and Panther. Mo-je Manido lured them away from the Red Path, the Path of Life that Ki-je Manido had made for them to follow—they no longer worked to live a good life. Things got out of hand, so he had to do something. He called on Animiki [Thunder] and asked him to make a great rain. Animiki agreed and began to rumble. Soon the world was flooded, everything was destroyed. Then Ki-je Manido felt bad.

So he asked Nanabozho to help recreate a new world. Nanabozho remade all things—plants, animals, and people—and he made a paradise in the West for people to go when they die.

Nanabozho asked Muskrat to dive to the bottom of Ki-je Gan, the Great Waters, and bring up a piece of the earth. Muskrat tried many, many times. Finally, exhausted, Muskrat succeeded and from this Nanabozho made Makinaak [Turtle] Island. Everything was very beautiful. Ki-je Manido asked Nanabozho to be the master of all animals and the teacher of man. Nanabozho taught our ancestors how to live: how to use, to respect, and to take care of all the plants and animals. Nanabozho taught all things how to deceive their enemies. He taught us about the ways to be Odawa and the dangers of straying from that path, the Path of Life, about how to use *mashkiki*, and about how to show respect for that power by always placing a dish of food or tobacco plus *mashkiki* in our medicine bags. It's also Nanabozho who taught us that on earth there is a right path that some follow but also many side paths leading to deserts, about how we must help our dead travel the Path of Souls, and about our responsibility to always stay in touch with our ancestors.

Ki-je Manido and Nanabozho gave us another chance to prove ourselves. All this happened during the Second and Third Fires. Then our prophets taught that the Fourth Fire would be the time when white faces would appear and that they would either be friends or bring death. It was death that came—physical and spiritual—to the Anishinabeg. But Ki-je Manido promised that by returning to the Red Path, the Path of Life—the traditional ways— that the life of the Seventh Fire will come and we will return to the ways things were in the beginning. We will again have *pimadaziwin*. With the Seventh Fire, the circle will be mended, the Old Ways will return, and my people will return to the good life. Ki-je Manido once more will destroy the imperfect world, including all people not following the traditional ways—those who stubbornly insist on following the path of technology, the ways of non-Indians that make people selfish and threaten existence. Those of us following the Red Path will return to perfection and be reunited with our ancestors.

Our great hope is that the community currently living— tomorrow's ancestors—will be wise enough to hear Ki-je Manido and follow the right path leading to this unity: the Red Path and not the path of technology. Our prophets also have taught that the worlds of the Fifth and Sixth Fires are to prepare and strengthen us.

No one knows when the Seventh Fire will happen. It's part of the Great Mystery. It may be in my generation. Things are very powerful now. It may be that we are just fanning the embers of it, and it will be for my children or for my grandchildren.

The world and people of the Seventh Fire only will happen when all Anishinabeg have faithfully returned to the Red Path, destroying all non-Indian values and all people who follow them, as these create imbalance. We will know of the Seventh Fire when a young man, actually Nanabozho, appears who will show us where to find the ancient birch bark scrolls of our origins that were buried during our long migration from the east. Then our spiritual and physical illness once again will be overcome.

Lone Wolf's account of the Seventh Fire suggests that the myth not only provides an exegesis of traditional Odawa mythic motifs (e.g., creation and earth diver themes) but also narrates the transformation of that tradition in the face of historical events. It also suggests that the myth has several levels of meaning. One level highlights the mediation of Mo-je Manido's threat through the creative collaboration of Ki-je Manido, Animiki, Nanabozho, and Muskrat. Then, too, the myth seems open to post-Christian interpretations. For example, the "good" of Ki-je Manido, Nanabozho, and the Red Path (especially as it has become emblematic of the American Indian Movement) is opposed to the "evil" of Mo-je Manido and the path of technology. On another level of meaning, while the myth articulates the reality of social change, especially articulated by the image of the white faces during the Fourth Fire, it also lays out the steps for constructive action leading to positive social transformation.

Normative behavior in the ritual reconstitution of the world, called for in the myth, has its roots in *pimadaziwin*, which was given to the ancestors in the First World. The past demonstrates that failing to uphold the norms of *pimadaziwin* is wholly destructive. Destruction thus is caused not only by the negative intentions and actions of others, such as Mo-je Manido. Additionally, disruption results when people adopt wrong intentions: selfishness, laziness, greediness, reliance on others—all that the path of technology connotes. All this recalls the emergence of a "new fire" imagery in the 1790s, which Gregory Dowd identifies as being "symbolic of both the presence of the Great Spirit and of annual regeneration" (1992:108).

The Seventh Fire offers a case for clarifying how some myths become fluid articulations of both the indigenous ethos and change-provoking events, providing vital sources for adjusting to shifting cultural landscapes. As I suggested in the opening of this chapter, what is implicit in the Odawa traditionalists' revitalization becomes explicit through allegorical analysis. When traditionalists reinterpret and reapply its allegorical component, the myth supplies a map of ways to generate social metamorphosis.

Mapping Metamorphosis

At this point it is fair to ask of "allegorical analysis": What is to be analyzed? Answering this question requires that we take a brief detour from the Odawa traditionalists themselves. Many of us commonly use the term *allegory* in the sense of replacing one meaning with another meaning. But a narrower definition, taken from the Classical Greek, is to assign a meaning to something. Assigning meaning to something is not necessarily the same as accumulating meanings, and assigning meaning may be altogether different from replacing meaning. This understanding of allegory supports the authority of the mythic message while also allowing for personal and collective interpretation and application. Although the mythic message may be open-ended, the authority behind it supports the mode of communication so the message can shift authoritatively to new applications (e.g., Muskrat, the "underdog" on superficial reading, is the hero who invites genesis; the ducks who are Nanabozho's feast are oppressed peoples who ultimately are vindicated). By calling on the imagination, allegory assigns meaning through implication. In mythic allegory, significance is assigned to an expression in the narrative, which creates a relationship between two ideas so that one idea parallels and echoes another. Because the words create something transcending the words themselves, it becomes necessary to understand the allegory within the set of words, such as "go [Nanabozho/the Odawa] to the place of flint [the Great Persons and ancestors] . . . they have within them the element of fire [power]. It is the only substance your father [those who oppose or threaten] fears." It is neither literally flint nor fire that threatens or strengthens, potentially, but power and one's purpose in using it.

My point here is not to exhaust the systematic manipulation of mythic allegory in the history of religions but simply to suggest that allegory is crucial to understanding religious systems in general (see, e.g., Auerbach 1953). Central to understanding the simultaneous retention and reinterpretation of myth through its allegorical content is an appreciation of the allegory's unique openness to personal interpretation and application, especially by "allegorical designators."[1] We can conceptualize these reinterpretations and applications as the primary means by which people keep the significance of their "text" (whether oral or written, as in myth, or performed, as in ritual) relevant and alive. To understand mythic allegory in this way raises an issue that leads us back to the Odawa.

Clearly Odawa traditionalists have a problem: How do they know that their interpretation, their "reading" of the "text," is the right one? Identifying a correct interpretation is a problem for all religious leaders who charge themselves with the responsibility to apply an authoritative message, an ethos that is a "given," to a new reality, a new context. As Michel Foucault (1972) poignantly argues for all peoples, individuals and groups, allegorical interpretation—or any other form of interpretation—usually involves religious elites who assign or reveal an interpretation to the "text" and then must convince the community of its meaning.

Among the Odawa, the classic role of the "religious expert"—that is, medicine people (broadly) and pipe carriers and Midé-wiwin members (more specifically)—is to be the master of interpretation. The religious expert motivates moving from theory to practice—being wholly religious—and so empowers others. Traditionalists today, who include Midé members, pipe carriers, others who specialize in specific types of healing, and elders who are community leaders, charge themselves with a cause similar to that of their prophetic predecessors. They see their ethical responsibility as advancing the Seventh Fire by enacting the ethical precepts of the narrative and supplying interpretation to meet the changing needs of their people. It is important to realize that the group and its changing social circumstances supply the interpretations, not the myth itself: too often, narratives are considered stagnant and are confused with the mode of their interpretation.

Common to the various interpretations of the Seventh Fire myth is the allegorical content. Part of this content is the allegory of positive change, or metamorphosis: the theme of the Red Path. Positive change can be personal, in that an individual can consciously choose to follow the Red Path, or collective. Odawa traditionalists see that their liminal social status can be metamorphosed by sacrificing modern technology, which they equate with the corruptive ways of non-Indians and regard as leading to the world's destruction.

For Odawa traditionalists, the path of technology is an allegory that triggers images of additional social ills: alcoholism and other socially disruptive behavior associated with non-Indian values, ethnic oppression and social marginalization, assimilation, and threats to tradition and identity. Despite social change, however, traditionalists are culturally persistent. Great Elk noted, for example, that "we believe life continually changes but it also stays the same because a person or by extension a group has the power to influence the direction of change through quiet persistence. It takes patience and work to remain Odawa." For the traditionalists, change can be either positive or negative, depending on one's ethical response to the call to act; the fact of change itself is the only given. Thus they see the periodic transitions between "fires" as designating how various persons, human and otherwise, act as agents in society in morally responsible ways. Each fire marks a historical consciousness, a play of human intelligence, understanding, and tradition.

Like the path of technology, fire, especially the actions of the "people with white faces" during the Fourth Fire, is an allegorical designator for the potential negativity of change. The Seventh Fire, however, designates positive change through the actions of traditionalists (ethical persons). Traditionalists themselves function as allegorical designators by equating their own significance with that of the gift of "the youth"—Nanabozho, the returned culture hero, culture bringer, and transformer—who finds the reorienting birch bark scrolls, thus supplying social solidarity and identity.

The myth establishes a sense of time in which the past, present, and future can be experienced as an intersecting series of seven fires. Although the ancestors "saw" the coming of people with white faces during the Fourth Fire and "knew" they would threaten destruction or bring death, Odawa traditionalists likewise "know" that the architecture of life is circular, that death leads to new life, and that proper behavior produces powerfully constructive and creative events, the causes of which always are interpreted interpersonalistically. Black Bear illustrated this in his own allegorical way: "We see life as a great flowing river. The water is always there, although the individual droplets of water may not be the same from moment to moment. Yet the river—life—is the same. Your society demands scientific proof for anything to be true, but we believe all things are possible if we act together." Traditionalists are not surprised that with the coming of the Fourth Fire the white faces brought death, particularly by making the people stray from the path of the Old Ways to the path of technology, much as Mo-je Manido did to cause the end of the world of the First Fire.

Traditionalists acknowledge two fundamental facts: that through ritual action the past informs the future about the present, a reality that can be articulated in myth, and that such ancestors as Pontiac and The Trout were catalysts for moving the world forward. Additionally, they interpret the current world as being in the Fifth or Sixth Fires, but they do not know which one. Consequently, they understand the Seventh Fire as presenting the challenge of putting the theory of empowerment, allegorically designated by fire, into practice.

For these Odawa, the goal of creating a new world—an empowered identity and status, with recognition of their sovereignty—is accomplished by revitalizing the Old Ways and strengthening their future. Traditionalists assign a symbolic meaning to the time when all Odawa will again "walk the path of the Old Ways." Paraphrasing Lone Wolf, when this unification of purpose is realized, the "web of combined *manidos*" will be the strongest, the technological world (i.e., disruptive non-Indian ways of doing things) "will die," the ancestors will be "reunited with the living," and the world of the Seventh Fire will emerge "in the image of the original perfection." By being linked with the First Fire, the advent of the Seventh Fire means the genesis of revitalization, a return to the *pimadaziwin* enjoyed by their ancestors. But the whole process is progressive, forward-looking.

In different cultural contexts than the Odawa's, Jonathan Z. Smith (1982:90–101) has made a similar argument for people's reinterpreting and reapplying the allegorical content of traditional myths under the pressures of culture change. Such use of myth, he shows, is related to an allegorical tradition that lends itself to a revitalization movement. We can see the relationship between an allegorical tradition and a revitalization movement if we approach the narrative as a deliberate presentation of what Smith calls a "situational incongruity" (1982:90); that is, we must search for an incongruous arrangement or situation that exists within the narrative itself.

The myth of the Seventh Fire expresses a situational incongruity in that contemporary Odawa life is unlike the ancestors': socio-cosmic harmony, established by the actions of ethical Great Persons, has been disrupted. The myth communicates the traditionalists' conviction that the world periodically changes and that the most profound change has resulted from a conflict with others: a clash between their own and Euro-American systems of structuring, ordering, and operating in the world. Modern techno-logical and capitalist principles are incongruous with traditional Odawa ethics (personing, gifting, and empowering) and principles for ethical living (*pimadaziwin*). Echoing and enacting the legacy left to them by earlier prophets and by Nanabozho, traditionalists ask how they can make other people, especially non-Indians, act out their ethical obligations.

Brown Otter succinctly stated the incongruity of Odawa life: "We once ruled ourselves and were sovereign, and now others rule us." Like the earlier prophets, traditionalists such as Brown Otter contend that they lost their sovereignty because others did not and do not understand how the mediating function of gifting creates proper relationships. In today's world, the traditionalists insist, they must establish and maintain proper relationships on several levels: between themselves and their ancestors, between the community and the Great Persons of mythology, and between themselves and other Odawa, other Indians, and non-Indians. When these relationships are based on ethical cooperation and interaction, Odawa traditionalists will have rectified an inappropriate relationship with Ki-je Manido. Black Bear anticipated the reunification: "All life has balance if we act wisely and listen to Ki-je Manido, who guides us and keeps us unified—*Odawa.*" Because of the active intervention and involvement of many forms of power in the world, especially in the social sphere, Ki-je Manido becomes an allegorical designator for the constructive use of power to generate ethnic solidarity and identity—the focus of a newly created world, a complete revitalization.

Actually, two incongruous situations arise in the Seventh Fire myth. Lone Wolf suggested this double incongruity: "Besides the general disruption caused by Anglos and our loss of sovereignty, some Odawa have been wrong to stray from the Red Path and allow non-Indian values to prevail, which has changed the world and our identity." The impending reconstruction of the present world, he continued, will result when the Odawa reunite and so survive "by returning to the Old Ways." He emphasized that an alternative was presented in the world of the Fourth Fire: the coming of the "people with white faces" was a given, but their continuing misuse of power and abuse of land, with some Indians accommodating these actions, have been unexpected and have resulted in a negative balance of power. Like Nanabozho and the earlier prophets, this elder expressed a commitment to setting right what traditionalists see as an unequal social world and to reconciling the incongruities voiced in the myth through constructive ritual action.

The traditionalists' apocalyptic focus is located elsewhere than in the immediate sociocultural setting: its roots are in the long tradition of Nanabozho's lessons and the prophets' intertribal discourse. By way of comparison, we can see how some non-Indians have resorted to an apocalyptic tradition as part of revitalization strategies. For example, D. S. Russell's (1978) examination of the apocalyptic literature of Judeo-Christian history shows that in periods of crisis arising from a conflation of cultures in which pressures to conform arise, there is a tendency to rediscover apocalyptic messages as part of human rights movements pursuing justice. This was the case with the earlier Indian prophets, and it holds for contemporary Odawa traditionalists as well. Apocalyptic messages foster social solidarity and identity, and they become one means of fomenting social activism directed at redefining identity.

An apocalyptic doctrine does not require a narration of the literal end of the world. In a narrow sense the term means "to uncover" a concealed message meant for a specific person, group, or community. Apocalypticism, in this sense, refers to a conviction that a message derives from the beginning of time but that the first people did not understand its meaning. The course of action focuses on a select few in the present world who have uncovered the meaning of the mythic message and take upon themselves the responsibility to enlighten others. In the case of the Odawa, these select few are the traditionalists. Apocalypticism—the act of uncovering the mythic message—is a reciprocal and cyclical process of empowerment and is increasingly encompassing.

Generally speaking, four elements occur in the apocalyptic genre of myth. First, a sense of time becomes historical instead of ahistorical. Second, a sense emerges that a transformation will arrive at a very precise and expected moment, much like a German train, and that one should "be on the platform" when it comes. Third, a sense of duality is expressed as a radical separation of purity and danger. Fourth, a select group develops a conviction that its members know the true meaning of the message.

The Seventh Fire myth voices all four elements of apocalyptic mythology, taking the myth beyond a pure "prophetic" purpose to one for achieving revitalization.[2] A sense of time has become historical: Odawa traditionalists are moving to achieve the Seventh Fire, and its advent can be hastened by actively following the Red Path. The myth expresses a sense of precise timing: The transformation will come at the moment that "the youth," the culture bringer and Great Transformer, Nanabozho, returns and all are following the Red Path. A sense of duality is communicated as a radical separation of purity—the Red Path—and danger—the path of technology. Lastly, traditionalists carry forth the conviction voiced by the earlier prophets that they have uncovered and know the true meaning of the mythic message. Traditionalists see the message as describing a modern world divided by the conflicting powers of the non-Indian state and the Odawa's traditional ways; out of this conflict will come a newly balanced, reunified, and revitalized Odawa identity. The fire allegory designates a simultaneous social transmutation and cultural retention (fire = gifting = empowering = personing). Although threatening, the force of change can be positively manipulated by the compassionate acts of ethical persons.

An apocalyptic meaning underlies the Seventh Fire narrative: the path of technology allegorically designates all dangerous, threatening, and destructive actions, especially by non-Indians; the Red Path designates constructive actions that are interpersonally and culturally unifying. One inherent incongruity that traditionalists identify is the failure of so many people to see the constructiveness of the Red Path and the destructiveness of the path of technology and their refusal to make the proper choice. Traditionalists find new ways to interpret, within an apocalyptic tradition, the embattled mythic themes of ethical opposition versus constructive intentionality and transformation. That they extend an apocalyptic meaning to social activism is not a novel cultural phenomenon: it was clearly evident in the actions of the prophets and has been documented repeatedly, in many cultural circumstances, in the anthropological literature.[3] For Odawa traditionalists, apocalypticism informs the vital message contained in the myth of the Seventh Fire, which lends to its revitalistic function.

The fundamental purpose of the Seventh Fire myth, beyond its apocalyptic meaning, is to supply a map for the transformation of Odawa identity and social status. Traditional Odawa ethics (personing, gifting, and empowering) dictate that medicine people, elders, political leaders, and others in positions of community authority guide people to a common ground and combat disorder, as did the prophets (who significantly are referred to in the Seventh Fire myth), and as do the Great Persons of mythology, especially Nanabozho. Traditionalists see themselves as exemplifying the Red Path; adopting this role, they have become the "great persons" who will drive this new world transformation. Traditionalists foresee, not necessarily a literal end of the world, but rather a change in their social identity and a return to their own sovereignty. Constructive ritual action, as articulated in the myth of the Seventh Fire, fuses ethos and worldview and provides a vital social cohesion.

The traditionalists aim to improve poor sociological conditions by "healing" the community through enhanced solidarity and identity, and by strengthened spirituality. They contend that their enhanced social solidarity and identity, and their strengthened spirituality, will lead to total transformation, "the world of the Seventh Fire," the new age of paradise, when they will purge their world of oppression and metamorphose out of their social liminality to a concrete and centered identity. Traditionalists stress that if one accepts oppression, then the superiority of the oppressor over the oppressed defines identity. For them, the importance of annihilating oppression will give birth to a new identity based on proper (i.e., unifying, empowering, and purifying) relations.

Many elders stress the need to purify one's "heart" to be connected with the totality of power, the "heart" or center of the great power person, Ki-je Manido. And they stress that proper "thinking" is accomplished with one's heart instead of one's brain. As Soaring Eagle put it:

> We try to know so much, and we try to control instead of listening to and seeing the greatness of power, which is true reality, and realizing that the community needs to prepare for the end of society and this world as we know it, and to live as Odawa. We need to listen carefully and trust our hearts, through which we can hear Ki-je Manido. Heart versus brain. These days, most people in their desire to control everything don't listen to their heart, Ki-je Manido, but to their brain.

When Odawa traditionalists "uncover" the unifying power of "heart," they can unite with the power of the many *manidos*: a powerful, constructive, and revitalizing event.

Conclusion

Our allegorical analysis of the call to action underlying the Odawa's myth of the Seventh Fire and its application to changing social circumstances has required us to consider its various meanings. One significance of the myth's message is that it prescribes an ethical or moral canon for the recreation of sociocosmic harmony (e.g., the Odawa ancestors did not behave properly in the First World; it is the contemporary traditionalists' responsibility to set things right). Another significance of the message is its focus on the power to create a newly transformed world (e.g., the Great Persons' recreating the world, Nanabozho's uncovering the birch bark scrolls, traditionalists' social activism itself). A third significance is the message's description of a world divided by conflicting powers and a world metamorphosed out of this conflict into a perfected world (e.g., the transformation of the world and the achievement of *pimadaziwin* with the advent of the Seventh Fire). We now can see how the myth of the Seventh Fire articulates Odawa revitalization, which highlights expectations about behavior as mapped by the actions of the Great Persons of both mythology and ancestry. The myth expresses the essential ethics that structure life for these Odawa.

We have come to appreciate how the lives of Odawa traditionalists are organized and maintained through acts of gifting as a means of establishing solidarity. The importance of gifting is to mediate personal, social, and cultural differences. Modeled after the lessons of Nanabozho and the prophets, the Seventh Fire myth contains an allegorical map of how to transform an Odawa identity given periods of adversity.

Allegorical analysis shows how Nanabozho, Ki-je Manido, and other Great Persons, as well as images of power, acts of gifting, and fire, are allegorically interchangeable. Assigning significance to fire and its corollaries—personing, gifting, and empowering—provides Odawa traditionalists with a way to act constructively in order to metamorphose the nature of change through time. The myth of the Seventh Fire—as testimony of the terrible consequences of the inculcation of non-Indian values and threat of technology to Odawa tradition—clearly is a case of new revitalistic mythmaking.

The next chapter focuses on how the messages contained in myths such as the Seventh Fire work to move the theoretical meaning of behavior into constructive ritual action. As voiced in myths—especially the Seventh Fire, which consciously calls for empowering transformation—the Odawa traditionalists' ritual enactment of the ethic of gifting is the practical medium for bonding I and Thou, We and Other (personing). For them, the Seventh Fire myth is socially reorienting, a map for new and collectively determined statements of community and identity.

Part Three

The Source
of Collective Determination
Religious Action and What People Do

Charles Meyers

Chapter 7

What Do We Do about the Others?
Contemporary Rituals of Community

Religion, like art, *lives* in so far as it is performed.
Victor Turner

This chapter begins to explore how rituals put into practice the traditional Odawa ethics communicated allegorically in myths. Those ethics, which we have been calling personing, gifting, and empowering, establish through their interconnection a system to mediate the danger that others threaten and to generate *pima-daziwin*. The traditionalists' rituals express these organizing ethics in two separate but related ways: personal prayers and communal ceremonies, both of which create a community with empowered identity. In these performances, traditionalists diminish—or annihilate altogether—differences between individuals and groups. For traditionalists, ritually interacting with the *manidos* produces a profound metamorphosis: they regard the presence of the *manidos* and encounters with them to be the source of dramatic transformation. Such religious attitudes give the traditionalists' social action its real salience and power, as Lone Wolf affirmed:

> Personal prayers and ceremonies are very important to us. They show commitment to our ways of being Odawa. I wake up every morning and go outdoors to a little place in the yard and, facing east, give thanks and offer tobacco to the *manidos* for the good morning. People forget to give back. It's just like cooking and eating. I only prepare what I can eat, and should there be anything left, I bury it with tobacco. I do this because it's proper. Everything we eat has been sacrificed for us and has sacrificed itself for our

gain. It's only right that thanks be given for that sacrifice and that the remains be treated respectfully. I return it to A-ki with thanks and make a sacrifice of my own of tobacco to Ki-je Manido and all the powers to show my appreciation.

Often portrayed as Great Persons of mythology, the *manidos* supply ways to establish ethical relations through ritual: their purpose, according to Odawa traditionalists, is to show how ritual actions restore right relationships. The goal of such rituals raises questions of how traditionalists do this and, perhaps more important, why they strive for it. For these Odawa, interactions with the *manidos*, coupled with their own ingenuity, reconstitute and reaffirm tradition, which allows these ritual encounters to be transformative and revitalizing.

As with the historical prophets, ritual empowerment through encounters with the *manidos* demonstrates the individual's commitment to community solidarity. Through ritual performances, encounters with the *manidos* establish a bond between the person and others so that a community emerges. The community in turn voices responsibility to its members. Traditionalists approach rituals as the most significant way to mediate interpersonal distance that threatens a collective, yet local, identity with social division. They regard rituals—personal and collective actions directed to and conducted with the *manidos*—both as ahistorical acts tied to the classic practices of medicine people and as contemporary practices with vital social, economic, and political effects.

Ritually seeking the guidance and constructive intervention of the *manidos* reflects the older, historical Odawa social pattern. In winter the larger group splintered apart to pursue subsistence, separating the individual and leaving him with an orientation of me-and-the-world-at-large. Here the individual sought the aid of powerful beings. In summer, with the reuniting of clan networks, this individual orientation shifted to we-and-the-world-at-large, when the collective sought the aid of powerful life forces. With these shifts in personal orientation and social organization, ritual established proper relationships between human persons and between human persons and more-than-human persons such as the ancestors and especially the *manidos*.

Ritual gifting is a medium of empowerment between persons, human and otherwise. It allows participants to transform ordinary time and space and to mediate disagreements and misunderstandings stemming from interpersonal distance. Interacting with the *manidos* through rituals is a traditional way to effect proper relationships between all ethical persons and to transform others who are unethical to being more benign (the process of personing). Encounters with the *manidos* mediate the relations among humans (gifting) and between human persons and more-than-human persons. An essential means of countering threats of social disruption, ritual encounters with *manidos* perpetually work to restore the unity of all persons, human and otherwise (empowering).

Traditionalists use rituals as a channel to direct the neutral power gained from encounters with the *manidos* for benevolent acts to achieve *pimadaziwin* and so create an identity that is collectively determined. Mythic messages show how all persons, human and more than human, can be powerful, but power is relative; when power is unequal or used in antisocial ways, it creates uncertainty about others' intentions. The traditionalists' rituals address a reality that is ontologically and phenomenologically organized as I/You and We/They, where actions confirm who I am to You and who We are to Them. A world structured by a duality between ethical and unethical persons calls for a system to guide proper behavior and mediate conflicting disagreements. The problem of "others" dictates a rationale for traditionalists to use ritual action to mediate personal forces of good or ill. Carrying on the legacy left to them by the prophets and the lessons of Nanabozho, traditionalists comprehend "otherness" through ritual encounters with each other and the *manidos*: a repeated announcement of one's ethical responsibility.

Contemporary Personal Rituals

Those Odawa who call themselves elders, or are so called by others, complement the religious expert's physical and spiritual healing. Elders work to enhance the community through their assigned significance as the keepers of traditions, especially of oral history. Being an elder has little to do with age. Instead, it is a title that both reflects and acknowledges a person's moral integrity.

Lone Wolf remarked that "the elders teach things. I'm Anishinabe, even though I grew up believing that Indians were 'dirty, drunk, and worthless.'" When I asked if he was an elder, Brown Otter said: "I've been called that. I just keep learning and sharing this with others." Gray Squirrel said: "The elders are the keepers of traditional knowledge and the teachers of how to use that power. Their life experience and actions, not their talk, and their willingness to share with others make them elders." Instead of writing down their knowledge, elders pass it on orally because, as Lone Wolf said, "I like to see what people are hearing from me. If it's important, they'll remember."

Classical Odawa religious experts—that is, medicine people and pipe carriers—understand their special skills as powerful gifts gained from communicating with a *manido*. Fulfilling his or her responsibilities to exchange the powerful knowledge gained from these encounters, pipe carriers and medicine people act for the benefit of the group. Most especially, these religious experts are the master interpreters, the exegetes, the allegorists. Charged with this responsibility, they are the ones who identify power as spiritual, physical empowerment and healing (*midéwiwin*) and, therefore, the prime source of *pimadaziwin*. Thus these religious experts invigorate Odawa social identity.

The community acknowledges religious experts, such as medicine people of the Bear clan, who specialize in knowledge of herbal healing, as having a profound relationship with and understanding of the *manidos*. Religious experts and elders are the spiritual leaders of the community and are regarded as "vision people" with special power. The pipe carrier, particularly, has had a revelatory message from the *manidos* of the nature, substance, and destiny of the world, and of the individual's and community's place in the world.

As one type of specialist in healing, the pipe carrier's responsibility is to protect the sacred pipe, a religious symbol and vehicle that empowers persons, human and otherwise. During communal gifting ceremonies led by the pipe carrier, the power that results from "knowing" the *manidos* is transferred to the community. Through the vision, the pipe carrier facilitates religious expression to address community problems and adapt to a world in constant motion.

Pipe carriers, medicine people, and other elders regard the ability to teach to be an honor that results from knowledge; for them, knowledge is power that can heal and renew identity and solidarity and generate empowerment. Like the prophets, these agents in society are vital critics of social relations who draw their strength and inspiration from the entire Odawa religious sphere, a framework they use to challenge people to renew sociocosmic solidarity. These traditionalists contend that renewal may be either personal spiritual and physical healing or community regeneration. However their efforts are directed, the ritual role of these agents in society is resonant with the leitmotifs of the earlier prophets and of Nanabozho.

Prayer for Odawa traditionalists includes visions and dreams. From an early age everyone is trained to remember dreams, which are interpreted by religious experts. The *manidos* encountered in dreams guide the dreamer to wisdom, which is a means for personal empowerment. Dreams are discussed freely between Odawa people, and often those faced with an important decision will say, "I'll have to dream on it." Ritual dreams are understood as a direct personal link with the *manidos*.

Vision quests or fasts, what the Odawa call "going up on the hill," also create a link to the *manidos* and with one's personal *dodem* (the more-than-human person from whom the individual and his or her clan claim descent). Today individuals of all ages and both genders engage in vision quests, often repeatedly (formerly, it was restricted to boys as part of their puberty rite of passage). Traditionalists stress the need to be trained in this rite by a religious expert. This teacher prepares the person to communicate directly with the *manidos* and find more succinctly one's own source of power so as to attain personal *pimadaziwin*. Before going up on the hill, a person must uphold the seven ways of being Odawa, thus enhancing his or her own power, which when passed on will contribute to collective *pimadaziwin*. The goals of these seven ways of being Odawa—purity in heart, body, and soul; humility; honesty; loving-kindness; and respectfulness—may take months, even years, to achieve. As reassurance, the teacher may accompany the person on the quest, which is always held at a power place dreamed of by the questor. "Many things can happen," said Lone Wolf, who was preparing for a vision quest:

> You have to have seven things purified and in balance: mind, heart, and body, plus be humble, honest, loving, and respectful. If one's out of balance, Ki-je Manido and the other *manidos* will know. They will show me something, even if it's that my life isn't together yet. I may have some subconscious stuff still there that I haven't reconciled yet. And if so, they will show me that I've got more work to do. I may have to meditate some more on the proper ways to be Odawa and live a good life. This is what we think about when we go up on the hill.

Lone Wolf explained that the person on the quest abstains from all food and often even water for several days (usually four), although the teacher may bring along "medicine water" in case of emergency. He also stressed that one cannot anticipate or direct the result of the fast: if an attempt at impure manipulation happens, "the *manidos* will not speak through the dreams."

The form a *manido* may take when encountered during a vision quest is uncertain and often surprising. While preparing for his quest, Lone Wolf told about a friend who went up on the hill because he was unsure of the direction his life should take.

> This man was sitting quietly when suddenly a little yellow finch flew into the branch of a tree in front of him. The two began to talk, and they understood each other perfectly. It wasn't as if the bird spoke English or Odawa or the man spoke the bird's language, or anything like that. They suddenly just had absolute knowledge of each other. And the little bird told my friend that he must prepare himself to be a great leader and go back to his people and guide them. And you know, he did. He's now a very important elder and pipe carrier. But it was funny to think about a little bird talking to this guy. He's a big, huge fellow. Bear I might have expected, or Elk. But not a little bird.

Contact with the *manidos* during vision quests and the message gained are powerful sources of metamorphosis and empowerment—two paths to *pimadaziwin*.

Vision fasts are essentially purification rituals that recreate a connection with all-powerful dimensions of life through the ritual experience of suffering, "death," and renewal. The *manidos* encountered in a vision are guides for powerful personal transformation through this ritual. Traditionalists see that a person who is "ill" because he or she lacks the qualities of the seven ways of being Odawa must be trained to purify himself or herself, a state of being that is crucial to successful communion with the *manidos*. Paraphrasing Lone Wolf, traditionalists also understand that:

Before direct communication can happen, the individual must "suffer" (fasting for many days is a form of self-sacrifice).

Through the dream, the person "knows" (gaining knowledge is empowering), "sees," or is "enlightened by" the *manidos*, and the person's empowerment results from gifting.

The person is renewed (in the sense that the individual's identity is ethically transformed or enhanced by personing).

Thus when traditionalists say a person "died up on the hill and a new person came down," they mean that the individual reemerged with new strength and wisdom gained from the *manidos*. He or she is then charged with taking this power back to benefit the community. Traditionalists regard the knowledge and power gotten from vision fasts as one's moral duty to apply for the benefit of society. For example, knowledge of the power of herbal medicine to cure, *midéwiwin*, originally descended through Great Medicine Bear (Ki-je Midéwiwi Makwa), one of the Great Persons of mythology.

Elders indicate that some unethical people—unlike religious experts, who act with benevolence for the sake of community welfare—deliberately use knowledge for harm, thereby disrupting sociocosmic harmony. The most widely known example of such people are bear walkers (*me'coubmoosa*), who constitute one type of socially internal "otherness." Most people know who bear walkers are and try to avoid crossing them. They often express real fear of the bear walker's power to harm and skill to change from human form into a malevolent bear. One elder insisted that I not study bear walking too intently as he truly feared for my safety. Lone Wolf described having been bear-walked when he was a teenager, "way before I began to follow the traditional ways":

One day, I became seriously ill and spent several weeks in the hospital only to have the doctors scratch their heads with confusion about what was wrong with me. I couldn't move my whole right side and had trouble breathing. So one of the elders in the community, after hearing I was sick, visited me in the hospital and reported that my problem was that I'd been bear-walked.

A pipe carrier, responding to his need, went to the hospital and conducted a series of empowering rituals. Lone Wolf said of the experience: "I've never been the same. I really changed. It was then I stopped drinking and started to think about people other than myself. I started to respect the traditional ways again. I discovered my own center of power." Although he did not die physically, he died metaphorically and was reborn.

When bear-walked, one is guided to self-curing by a religious expert, who consults with the "patient," meditates on the source of the problem, and conducts a pipe ceremony to communicate with the *manidos* and ask for guidance in addressing the problem. The process enables the individual to heal himself or herself through a series of actions. Smudging is the first step: opening two windows and smoking out the house, especially the corners, beginning at the lowest level in the southeast and proceeding clockwise. Smudging with sage drives out malevolent spirits; smudging with tobacco invites in benevolent beings. The second step is to hang a piece of red willow tied with red yarn over an entryway. Third, one puts salt around all windowsills and doors leading outside, an act to keep other malevolent spirits out. The fourth step is to place four branches of cedar tied together on each of the four sides of the house. If the bear walker's malevolent purpose is particularly powerful, an individual may require stronger measures and "medicines," including "shooting" the bear walker and then reviving him or her in a purified state. The bear walker epitomizes powerful malevolent acts: the religious expert exemplifies the ethical obverse.

Contemporary Collective Rituals

The central aims of collective rituals, as presently practiced, are twofold. First, they preserve healing traditions, especially as they perpetuate collective *pimadaziwin*. Second, religious experts have told me repeatedly that such rituals are used to transmit knowledge of the coming of the Seventh Fire (i.e., renewed identity) and other secret knowledge still mnemonically recorded on birch bark scrolls. Religious experts retain their responsibility as master interpreters of this sacred knowledge, and they heal by keeping and using sacred water drums and medicine bags to recreate the connection of the person and the community with the *manidos.*

The pipe, one of the contents of the *pinjigosaum* or medicine bag, is a central component in most Odawa communal rituals (on American Indian pipe ceremonies in general, see Paper 1988). Laying down or burning tobacco or sweet grass extends the pipe ceremony. The ritual participants smoke the pipe while all are joined in a circle. The pipe carrier chants a prayer and holds the pipe to the *manidos.* As the pipe passes to each person, he or she absorbs the many powers called on by the pipe carrier: combined powers from the collective, the ancestors, the environment, the earth, and the plethora of *manidos.* The pipe passes around the circle in "the direction of the sun" (clockwise). After each person has smoked and silently prayed, he or she swings the pipe in "the direction of the sun" and passes it to the next person. Pipe carriers are special people with enhanced power, but the power of the ceremony does not derive directly from them; its source is the *manidos.* The pipe carrier simply is charged with keeping and protecting the pipe. "Ki-je Manido and the other grandfathers speak through the pipe," explained Soaring Eagle. Pipes are usually made of cedar (recalling the myth of the Medicine Tree; see chapter 4) and have stone bowls with decorations that, according to Soaring Eagle, "represent the four vertical and horizontal directions of space" and eagle feathers representing "*manidos* associated with the sky and earth, like Mishomis, Nokomis, and Animiki [one of the Thunders]."[1] Soaring Eagle continued:

> The pipe represents the unity of heart, mind, and body that is possible within each person. The bowl is Grandmother's, Nokomis's, heart—just like the drumbeat. It creates a center, the bond between A-ki and Nokomis and Mishomis. Each section of the pipe points to each section of the person, and smoking it guides them in purifying themselves, unifying their body, mind, and heart. Each grain of

tobacco put in the bowl represents all forms of life. Add fire so a person smokes the sacred tobacco, and while praying, the breath of Ki-je Manido enters them.

Here the "breath of Ki-je Manido" is power: the empowerment derived from knowledge gained through ritual interactions.

Like the pipe ceremony, sweat lodge rituals are for collective purification and empowerment. During the ritual, the participants chant: "Bathe in the breath of Ki-je Manido [the steam] and be reborn." Brown Otter said:

Sweats are held for spiritual purification. The problem in this community today is two things: People have strayed from the Right Path; they aren't living a good life. They've been indoctrinated into Catholicism and they think that we who practice the Old Ways are practicing magic—voodoo or something. Also, it's hard to have a sweat or any other ceremonies without having land to build the lodges on and conduct the ceremonies.

Despite these worries, Odawa traditionalists do engage in two different types of "sweats." A person may take part in a sweat lodge for either spiritual or physical healing; sweat leaders specialize in one type or the other. Sweats are also conducted for an individual's or a group's empowerment.

In group sweat lodges, men and women generally take part separately. Laughing Gull said: "Many people think women don't need to take sweats at all because they're purified every month." For a sweat lodge ceremony, the sweat leader builds a round lodge covered with cedar with a central fire (a structure again recalling the myth of the Medicine Tree). People enter the lodge through an east door and sit in a circle around the fire, with four people named as the "Keepers of the East, South, West, and North Doors." Tobacco passes to each participant. Lone Wolf described his first sweat lodge ritual.

When I entered the lodge, I could feel incredible power coming both from all the people there and from somewhere else. When the pipe passed to me, however, I couldn't see anyone else in the circle except for the Keepers of the Doors. Suddenly there was a green light that radiated from the ceiling over the hearth. When the ceremony was through and I came out of the lodge, it was very dark, but I looked up into the trees and could see every branch, every leaf. I suddenly looked down at my side and saw a bright concentrated light right alongside my leg. I thought I was hallucinating, maybe from the heat and being dehydrated. I said to the guy standing by me, "Hey, you see this?" He said, "What?" I said, "Up there; the lights in the trees. This, by my side." He said he didn't see it but it must be very powerful and I should go and talk to the healer about it. So I did. He said this kind of thing didn't happen very often and it may never happen to me again. But this is exactly what the sweat ceremony is all about. He told me, "You have been shown that you can harness great power. The light by your side is your spirit helper."

Through the sweat lodge, the sweat leader guides the individual and the group to encounter the benevolent *manidos*. "Bathing in the breath of Ki-je Manido" is an empowering ritual act that affects a rite of passage: a transition from one moment to another and a change in being. Sweat lodge rituals cleanse a person's impure state. Personal power is enhanced through group solidarity, and vice versa. Each person emerges from the lodge with a changed state of being and identity, which makes the ritual a classic rite of passage. For those who receive a vision during the ceremony, solidarity simultaneously is established with the group and directly with the *manidos*, sometimes in the form of light. The group comes together and establishes a proper relationship; the individual is empowered not only by other individuals but more importantly by the *manidos*. The ritual concretizes power as a gift that transpires among a community of ethically empowered persons. The community of participants itself, therefore, becomes an organizing center, a lightening rod for empowerment.

Other contemporary communal rituals are more visible than pipe ceremonies or sweat lodges. Probably the most widely held community ceremonies are dances, either local band "homecomings" or interband powwows.[2] These are gatherings in which both dancers and traders exchange gifts to strengthen social ties. Black Bear said: "The sound of the drum is the heartbeat of our Grandmother, and when you're dancing you try to get into the rhythm—get in harmony with A-ki." Gray Squirrel said: "Powwows are a strong spiritual event where you can show Grandfather and all your ancestors that you're doing what you can to keep traditions going." The arbor, an open-framed circular lodge made of cedar posts and covered with cedar bows (once again recalling the Medicine Tree), is in the center of the dance circle and is where the drumming occurs.

Powwows open to both Indians and non-Indians generally include dances called "intertribals," in which everyone is invited to take part (except menstruating women, who "on the honor system" stay outside the dance circle because of their "enhanced power," as Laughing Gull explained). These rituals also include other dances in which only Indians may participate, such as honor songs. Today powwows play a key role in the revitalization of Indian traditions.[3] Although non-Indians appear to be welcome at Odawa homecomings, they are guests nonetheless: the Odawa traditionalists understand the ritual to be essentially Odawa and use it to assert a unique identity and create solidarity.

Although male "fancy dances" and grass dances, like female shawl dances and "jingle-jangle" dances, have become quite popular, these performances are not indigenous to the Great Lakes but to the Plains tribal groups. "Part of their popularity is the young people's attraction to the associated dress," explained Great Elk. Only what are called "traditional dances and dance dress" are indigenous to the area; the Odawa do not use the term "costume." Those who are called or call themselves "traditional dancers" are the pipe carriers, medicine people, and other elders. Their talent and skill are crucial to the success of the event. Each dancer's regalia is unique and usually stems from the person's dreams and *dodem*, which his or her movements also express.

By consecrating the land, building the arbor, and lighting and tending the central fire, traditionalists begin the ritual of pow-wows well before the actual dancing. Dancing begins with a Grand Entry early in the afternoon, with a second in the evening. Dancers line up and enter the dance circle through an eastern-facing opening, thus reaffirming the east as the direction where life starts. They then dance "in the direction of the sun." The first dancers to enter the circle are the head dancers, whose positions are by invitation and are a gift from the group that acknowledges an individual's importance to the community. Head dancers always are traditional dancers who are charged with the responsibility of ensuring protocol, solving problems, and resolving conflicts. They need extensive knowledge of specific dances and styles, customs, and protocol such as the proper action to take when an eagle feather is dropped. In the latter case, for example, all dancing stops and the dancers leave the circle, except for a few male head dancers who perform a dance that ritually neutralizes the feather's power. It is then picked up and given to the host dancer, who decides to whom it should be passed. The feather is never returned to the person who dropped it.

Invitation as a head dancer, who enters the arbor first, is both an honor and ethical responsibility, as it calls for extensive gift giving in exchange for prestige and community accolade. After the head dancers come the veteran dancers, who represent all Odawa people who have died in battle, including veterans of U.S. wars. Then come the flag bearers, who carry the Canadian and U.S. flags (sometimes upside down to honor the American Indian Movement), a veterans' flag, and a tribal flag with eagle feathers honoring the *manidos* who guide Odawa life. Then come the men whom the people themselves call traditional dancers. Behind them come the male "fancy dancers" and grass dancers. The women follow, and the children come last. The entire group makes a loose clockwise circle to honor the *manidos*, after which they stop to sing the flag song, a song in Odawan directed to the tribal, veterans, U.S., and Canadian flags. After the flag song, an elder gives an invocation and the dances begin.

The drum controls the dances themselves. A group of musicians and singers called "the drum" play one large drum in the center of the dance circle under the arbor. The songs and dances are highly structured, and the order is determined by the head singer. Drums must have an extensive repertoire. Not knowing a song or prayer called for by the head dancers causes an embarrassing loss of honor and prestige, and it requires passing the right to another drum.

Different chants combine with the rhythm of the drum to determine the dancers' patterns of movement. While the women tend to be sedate and the men flamboyant, a visible transformation happens in both. As Laughing Gull explained, power is transferred "through the energy of one person to another," which results in group enhancement, and it moves "directly from the *manidos* to the person through the energy of the dance itself."

As one type of collective ritual, powwows traditionally ensured successful hunting or victory in warfare (an elder told me that the word *powwow* is derived from the Algonkian word for "dream"). Today Odawa traditionalists use powwows to express unity, solidarity, and social identity. Like all rituals, they happen in a concentrated and consecrated time and space, creating a bond between human persons and more-than-human persons, especially the ancestors and the *manidos*. Powwows establish proper relationships among all persons (personing). Being a place to both trade and dance, they enact and reinforce the ethic of gifting to mediate social distance and disagreements between people. At powwows, ritual dances establish and maintain the life-perpetuating connection with the *manidos*, which sustains collective *pimadaziwin* (empowering). The power of dance, the drums ("the heartbeat of the earth"), and the central arbor make real the concentrated creative power within each person and through which communal solidarity is voiced. The unity within each person extends out to the group and remains an active source of solidarity throughout the year (harking back to Lone Wolf's comments in chapter 3). Through dance, the participants purify themselves, change their state of being, and unite with other people and the world at large.

Through the power of the dance, a person, in harmony with "the circle of life," momentarily separates from his or her everyday identity and becomes part of the identity of a unified and harmonious world, both social and cosmic. Differences are annihilated. The dancer "becomes" the eagle or some other powerful life form. Each dancer creates a different image and identity through a different visual channel. Powwows teach the proper expression for a specific person and reaffirm group membership and kinship relations. This experience is crucial for young children, whose attention spans may be too short to take part in other communal rituals; therefore the elders teach "the Old Ways" through dance with special enthusiasm.

Giveaways, as part of complex ceremonies such as powwows, are another type of community ritual. For example, at an annual powwow, the group recognized a young woman who had lost a child the previous winter. To honor the child and acknowledge the support of the group, this woman led a ceremony in which she gave gifts first to the host couple, then to a veteran dancer, next to all the dancers, and then to the children. Before she distributed her gifts, however, she offered a prayer, a gift, to the *manidos*. She held tobacco out before her to the north, behind her to the south, and to her right (east); lastly she swung her arm over her head to the west, reenacting the pipe ceremony. This action reaffirmed "the connection of the Four Worlds and Four Doors [cardinal directions]," as she explained, and both her own and the group's central position in this cosmographic architecture (as does the sweat lodge).

Here is another example of a giveaway: One of the first ceremonies in traditional weddings is for the "warriors to capture a tree to give to the wedding couple as a gift from the earth (A-ki)," explained the mother of a bride. The men find a young tree, dig it up, and give it to the wedding couple as a sign of their union with each other and with the earth. An eagle feather (a power sign associated with the *manidos*) is placed at the top of the tree, and the women cover the roots with earth before a pipe ceremony begins.

An extremely popular form of communal ritual is the naming ceremony. Most traditionalists desire an Odawa name. Like giveaways, naming ceremonies occur in many circumstances, and a person may receive several names throughout his or her life. The community gives an Odawa name to honor special deeds. Most often the name results from dreams. In a community naming ceremony, the individual calls on a "vision person" (i.e., a religious expert) to fast and confirm the appropriateness of the name and to conduct the ceremony. People also may have secret names used in prayer to generate a direct connection with the *manidos*. Lone Wolf said he received his Odawa name, Nazhikewizi Ma'iingan, after his teacher dreamed it was his "proper identity." This is a particularly noteworthy name, he explained, as it refers "to the separation of animals and humans but also to their continuing bond." Lone Wolf said that besides this name he has a Christian name, a family name, and "two other names that I can't say but that I use in the mornings when I go out to pray with Grand-father." Today there is particular importance put on naming ceremonies, which usually happen in the spring. Most people have Christian names on their birth certificates and driver's licenses. The gift of an Odawa name is a means of cementing one's position in and identity with the community. Accumulating names expands one's personal definition and social identity as well as asserting the integrity of the collective.

By far the most visible communal rituals are feasts (explored in greater detail in the next chapter). Various seasonal feasts stress the importance of ethical gifting. For example, fall feasts commemorate the tradition of groups coalescing for the summer months and then sharing a harvest before separating for the winter. Similarly, summer berry feasts commemorate the tradition of groups rejoining and reconfirming kinship ties after separating for the long winter.

Today, among these other socially constructive and healing actions engaged in by Odawa traditionalists are elders' councils and spiritual gatherings. These collective activities affirm and strengthen traditional ethics, especially those we have been calling personing, gifting, and empowering. They reserve time to recount oral tradition, and they provide a place for participants to remove themselves from their everyday lives and live the traditional ways. We can understand their purpose as generating a nonsecular space-time for people to reassess their current lives, to become empowered through the guidance of the elders, and to return to their everyday lives with a new identity. In other words, they consciously aim to restore right relationships, which makes them a powerful ritual event. During these gatherings the elders not only speak but also, through their ritual actions, show the power of ethical behavior to create proper relationships. The setting allows all participants active involvement in this revitalizing process. Everyone receives attention, but the main focus is on young people and those struggling with substance abuse.

Elders' councils and spiritual gatherings, which usually take place in the summer months, follow a general pattern. Various numbers of elders, pipe carriers, and people from throughout the community gather for four days, preferably in a secluded, wooded area. Resources such as food and firewood are pooled, tents are set up, and a cedar-covered arbor is built. One person is charged with building a fire in the center of the arbor and tending it for the four days and nights. Each morning begins with a sunrise pipe ceremony, followed by breakfast. The day is spent on general recreational activities, such as walking and canoeing, unstructured storytelling of life experiences, one-to-one chats with elders and pipe carriers, recounting of oral tradition, demonstrations of traditional crafts, and instruction in the Odawa language. Gossip is passed about what is regarded as the unethical behavior of other people, especially those Odawa who direct their efforts toward non-Indian "wannabes" and people who claim to be keepers of Odawa traditions who are not Indian at all. After dinner, everyone gathers under the arbor.

Each person enters the arbor through an eastern door, walks around the fire "in the direction of the sun" (clockwise) three times, places tobacco in the fire with a silent prayer, then sits down. The organizers of the council pass a bowl of burning tobacco and sweetgrass to each person, who bathes in the smoke and thus is purified. Each person then receives a gift of tobacco, often in the form of cigarettes. Next the elders pass an eagle feather, the medium for both purifying the individual's thoughts and empowering him or her to speak honestly. Everyone present knows that the source of the person's voice is a *manido*, whose knowledge is transferred through the feather to the speaker. No social pressure exists for any individual to speak, but those who wish to do so get up one by one, go to the central fire, and while holding the eagle feather present their concerns to the group. Most statements are confessions of personal transgressions from traditional ways of behaving. For example, at one elders' council a woman told how she lost three children because of alcohol abuse. At another, a man just out of jail discussed how he beat his wife while under the influence of drugs. At a third, a person revealed that he had gotten drunk recently. (Compare the role of ritual confession in the actions of the prophets, described in chapter 2.) Following these confessions are formal discourses by the elders and pipe carriers that address the people's problems and concerns. Afterward, the group disperses, and small groups gather around campfires talking informally, sometimes the entire night.

It seems appropriate to regard spiritual gatherings and elders' councils as ritual events that reaffirm the ethics of personing, gifting, and empowering. Like all rituals, they happen in a concentrated and consecrated time and space, when transformation of both the person and the community happen through insight. As a healing event—a call for *pimadaziwin*—they are a medium for restoring right relationships. "They're a time of intense training," said Gray Squirrel. "Many ideas are offered and the Old Ways illustrated." The motive for holding these meetings stems from the deep concern that "traditions are being lost, and the loss of traditions means the loss of power and therefore our spiritual wellness and identity," as Lone Wolf put it. Spiritual gatherings and elders' councils are directed to young people particularly because they are "the community's most valuable resource."

In all these ritual contexts one can witness how elders, by showing more than telling, use techniques of communicating with the *manidos* to guide people to proper relationships. These gatherings of traditionalists are thus ritual or religious events. By sharing their knowledge of these powerful communications, persons are giving gifts to each other. Thus the setting empowers the entire collective. Such activities as elders' councils and spiritual gatherings allow the group to discuss problems, issues, and difficulties, and to use them as a means of both personal renewal and collective solidarity. The elders and religious experts do not merely ask people to rid themselves of their problems and show them how through their own behavioral example; they also use the problems constructively as a means of total sociocosmic renewal, as did the earlier prophetic actors in history. For example, they integrate the problems of alcoholism and social marginalization into the action of generating a completely revitalized identity.

Gifting and Solidarity

Odawa traditionalists stress ritual acts, especially gift exchange, as the primary medium for creating constructive relationships, establishing social solidarity, and carving a collectively determined identity. For them, one must enact the ethic of gifting to maintain proper relations. Persons have been and are respected for their knowledge and achievements, which reflect and create their ethical being. Gifting is the primary social act that lends respect and prestige; it is also empowering, which lends to the process of personing.

As a continuum of sharing and reciprocity, gifting follows set rules for bonding the giver and receiver. On one end of the continuum, personal survival often depends on sharing between kin members. On the other end, reciprocity is one form of gifting that can dramatically enlarge family units to include clans, bands, other tribes, and non-Indians. As a continuum of sharing and reciprocity, gifting extends to include the exchange of wealth, labor, and food within the family group, between groups, among the ancestors, and ultimately to all more-than-human persons.

In their rituals, Odawa traditionalists enact the ethic of gifting to unite groups through the social duty of exchange. As with many peoples, what is exchanged can be goods and wealth, real and personal property, or things of economic value (Mauss 1967), such as concrete lands and rights through upheld treaties. Because traditionalists establish intragroup and intergroup bonds, as well as bonds with the *manidos*, through acts of exchange, such institutions as marriage, initiations, and the *dodem* system unite, cement, and expand interpersonal alliances. Because all such activities include ritual gifting, reciprocal exchange becomes the main social means of creating solidarity. Traditionalists understand clearly that failing to build reciprocal exchanges results in an individual's loss of status and dignity and, on a larger scale, deteriorates alliances as well as communities, social organization, and collective identity.

For Odawa traditionalists, to establish proper interpersonal relationships, contracts, and alliances, receiving is as important as giving. They regard a person's or a group's refusal to either receive or give as slamming the door on friendship, which annihilates social relationships and therefore introduces danger. For traditionalists, gifting is a powerful means of reducing the distance between ethical persons and unethical "others"—We versus They—and of mediating the potential hazards of social distance, such as that created by competition and hostility.

Examples of powerful actions associated with the Odawa's ethic of gifting are the traditionalists' healing rituals. Elders explain that curing, for example, is a process of gifting: the person to be healed gives the religious expert a gift such as tobacco or silk to honor that person's position as initiating donor. The religious expert acts as the mediator between the person and the *manidos* in times of personal crisis. The gift exchange between the person seeking guidance in healing himself or herself and the religious expert differs only slightly from the religious expert's ceremonial gifts of prayers and tobacco to the *manidos*. Using the healing event as an example, the function of gifting can be illuminated by applying a modified version of Marshal Sahlin's (1972) theoretical model as a heuristic device to show how social distance conditions the way persons interact, and how the range of interactions drives aspects of the traditionalists' lives.

A (the person in need of spiritual or physical guidance for renewed health and empowerment) gives to *B* (the religious expert), who acts as the mediator to transform the gift into something else (knowledge, revelation, and guidance transformed into power) in exchange with *C* (a *manido*). Because the power given by *C* through *B* stems from *A*'s initial gift, the gift acts as something of a catalyst for the transferal of power. This process of exchange creates a closed loop ($A \leftrightarrow B \leftrightarrow C$). The presence of an intermediary party, *B*, is necessary to maintain interpersonal equity and ensure that the gift is used for benevolent acts. "The use of power can become harmful," warned Black Bear, if this closed and circular relationship is not cemented and reciprocal in its purpose:

> A person's gift can't be allowed to become another's power to do bad things. Life has to have balance—male/female, human/*manido*, person/person, and among our many groups. When things get out of balance is when we're in trouble. This is why I honor you for your gift, I honor Ki-je Manido with my gift, and we're both honored by Ki-je Manido's gift of power to us. It is also why we seek the Red Road: the right way of living that Ki-je Manido set out in the First World. The Red Road keeps things in balance if one accepts the calling and uses well the power of what Ki-je Manido has given. This is the path toward a good, long, and healthy life—what we call *pimadaziwin*.

Conceptualizing the exchange process in healing ceremonies through the above model suggests that degrees of empowerment and solidarity result from different types of exchange. In this type of exchange, gift giving itself provides an initial act of social organization. For traditionalists, gift exchange structures relationships between human persons and more-than-human persons (A to C and back to A through B). Sharing/pooling and reciprocity are the ethical acts of interpersonal exchange that concretely organize the traditionalists' internal community and external relationships.

Sharing and pooling are purely intragroup activities associated with kinship solidarity (Sahlins 1972:188). Pooling is when clan segments come together and amass needed resources within the kin group without the expectation of return. Family members simply gather and share resources for the common good and survival of the group. Because an unspoken understanding exists among traditionalists that the current "have not's" eventually may become the "haves," not having something to exchange never is held against anyone. Having something and withholding it is regarded as the most abhorrent behavior. The ethical duty of kin is to take care of each other with equality and altruism.

Reciprocity expands the personal level of exchange (sharing) beyond family relations to the broad collective level. While sharing solidifies and reaffirms kin relations, reciprocity extends these in-group associations to include non-kin members. Reciprocity has the power to mediate differences between disagreeing people—for example, traditionalists and those who oppose them—because it reduces hostility and averts dissension. By giving with the expectation of a return, traditionalists use reciprocal actions in ritual to mediate conflict. But enacting the ethic of gifting through reciprocity introduces tension in the system, for always the question exists, What if the recipients withhold the expected return? Because withholding undermines the ability to expand the social sphere and simultaneously maintain solidarity (Sahlins 1972:188), traditionalists expect positive or balanced reciprocity to alleviate, at least temporarily, tensions between groups, whether between individuals, clans, bands, tribes, or between Indians and non-Indians. Positive or balanced reciprocity can mediate greater social distance between groups than sharing/pooling can. Reciprocity creates alliances through a contractual agreement and addresses the structural tension felt between non-kin groups:

ethical persons versus others who pose danger. Both sharing and reciprocity are equated with the ethic of gifting, and both acts define ethical personhood.

A central theme of the Odawa traditionalists' ritual activity is the mitigation of social distance through giving. Individuals and social groups invoke the ethic of gifting to mediate the many dangerous and often chaotic situations that other people create. Gift exchange automatically creates a bond between persons because doing so is to give part of oneself, as the gift is part of one's personal identity; to receive is to take part of another's being (Mauss 1967). Thus gift giving is a perpetual exchange of power in the form of increased social solidarity. Odawa traditionalists insist that a person does not "own" things such as eagle feathers; they are a gift. And by giving them to someone else, the person shows compassion and generosity, which is interpersonally empowering.

For Odawa traditionalists, the ethic of gifting is the umbrella under which all acts of exchange on a continuum of giving and withholding derive. As suggested in part 2, myths—especially those about Nanabozho—map proper social action in relation to gifting. Nanabozho's actions express both the ethical challenge to maintain kinship solidarity and the greater challenge to expand social solidarity or networks. His message models both the mythologically ideal and the humanly or culturally real: theory and practice are inseparable. Ritual acts of sharing and reciprocity define, maintain, and reinforce the traditionalists' social and cultural orientation. The mythological model for ethical exchange behavior is mirrored, for example, in such ritual acts as greeting each other with "bozho!"—an abbreviated form of the name of the culture hero, culture bringer and Great Transformer, Nanabozho.

Gift exchange, for the Odawa, is a responsibility that extends from the ethical Great Persons of mythology to the present. Acts of gifting, such as exchanging *mashkiki*, are not impersonal: on the contrary, they are emphatically personal.

Conclusion

Odawa rituals are an important means of revitalizing a collectively determined identity. The two basic forms of ritual, communal ceremonies and personal prayer, show a continuity that extends from the origin to the present. This can be conceptualized as follows: having overcome his or her "illness" through "death" and "rebirth," the ritual participant transforms his or her human condition by "knowing" the concentrated power of the *manidos* through visions or dreams. Traditionalists regard personalistic dream knowledge as powerful "medicine" that it is one's duty to pass on to fellow community members and so help heal and empower the collective. Traditionalists understand that this exchange contributes to a state of existence closer to the Path of Life laid out in the First World.

Dreams are for many Odawa the ultimate personal ritual, the principle means for humans to elicit their own power directly. One's power is the basic source for communicating with, sharing the attributes of, and transmitting power among all ethical persons, human and otherwise. Traditionalists stress that this communication between persons keeps traditions alive because it illuminates or directs one to the Right Path, *pimadaziwin*. Since dreams are the essential guide for personal life, ultimately they function to maintain a healthy community life that results from ethical tradition and action.

Elders stress that collective rituals such as powwows, the "capturing of a tree" at traditional weddings, pipe ceremonies, naming ceremonies, giveaways, feasts, spiritual gatherings, and elders' councils all "unite the vertical Four Worlds and the horizontal Four Doors," as Laughing Gull put it, placing the ritual participants squarely in the center of this cosmographic map. Although people hold giveaways on many occasions, the purpose is to enact the ethic of gifting by showing generosity and compassion, to thank the human community for being part of it, and to thank the *manidos* for being a part of the larger community of ethical persons. Proper relationships are either reaffirmed or established through giveaways. As we have seen, the head dancers at powwows hold a giveaway in which they give all participants, whether actual dancers or supporters, token gifts: an act of exchange or thanks for participating. They give back something in exchange for the prestige and acknowledgment they receive from the community. The giveaway, therefore, is a process of mediation and social reciprocity. Receiving an Odawa name is like a give-away. It collectively acknowledges a person as part of a traditional Odawa community. The recipient's self-esteem is enhanced, personal power is increased, and identity is revitalized. Given this understanding, the next chapter focuses on feasts, particularly, as powerful rituals that simultaneously transform, retain, and empower identity.

Chapter 8

Invite the Others to Dinner
Ritual and Transformation

Humans respond not to events but to their meanings and can read into any event an endless variety of meanings.

Jerome Frank

This chapter illustrates the transformative and empowering nature of Odawa ritual practice by discussing gift exchange further and by applying metaphorical analysis to two forms of a ritual feast called the *gi-be wiikonge*. Much as we used allegorical analysis to examine myths and their use by Odawa traditionalists, metaphorical analysis here reveals how Odawa traditionalists similarly reinterpret rituals and reapply them to their revitalization movement.

One form of the *gi-be wiikonge* is commonly called the "Feast of the Dead," the other the "Ghost Supper." There exist many ethnohistorical descriptions, by both Indians and non-Indians, of the Feast of the Dead, but two stubborn questions surge throughout this literature: Was the ritual practiced in the Great Lakes area before Euro-American contact? And was it an Iroquoian practice imported into the region through socioeconomic relations with the neighboring Iroquoian-speaking Huron/Wyandot? Out of necessity, this is a problem we must leave to the archaeologists.[1] The same archaeological evidence together with ethnohistorical material, however, shows that the ritual was practiced in the Great Lakes region by the seventeenth century.[2] More important than the questions of origination and diffusion is that contemporary Odawa elders remember their ancestors as having practiced the Feast of the Dead and, as Black Bear said, they regard the ritual "as a collective burial rite associated with *midéwiwin*" (i.e., life-sustaining health that contributes to collective *pimadaziwin*).

The *Gi-be Wiikonge*

One of the first descriptions of the Feast of the Dead in the Upper Great Lakes region dates from the early seventeenth century.[3] This lengthy account by the Jesuit missionary Jérôme Lalemont describes as many as two thousand people from "all the confederated nations" attending a Feast of the Dead held in 1641 (Thwaites 1959:23:209–23). At this time, the Huron/Wyandot and Odawa had what we might call "most favored nation" trade agreements, and Odawa guests probably attended even if a Huron/Wyandot group did host this feast (see note 1 of this chapter). According to Lalemont's account, all the guests brought gifts to the hosts, including food, and the ritual had several other components: elaborate feasts, guest housing, dances, contests for prizes, a highly charged atmosphere of festivity, a ceremony for the election of chiefs, a ceremony for the dead, and extensive giveaway ceremonies.[4] Clearly, none of these activities was trivial or inexpensive for the hosts. During these events the women defleshed and cleaned the bones of the bodies of the dead in a special lodge. The next morning, while the women distributed goods, the men "attacked" the lodge and forced the women who protected the dead to sacrifice the bodies to them.

Nicholas Perrot, who began a forty-year career among the Great Lakes Indians in 1665, provides another seventeenth-century account of the "Outaouas" funeral rituals and the "feast of their dead" (quoted in Blair 1911:78–88). In his report Perrot describes how the Odawa covered a dying man with red paint, and how once he was dead the guests presented a gift to the wife, after which relatives and friends collectively offered a gift to the deceased. When the funeral ceremonies ended, the family distributed extensive gifts to the participants.

> A few days afterward the relatives of the dead man give a feast of meat and corn, to which are invited all the villagers who are not connected with them by marriage and who are descended from other families than their own—and especially those persons who have made presents to the dead. They also invite, if such are found, strangers who have come from other villages; and they inform all the guests that it is the dead man who gives them this feast.

Considerable presents in goods are given to all those strangers who
have previously made presents to the dead person; but these are not
given to his own tribesmen. (Quoted in Blair 1911:83)

Specifically describing "the manner in which the savages celebrate
the feast of their dead," Perrot writes:

If the savages intend to celebrate the feast of their dead . . . they
send deputies from their own people into all the neighboring
villages that are allied with them, and even as far away as a hundred
leagues or more, to invite those people to attend this feast. . . . they
[the guests] offer their presents . . . [and] as soon as the hosts call for
the dances to stop they take from their guests the presents which
they have made, and all their garments; and in exchange for these
the visitors are given, by those who invited them, other articles of
clothing which are more valuable. When all are assembled, they are
expected to dance all at the same time during three consecutive
days; and during this period one of the hosts invites to a feast at his
own house about twenty persons, who are chosen and sent out by
their own people. But instead of serving food at this feast, it is
presents which are offered to the guests. . . . only this sort of lavish
spending . . . can fully secure rest for the departed souls. . . .
Solemnities of this kind for the dead were formerly celebrated every
year, each tribe being alternately hosts and guests; but for several
years this has been no longer the custom, except among a few
[villages]. (Quoted in Blair 1911:86–88)

In 1857 Benjamin Witherall described the condition of three
burial mounds at Springwells (near modern Detroit) as he remembered them from his childhood in the early years of the nineteenth
century. His account suggests a Feast of the Dead site:

In my childhood I have seen the children of the wilderness deposit
the remains of their departed friends on its bosom [the mound].
They scooped out a shallow grave in the center of the top of the
mound, and covered the body with some sand, brought from the
neighboring sand-bank. After covering the body, the friends of the
dead man went into the river and waded about in a zigzag or
circular course, for some time, until they thought the spirit had
departed on its long, long journey to the setting sun. (Quoted in
Pilling 1961:24)

Although Witherall interpreted "their object in wading in the river" to be "that the spirit might not be able to follow their tracks in the sand," this ritual act suggests a reenactment of the myth of Medicine Bear's worldwide journey with the Pack of Life, spreading the messages of empowerment gained through *midéwiwin* and *pimadaziwin*, as well as the ritual responsibility to assist the deceased along the Path of Souls to the Village of the Dead. Repeated use of the ossuary, as described here, suggests a variation on the general Feast of the Dead pattern.

An early twentieth-century account by the Michigan historian John Wright stresses two other components of the Feast of the Dead as the northern Michigan Algonkians remembered its practice: the Feeding of the Dead and the Shooting of the Devil. The Feeding of the Dead involved sharing food between the living community and, more important, offering sustenance to the deceased. The Shooting of the Devil is described as being accompanied by everyone shouting *amo awda*, which roughly means "let us drive away the evil spirits" (Wright 1917:87–89).

The contemporary Odawa recount that their ancestors practiced the Feast of Dead. Lone Wolf described the ritual as retained in oral tradition:

> The *gi-be wiikonge*, or Feast of the Dead as you call it, happened in the spring and early summer when groups that had splintered to winter hunting places came back together for communal gathering, fishing, and planting. Often, somebody died in the winter during the long separation from the larger group. Because the ground froze, it was too hard to dig a hole for permanent burial. So the bodies were either wrapped and placed on tree platforms or in shallow graves. However, in the spring no one wanted to leave Grandfather behind, separated from families and communities. So when the families all regrouped at their communal territories, the band or clan leader would announce the time for a *gi-be wiikonge*, and group members who had lost a relative during the winter would return to collect the body. Obviously, the bodies themselves were in various states of decay, and upon returning to the summer place, those that were partly decomposed would be defleshed—usually by the women. While this preparation was happening, other people would dig—or redig—a huge hole in the ground, with niches made for the various families in the group. On the evening of the feast, the

leaders would have huge quantities of food cooked, torches would be lighted, and the group would descend into the pit and place the bones in their proper niches. All night, everyone would eat down in the pit, sharing their food with each other and with the dead— including with all the ancestors, in the case of a hole used before. At sunrise the mourners would come up out of the pit, the hole would be covered over, and no one would speak of the dead again.

Lone Wolf's account clearly describes a tradition that is retained in oral history. The question becomes how the Feast of the Dead was applied as a means to consolidate interpersonal relations, on both the social plane and that of the ancestors. The answer can be teased out with a brief examination of historical events.

Besides the economic disruption that resulted from the fur trade, which we have already reviewed (especially in chapters 2 and 5), another threat to traditional ways of living was the presence of the missionaries. One can imagine what the Jesuits thought when they first observed the Feast of the Dead, especially the defleshing of bodies. From their perspective, the desecration of the body, the "temple of God," was a satanic sacrilege that had to stop. They came, however, with a ritual feast of their own: All Souls' Feast, celebrated on the night of 31 October/1 November to commemorate the dead and actualize the Kingdom of Heaven, where the communities of the living and dead would be reunited. The Odawa drew a parallel in purpose between the two rituals and refused to abandon their ritual honoring of the dead to please the priests. Instead, they adapted their rite to their changed social environment. While obliging the priests they also reinforced their own religious tradition. Bodies no longer were defleshed but simply brought to the missionaries for burial, even in the winter. On All Souls' Eve, however, the Odawa leaders continued to host a ritual feast to honor the dead. They performed this ritual, which the Odawa continued to call the *gi-be wiikonge*, beside but separate from the Christian feast. The Odawa use the term *gi-be*, "spirit," instead of "Ghost Supper," because as Laughing Gull said: "We don't believe in ghosts like some non-Indians do."

Contemporary *gi-be wiikonges* happen primarily on the night of 31 October/1 November but also throughout November. The ritual begins before the actual feast when members of the community decorate the graves of relatives and friends. People go about to various cemeteries and burial sites, tidy up the area, and place ribbons and bows of cedar on the markers. Often bits of food and tobacco also are left. Then someone who has lost a relative or simply wishes to honor the dead announces that he or she is hosting a *gi-be wiikonge*, saying "I'm cooking . . . ," and prepares food in enormous quantities. Word spreads rapidly through the community. In the evening, people from near and far attend. Everyone, including dead relatives and dead friends, "eats." "It's real important to have lots of people come," Soaring Eagle said, "because the more who come and eat, the more spirits are fed." "You feed the guests in honor of the dead," said Lone Wolf. "Each person represents someone who has died. So it's real important to attend as many as your stomach can handle. Last year, I went to eight in one night."

Although the menu, which depends on one's financial means, differs slightly from house to house, generally the meal has various combinations of corn soup, wild game and fowl, potatoes, wild rice, and squash. One feature appears on all menus, however: frybread. Laughing Gull explained that to share frybread is particularly important "as it's something people can always give, despite how poor they are."

At the ritual feast, usually one large table is set where a group is seated and served by the host or hosts. People eat in no particular order in terms of some rank by age or gender. Those for whom there is no room at the table simply wait their turn, chatting, gossiping, telling family stories and traditional Odawa myths, and milling about. When the first group finishes, another group is seated and served. This rotation continues until the food is gone, which ends the ceremony. Considerable gaiety and few overt ritual components are present besides the consumption of food itself, except that the host quietly observes two additional ritual acts. For the first ritual, feeding the *gi-be*, the host picks someone nearest the age of the deceased being honored and serves this person either tobacco or special foods that the deceased particularly liked, thereby "feeding" and so empowering the dead. Second, the host burns a plate of food and tobacco or places a plate of food out on a table all night. Laughing Gull said the plate is burned or set out for the ancestor who most recently died, and "if it's gone in the morning, the spirit of the dead person has received it. The power of the food is transformed and passed to the dead person, making their spirit strong."

Lone Wolf explained his understanding of the *gi-be wiikonge*: "It's not only a time set aside to honor our dead, but the dead, the *gi-be*, are here. Gaiety and eating are important. If the occasion isn't fun, it'd be solemn, and we want to give thanks for all we have by showing our relatives and friends from other groups—both living and dead—that we're happy and prosperous, and we want to share that with them." Gray Squirrel offered how she approaches these feasts: "The *gi-be wiikonge* is an Odawa get-together when we can all break bread together. Sharing our food and exchanging our legends and oral traditions let us remember our dead, keeping them alive. Sharing our customs brings us closer to our ancestors and to each other. It's a very important dinner because it helps get us back on the Red Path, the way to live a good life." Clearly, these Odawa traditionalists understand that their identity depends on an ongoing interdependence with the dead. Identity is religiously bestowed, culturally maintained, and socially transformed. In this way, the living may substitute for the dead within the ritual context (see also Ettawageshik 1943; Andrews 1984).

The *gi-be wiikonge* establishes proper relationships between various subgroups: between the individual and the world at large; between the individual and other individuals (both human and more-than-human, including the dead); and between the individual and other members of the group. The feast also cements human relations because it supplies personal and collective orientation and empowerment, and it establishes alliances through gift exchange, especially the exchange of food.

"Foreign" Exchange

To create alliances means to relate with other people despite their differences. In the last chapter we began to see that Odawa traditionalists cement alliances by ritual acts of gift exchange that diminish the differences they see between themselves and others. Applying this understanding to the *gi-be wiikonge*, we can further appreciate the power of traditionalists' enacting the ethic of gifting. Johann Kohl's observation, documented in the nineteenth century, may be the best testimony to the contention of Great Lakes Algonkians such as the Odawa that exchange enacts the ethical principles associated with gifting: "As long as a man has anything, according to the moral law of the Indians, he must share it with those who want; and no man can attain any degree of respect among them who does not do so most liberally. The right men . . . give to the tribe not only what they obtain from the chase, but also all the presents they get from the Europeans, even to their tribute money" (1860:66). The ethic of gifting, which Odawa traditionalists approach as a continuum of sharing and reciprocity, establishes obligatory relationships between the person and the group and between groups.

Traditionalists see Euro-Americans who do not share the ethic of gifting as dangerous "others." From the traditionalists' view, the "foreigners"—the Euro-Americans—have produced and continue to threaten a crisis of nuclear proportion. For traditionalists, these Euro-Americans never have given with equality and still do not; instead, they withhold. For these Odawa, withholding is an act reflecting the worst behavior and ultimately creating an ethical dilemma: "Where is their generosity, and what should we be grateful for?" as Brown Otter asked.

Brown Otter's rhetorical question assumes more meaning if we first consider that the orientation to the world of hunter-gatherers—the Odawa's traditional subsistence pattern—is toward plant and animal more-than-human persons who are daily killed for food. To ease the existential dilemma thus threatened, the ethical hunter gives thanks for what he or she receives and simply participates in the normal flow of exchange between ethical persons. Unlike most Euro-Americans, the ethical hunter makes no economic distinction between means and ends. Hunting-gathering societies move to areas with better resources and engage in two primary activities associated with exchange. First, they continually enact rituals to ensure both the abundance of animals and plants, and they maintain a social structure based on the equal distribution of food for group survival (precisely what the earlier prophets saw breaking down and for whose return they called).

Second, they intensify food exchange in times of crisis as a means of reaffirming social bonds. Ritually enacting the ethic of gifting through food exchange extends ordinary social contexts of sharing, becoming a basic element in cementing social relations (see Price 1975:5, 12, 14, 21).

Between the seventeenth and early nineteenth centuries the Odawa became increasingly reliant on European trade goods and monetary support funneled through the missionaries for agricultural endeavors. By the middle of the nineteenth century the shift in economic orientation away from hunting and gathering was complete. Throughout this two-century period of economic transformation the Odawa's shifting worldview presented a potential conflict between the newly adopted agricultural orientation and the historically recent hunting-gathering orientation. The Odawa's special attitude toward food as gift, however, has remained both ritually and mythologically. Laughing Gull reaffirmed this retention of purpose: "We're really not supposed to eat alone. It would be like stealing. Nanabozho showed how food is a sacred thing that is to be shared, like all other sacred things, not consumed by yourself."

Between the seventeenth and twentieth centuries reciprocal exchanges became the practical medium for the Odawa to lessen the potential danger of interpersonal distance for the continuity and survival of the group. Exchange activities, especially those related to feasts, lessened social differences and potential disruption caused by outside influences. Reciprocal exchanges through feasting came to function in ways similar to personal and collective ritual performances associated with kin group sharing and vision quests. In the Odawa's ethical system of reciprocity, and especially ritual gift exchanges, gifts of food became a way to perpetuate the interchange and transfer of power, thereby solidifying and strengthening individuals, ranks, sexes, clans, and bands across generations (Clifton, Cornell, and McClurken 1986). The precedent for social network building through exchange was the message of gifting by the ethical Great Persons of traditional myths. As we have seen, in religious theory as mythologically expressed, a "master"—a mythological ideal—for each animal and plant species exists (Hallowell 1942:7):

So, individual rabbits might come and go—live, die, and be eaten or rot—but the Great Hare [an avatar of Nanabozho, is] the source of all rabbits, and so long as he [is] respected in prescribed rituals he [will] continue to supply the temporary, edible, manifestations according to man's needs. Even among the Source Beings, as I prefer to call them [instead of Hallowell's "masters"] there [are] higher and lower ranks, partly determined by their importance as a food supply, partly reaching deep into traditional mysteries. (Dewdney 1975:38)

This description underscores how myths and rituals work together as the precedent for network building. It also implies an important interrelationship between ritual and metaphor in Odawa religious experience.

Ritual and Metaphor

Lone Wolf's following remarks suggest how Odawa traditionalists transform religious theory into practice through ritual:

There are many misunderstandings. For example, the Midéwiwin ceremonies today generally begin before dawn and may last for hours, even days. Today there are four levels of initiation, all with increasing power, although some people believe there used to be as many as eight degrees and may still be in some. The cross is a traditional Midéwiwin symbol. The Midé used it way before the Black Skirts [Jesuits]. It has nothing to do with Christianity. It refers to the number four, which is our most sacred number, as it reflects the connection between all things: all four doors. Besides the Midéwiwin, there's also the Shaking Tent Society, the Shield Society, and the Wabeno. They're all meant for healing. When I was at my first Midéwiwin ceremony, I periodically had to walk away because the power overcame me. You see, the power of the earth that's concentrated in the Midé draws power in, also letting it out. In the Midéwiwin, heron feathers that honor the great Crane clan—who were our founders—and the *mégis* shell are important symbols. But most 'ologists think that the *mégis* is unique to the Midé. But anyone can wear one. I used to wear one on my dance dress. It's a symbol of our origins and of our unity. It refers to our vision of life as flowing like a great river. The water's always there, although the separate droplets of water may not be the same from moment to moment. Yet the river—life—is the same. All life is balanced.

Nanabozho has taught us that things are always in motion: They can change forms, in this life and the next.

As practiced by Odawa traditionalists, rituals are powerful constructive actions that voice the ethic of gifting. Both action and speech are communication processes by which traditionalists express what they find meaningful in their lives. By explicating what is otherwise implicit, metaphorical analysis particularly helps us to understand Odawa ritual practice, especially the transformation in the *gi-be wiikonge*.

Like myth and allegory (see chapter 6), metaphors operate linguistically to structure everyday life. They are part of everyday speech, which affects perception, cognition, and behavior (see Lakoff and Johnson 1980). Metaphors define reality, reflect cultural ethics, and sanction moral behavior. Since action is a form of language, and vice versa, an act itself metaphorically can define reality (see Burke 1989). Metaphors are keys that unlock a culture's construction of reality and its translation. The power and continuity of culture depends on a people's skill in drawing on and manipulating language to create images that both reflect and change reality. Such a process results in an adaptive cultural system, with metaphors either equating socially sanctioned references or substituting one for another, thereby forcing each participant to be an interpreter (Wagner 1986:6). As with the allegorical content of myths, the range of interpretation and application of a metaphor contained in ritual action depends on both personal and cultural experience. The relation between the metaphor and the ritual creates an open-ended system (Wagner 1986:5).

By interpreting and applying the metaphorical content of ritual, a culture moves from a state of potential, "as if," to an actual concrete state, "is" (Wagner 1986:8). The shift in cultural ethos from the subjunctive state of being, "as if," to the concrete "is" can extend beyond the performance of a specific ritual. This shift in orientation is possible because metaphors have the power to combine immediate personal and social experience with accumulated cultural experience, thereby contributing to collective personhood. As a universal discursive tool, and one that is most profound in oral traditions, metaphors simultaneously allow the intersecting presence of the past in the present, the presence of the present in the past, and the presence of the present in the future: a precise, circular cosmographic architecture. Each generation rewrites its expression of religiousness to fit its generational experience, but the basis of the reinterpretation always is its philosophical roots (Husserl in Grimes 1982:7).

Metaphorically expanding the ritual content to the broader frame of cultural experience, ritual can become a basis for social adaptation through activism in response to shifting contexts. As both a proposition for reconstituting identity and tradition and a source for resolving identity crisis, a metaphor represents itself and can expand exponentially to include and define larger cultural spheres, powerfully driving cultural motivation and action (Grimes 1982:11). Thus metaphorical reinterpretation and application, as with allegory, is a significant component in revitalization strategies.

George Lakoff, in collaboration with Mark Johnson (1980) and Mark Turner (1989), has demonstrated that several metaphors are universal, and we can look to those metaphors as a useful heuristic device to further understand the *gi-be wiikonge* within the general framework of the Odawa traditionalists' religious theory and practice. We can identify the following operative metaphors: *time is a changer*; *life is fluid*; *purposes are destinations*; and *events are actions*. As voiced by traditionalists, these metaphors allow us to see that the purpose of their contemporary *gi-be wiikonge* continues directly from the religious ethics embodied in the seventeenth-century Feast of the Dead. Both ritual forms are linked to the interconnected religious ethics that we have been calling personing, gifting, and empowering, as these ethics are expressed in certain mythic messages extending to the present version of the Seventh Fire. Metaphors structure Odawa identity through ritual relations with ancestors, both in the past and present. Metaphors, like allegories, are central to the traditionalists' religious action and social adaptation because both voice the dynamic effect of their orientation to and reaffirmation of reality.

For traditionalists, the mythological theme of illness-death-renewal and the coming of change for a better life parallels the ritual rite of passage and transmutation of being in the shamanic experience. Because life is constantly moving (*time is a changer*, *life is fluid*), a ritual return to the beginning is always necessary before the person, the community, or the world can transmute the present and emerge with renewed identity. This is possible because, as Lone Wolf said, "All life is circular and continually changes. It has many phases. But all things in all their different phases are related to each other." For traditionalists such as Lone Wolf, myth and oral tradition are kept relevant and immediate through ritual enactment. Traditionalists engage in rituals precisely because these actions contribute to cultural revitalization: renewed identity, social solidarity and sovereignty, ethnic cohesion, and a reconstituted meaning and significance of tradition. Communal ceremonies, particularly, show band and tribal identity, cohesion, and solidarity. The annual *gi-be* feasts voice the religious ethics that are reaffirmed mythologically, especially the socially building value placed on gifting. As happens with other cultures' religious traditions, individual Odawa traditionalists may or may not be able to point out specific metaphorical applications or meanings, but this should not suggest that they do not generally understand and apply metaphors within ritual. Additionally, among those traditionalists who can explain religious metaphors, not everyone may apply them in the same way. The interpretation and application of metaphors in response to changing social situations depends on both personal experience and collective history.

The first of the four universal metaphors, *time is a changer*, expresses here a basic awareness by traditionalists that other Indians, Christianity, and Euro-American processes in general have affected their religious practice and that rituals such as the *gi-be wiikonge* are modifications of more ancient forms. Gray Squirrel affirmed this transformative purpose of ritual: "With the coming of the missionaries, the ancient traditions were gradually affected by Catholicism. The Odawa Nation, for its part, was adept at adjusting. It was part of survival and helped further trade." The second metaphor, *life is fluid*, expresses the traditionalists' sense of cultural persistence despite change. Great Elk: "We believe that life continually changes, but a person or a group has the power to influence the direction of change through quiet persistence." Combined, the third and fourth metaphors, *events are actions* and *purposes are destinations*, voice the creative and adaptive effects of Odawa ritual performances as they lead to community empowerment. Black Bear expressed this metaphoric aspect of ritual action: "It's important to know one's purpose. We know our purpose through our dreams, our traditional legends, our happenings like *gi-be* feasts. Knowing our purpose gets us to our goal of the Right Path of peaceful unity: A oneness with the earth; with A-ki, with the *manidos*, and with each other."

The seventeenth-century fur trade illustrates how the Odawa view events as actions showing personal intentionality. The Odawa approach to history—as the intentional actions of persons instead of impersonal causation—explains how they interpret and apply the Feast of the Dead. It became one vehicle for creating and maintaining new forms of interband, intratribal, and intertribal solidarity, expanding and redefining social identity in the process. The *events are actions* metaphor shows how the Odawa understood the fur trade to have personal and social instead of merely economic components. The Feast of the Dead empowered a new sense of personal action to expand group identity. Band identity extended outward to include other bands and even other tribes so that social distance expressed as "otherness" was transformed into a vital new voicing of community and identity. Through acts of ritual gift exchange in the Feast of the Dead, the seventeenth-century Odawa made this ritual one means of mediating the opposition posed by others and of transforming social distance and hostility. In a practical way, these Odawa engaged the ritual to reduce the disruptive competition for resources that the fur trade created, and to help contain intertribal conflict.

Besides understanding the mediating function of the Feast of the Dead, contemporary Odawa traditionalists realize that missionaries affected the feast's history. In particular, they note the priests' hostility to the ceremonial defleshing of the dead's bones and to the communal graves. Traditionalists also stress that their seventeenth-century ancestors, who faced both the fur trade and the missionaries, understood the similarity in purpose of their Feast of the Dead and the missionaries' All Souls' Feast. Rather than simply abandoning their ritual relations with the dead to please the priests, they instead transformed the rite to adapt to missionary demands while simultaneously reinforcing the integrity of their own religious action.

Without question, the *gi-be wiikonge* is a simpler form of the Feast of the Dead. However, both rituals derive from the Odawa traditionalists' conviction that their identity depends on their interdependence with each other, with their ancestors, and with the *manidos*. Behind the traditionalists' explanations of the purpose of each form of *gi-be wiikonge* lie powerful metaphors. The community is empowered by using two metaphors to reinterpret and reapply the general purpose of the seventeenth-century form of the Feast of the Dead to the contemporary *gi-be wiikonge*. First, the metaphor *purposes are destinations* defines the feast as contributing to unifying the communities of the living and dead, and that community with the *manidos*. Second, the metaphor *events are actions* focuses on the feast itself. The ritual sharing and eating of food bonds the living community members with each other and the community with its ancestors and the *manidos*.

The *gi-be wiikonge*'s ability to drive community activism also involves the metaphors *time is a changer* and *life is fluid*. In the first case, traditionalists do not question that one's status as a person changes with death. In the second case, however, traditionalists contend that while the nature of the relationship between the living and dead changes with death, the relationship nonetheless continues to exist. For these Odawa, the dead paradoxically stay alive and still need a constructive interdependence with the living. The purpose of the ritual to maintain this interdependence was as true for the seventeenth-century *gi-be wiikonge* as it is today.

Today the ritual event itself—the action of decorating the deceased's graves, then sharing and eating food—expresses the metaphoric rationale. The action is metaphorical because sharing and eating unite two levels of meaning. Sharing food is a gift between persons, living or dead, human or otherwise. By metaphorically elaborating the ritual content one step further, the offering and sharing of food itself becomes a means of uniting people in compassionate and nurturing associations. Sharing food is a conventional event that suggests one way in which the community can be empowered.

Lakoff and Turner, however, suggest an important point concerning the metaphorical character of the *gi-be wiikonge*. As with all metaphors, the concept is not necessarily entirely metaphorical; part of it can be interpreted metaphorically while another part can be understood directly (1989:58). The traditionalists' communion with each other and the dead through the act of eating is metaphorical. But food as sustenance is a biological fact and understood directly. The *gi-be wiikonge*, then, involves a metaphorical chain highlighting the ethical action of sharing and eating. Food as gift metaphorically designates a whole series of connected events:

Food as gift is sustenance that leads to personal strength (personing).

The combined strength of individuals results in communal vitality that is reinforced by acts of gratitude and compassionate sharing (gifting).

These collective acts of compassionate thanks create empowerment and solidarity (empowering).

Here the source domain of food as metaphor is the biological fact that survival depends on eating. Understood within the conjoined ethics of personing, gifting, and empowering, however, food is meaningfully transformed by a person's ethical and compassionate giving: an act of humanism in the fullest connotative sense of the word. The importance of this event extends from Nanabozho's redistributing food in the newly created world. Therefore the power of the *gi-be wiikonge* for Odawa traditionalists, as it is metaphorically communicated, derives from three sources: the power of metaphor to structure experience, the ethical skill to make constructive choices, and enlightened reasoning (Lakoff and Turner 1989:64–65).

The ritual transformation of the *gi-be wiikonge* shows a pattern drawn from the past and projected onto the expectation for the future. Traditional economic pursuits dictated a particular social pattern. Annually, the individual was separated from the group during the winter, then reincorporated into the larger kin group during the summer. This seasonal transition involved a process of shifts in personal orientation from individualism to communalism. Separation, transition, and return were all real and patterned experiences. Transitions in personal orientation called for an ethos and worldview based on shifting membership.

The social orientation of contemporary Odawa traditionalists allows transformations in identity so that, for example, a person can simultaneously engage in part-time menial labor and be a member of a tribal council, a substance abuse counselor, an initiate in a secret healing society, a pipe carrier, a medicine person, and an elder. During events such as the *gi-be wiikonge*, members from different socioeconomic backgrounds can take part together, and at least for the period of the ritual event social differentiation disappears, as do disagreements between people and factions. People are unified: they become equal and mutually appreciative, which is a powerful source of social cohesion and community identity. The social group changes itself by empowering its members. For a moment, at least, the group is redefined.

Ritual is the agent the Odawa traditionalists use to unite redefined persons and social groups. By abolishing social differentiation, the *gi-be wiikonge* restores right relationships. This socioreligious reorientation has a profound psychological and physical effect, and traditionalists apply this experience to secular social issues such as their revitalization efforts to counter pressures for social change.

As part of an all-encompassing revitalization process, the *gi-be wiikonge* becomes political. The ritual feast is politically important because it links individuals as social groups: it extends personhood, defines others who threaten social upheaval, and even diminishes their threat. The *gi-be wiikonge* is a change-provoking ritual event that fuses ethos and worldview.

Both the *gi-be wiikonge* and the myth of the Seventh Fire are powerful agents of the traditionalists' identity, social cohesion, and sovereignty. The allegorical content of the Seventh Fire myth and the metaphorical component in the *gi-be* feast appear in Lone Wolf's explanation of the reason for the Feast of the Dead: "It was one of the primary ways to join the scattered bands, and since the journey to the Village of the Dead was dangerous, the common burial allowed all the dead to travel together and help each other, along with having our support, which is what Nanabozho taught us was the right thing to do." The force for change to social solidarity, which Lone Wolf suggests, creates a reality based on unifying the mythological ideal and the humanly real. Human limits are tested continually in the ritual event. The ritual actors powerfully transform the social condition through meaningful actions unifying the past, present, and future. The *gi-be wiikonge*, whether as the seventeenth-century Feast of the Dead or the contemporary "Ghost Supper," combines with the ethics of personing, gifting, and empowering. Their interconnection forms a system for mediating the dangerous problems caused by unco-operative others, and this combination becomes a motivating source of action.

Because history for Odawa traditionalists results from the events of persons acting for good or ill and not from impersonal causes, they approach the *gi-be wiikonge* as a significant way to address relationships between ethical humans, between human and more-than-human persons, and between themselves and threatening others. How traditionalists transform status by enacting the ethics of personing, gifting, and empowering is mapped out in the positive ritual actions of the Great Persons of mythology. For traditionalists, ritual is the mode to achieve social solidarity and revitalization. They see the *gi-be wiikonge* as one source for a powerful new voicing of community; as a conjoining event that brings together potent forces that both reflect and propel positive change, and as a significant way to reconstitute meaning and identity.

Conclusions

The transformation in the *gi-be wiikonge* shows the power of metaphorical reinterpretation. This ritual establishes and maintains bonds between communities through ethical acts of gifting that create powerful new relations. The *gi-be wiikonge* proves that gifting shows ethnic compassion. The ritual expresses a mythologically reaffirmed religious ethic: seeing the past in the present and projecting it into the future, establishing an "every-when," comes powerfully alive through ritual. Thus the ritual provides traditionalists with a means of adapting to a socio-economically changed environment. Ritual—which recreates the right relationship—is one medium for responding to shifts in social circumstances.

We should now appreciate how the *gi-be wiikonge*, based on exchange activities associated with the ethic of gifting between human persons and more-than-human persons, became the yardstick by which the Odawa understood the fur trade and made sense of agriculture, Christianity, and their relationship with Euro-Americans generally. In its current form, the *gi-be wiikonge* provides traditionalists with a way to use religious ethics to build a new sense of band and tribal identity, as well as sovereignty. Great Elk put it clearly: "Participating in traditional culture and being regarded as an elder are important. They're an honor that must be recognized. They give us a sense of identity and sovereignty. So do events like *gi-be* feasts." Ritual acts of exchange in the *gi-be wiikonge* have been one medium for responding successfully to threats to identity.

In one way or another, traditionalists continually ask: If social relations are organized by the mediation of disagreements through gifting, then where was the exchange and therefore compassion shown in the social behavior of the Euro-Americans? They have an answer to their own question: little if any positive reciprocity existed. From the traditionalists' perspective, "foreign" exchange did little to uphold ethical responsibility. Nevertheless, the Odawa continued to demonstrate their ethical responsibility through rituals, especially in the annual *gi-be wiikonge*.

The contemporary *gi-be wiikonge* is an example of a ritual that creates community identity by reinterpreting an earlier ritual with which it shares a common purpose. Similar to the traditionalists' drawing on mythological themes in their Seventh Fire narrative, both the contemporary *gi-be wiikonge* and its historical antecedent, the Feast of the Dead, reflect an apocalyptic situation. Contemporary apocalypticism reflects threats of intrusion by cultural "others" and increased Indian factionalism. Lone Wolf expressed the foreseen event of overcoming these threats of social disruption: "The Seventh Fire will happen when all Anishinabeg faithfully return to the Path of Life, putting aside all non-Indian values and all people who follow them, as these create imbalance or lead away from the Right Road." Myths like the Seventh Fire and rituals such as the *gi-be wiikonge* show the terrible consequences of not following tradition and voice a crucial ethical lesson: the Odawa have been wrong to "stray from the Right Path and allow non-Indian values to prevail, which has changed the world," as Black Bear put it. Traditionalists know that the impending transformation of the world will result when the Odawa reunite and survive "by returning to the Old Ways." Their enactment of religious precedents for proper ethical behavior drive this transformation. As the traditionalists understand it, sharing food in the *gi-be wiikonge* ethically enacts empowerment as voiced in the messages of some myths.

We have seen how Nanabozho recreated the world and redistributed food, making life possible. Nanabozho and, by association, food point to the possibility of constructive transformation. In mythology, acts of respect articulate the Odawa's relations with plant and animal persons, and these allegorical relations gave the Odawa a rationale for adapting to the challenges that have threatened their social unity and cultural identity.

Traditionalists understand that if food is a gift from Nanabozho, one of the ethical Great Persons of mythology, it is a source of personal and communal power. Considering food as a metaphorical medium to bond human communities, and to maintain their relations with the dead and with more-than-human persons, traditionalists assign ethnic unification as their purpose for ritual feasts. Food, as an empowering gift, allegorically designated in myths and metaphorically enacted in ritual feasts, becomes a powerful tool for ordering life, strengthening identity, and achieving sovereignty.

Ritually enacting the ethic of gifting in the *gi-be wiikonge*—as a continuum of sharing and reciprocity—expresses all that the Seventh Fire's message voices: the world periodically becomes disrupted and needs to be set on a proper course based on ethical principles of just and proper behavior (personing, gifting, and empowering). The next chapter, therefore, explores how some Odawa engage these ethical principles of justice as a source for asserting collectively determined and transformed identity, most particularly because they are confident about how the U.S. legal system works, even though they are skeptical about its purposes.

Chapter 9

Is Law a Medium for Collective Determination
Rituals of Authority versus Rituals of Equality

We the people of the United States, in order to form a more perfect union, establish justice, insure domestic tranquillity, provide for the common defense, promote the general welfare, and secure the blessings of liberty to ourselves and our posterity, do ordain and establish this Constitution for the United States of America.

Preamble to the U.S. Constitution (1789)

To change their current sociopolitically marginalized status (i.e., liminality) into a sovereign one, Odawa traditionalists extend their religiously charged activities to the legal arena. This extension of their activities focuses especially on the purpose of ritually enacting the existential postulates—personing, gifting, and empowering—to establish just relations. The transformative and empowering nature of their rituals allows for this kind of ethical application. By confronting U.S. law, these Odawa both comprehend an altered cultural landscape and assign new meanings to the changes. Extending their ritual activities to the legal setting affirms a collective "personhood": it is a constructive measure to restore a vital collective identity—*pimadaziwin*.

Particularly, traditionalists view communal access to time-honored sites and use of land for ritual activities as immediately important actions to redefine their identity and attain both ideological and political sovereignty. As Brown Otter put it, "We are supposed to practice our traditions. They're not something that are simply written down in some book. But it's kind of hard to practice when the government, and other Indians who follow, claims it owns the lands of our ancestors and therefore thinks it can keep us out." Traditionalists such as Brown Otter identify unjust behavior on two fronts: Anglo-American jurisprudence and other Indians whom they view as kowtowing to its "authority."

To truly revitalize traditions and regain a sovereign and collectively determined identity, these Odawa must face the U.S. courts and congressional acts, especially the American Indian Religious Freedom Act (1978) and the Native American Graves Protection and Repatriation Act (1990). In large part, traditionalists regard their success at reinvigorating a sovereign social identity, and therefore restoring *pimadaziwin*, as depending on whether federal statutes and legislation apply to nonrecognized groups, and if not, whether First Amendment guarantees hold for collective religious practice. Traditionalist Odawa now know the U.S. system well and are confident enough to meddle with its laws. They are taking the old colonialist tactic of forcing ways of doing things on the conquered and turning it on its head: traditionalists regard themselves not only as operating through the very system that they see as conflicting with their own but also as doing so to illustrate precisely how unjust that system has been and continues to be.

Focusing on Odawa traditionalists, this chapter examines the nature of these intercultural relationships, specifically as they are formed by U.S. law, and explores the legal implications for groups of non-federally recognized Indian peoples. These traditionalist Odawa clearly identify a conflict between their traditional understanding of justice and U.S. written law. They also aver that Indian case law, especially case precedent based on First Amendment free exercise claims and subsequent legislation, has not addressed the questions of whether either statute or legislation applies to all Indians or only to recognized groups, and to entire communities or only to individuals. These questions are particularly pressing regarding case precedent based on First Amendment free exercise claims and subsequent legislation, and case precedent established before the recognition petitioning procedures that were administratively promulgated by the Department of the Interior through the Bureau of Indian Affairs (BIA) in 1978. Traditionalists see the U.S. legal system as continually undermining their unique identity and rights, as well as their collective demonstrations of those rights and identity. For example, relative to a land issue that some

Odawa currently are facing, traditionalists ask whether case precedent and recent statutes and legislation apply to state and privately owned property or just to federal lands. They also claim in this situation, which is discussed below, that if the law does apply to private lands but not to nonrecognized groups, then as a U.S. citizen an individual could make a legal claim based on First Amendment free exercise infringement. Traditionalists ask: If such a claim were made and the claimant won, arguing for both self-interest and that of the Odawa, then would the court be recognizing the legitimacy of the group—even if by default? (Keeping to the Odawa's story, we will not examine these questions and claims from the absolute standpoint of U.S. law but from the view of the Odawa themselves.)

The Traditionalists' View:
Rituals of Authority versus Rituals of Equality

Traditionalists understand that the U.S. Constitution, which includes the rights of due process and equal protection, was the starting point for the statutory enactment of American society. They also understand that these provisions are not the only guidelines that have shaped their relations with the U.S. government. "Who's protecting who? And from who?" asked Brown Otter. "The U.S. protects itself with its laws. We see 'law' as a matter of reestablishing equal and just relationships—not a matter of authority, per se." Laughing Gull noted that "the U.S. legal system doesn't ask what our needs are. The law decides for us what programs are going to be started in our own backyards, whether we want them or not. Non-Indian lawyers simply dictate without our involvement or consent. They just hide behind their little laws." These statements suggest that some Odawa characterize U.S. law as being structured to protect an order created by people: We [Euro-Americans] are protected from Them [the Odawa] by Law. They also would agree with the conclusion that when put into practice, this American order masks aggression that allows injustice to operate under the guise of laws commanding obedience (Ball 1985:23, 25). Odawa traditionalists view American Indian case law as legitimizing the continuing attempts by American policy makers to suppress collective Indian religious exercise; practice that is fundamentally place oriented and site specific.

The traditionalists' view of U.S. law is articulated best in terms of "fences," "bulwark" and "ownership." Traditionalists see opposition to their ethical principles in the fact that "the doctrine of [land] use . . . became fundamental in American law and politics. In their stress on use, Puritan moral theologians anticipated John Locke's theory of property: [Euro-Americans] have been granted dominion over the earth; they have a God-given right and responsibility to use it; and they gain a property right in that with which they mix their labour" (Michaelsen 1986:257). Traditionalists regard the United States as having framed its law in a way comparable to its fencing of property. From this perspective, U.S. law establishes value-laden moral and civil stipulations that separate people from their own identities, from each other, and from the universe of ethical persons. For traditionalists, the U.S. legal framework conflicts with their method to establish and maintain proper interpersonal relationships, particularly as each person is ethically charged with upholding collective *pimadaziwin* through ritualized purposeful action, especially empowering acts of gifting.

The traditionalists' profound association between land and identity, clearly different from Euro-American notions of "property," is suggested in a story told by Old Man (Akiwenzii) of how his family lost their traditional land and allowed the first non-Indians to move into the area:

When we were married, my father gave me and my brother each a lot of his land, both up on the bluff and along the waterfront. One day, soon after my wedding, my wife and I were out on the lake canoeing, and suddenly I heard a commotion on the shore. It was my father calling and waving. But he wasn't alone. He was with a *sogonosh* [Anglo].

We paddled in to shore, and my father came up to me and said, "This man is a good man and he wants to buy your land. You're newlyweds and soon will have children, and you need the money."

I thought to myself, "Sell our family land? How can you sell land?" But being respectful of my father, I did what he wanted and sold this man the land Father had given me along the lake. I didn't give him our land on the bluff and that's where I have lived since. I helped this man build his house; they were the first non-Indian family in the area—but soon there were many more.

One day, my brother came to me and announced that he'd sold all his land to some non-Indians. "Sold all your land?" I said to him. "How could you sell all of it? What do you have left? Where are you going to live?"

He simply said, "I needed the money."

"Needed the money?" I asked him. "For what? If you needed it that bad, I would have given you money."

But he didn't respond, and do you know, my brother went out every day after that and got drunk until all his money was gone. We never should have sold any land. It was a great loss to all our relatives. We lost part of what made us who we are but aren't anymore.

Here we see clearly the fundamental interconnection between identity, land, and ethical social relations. Old Man's sentiments echo the problematic influence of land deals with Euro-Americans on ritual acts of reciprocal gift exchange. He certainly expected reciprocity, but whereas land is permanent, money is transient. Therefore nothing tangible and indelible was reciprocated by the non-Indian. To Old Man, exchanging land, which is permanent, for money, which is transient, could not be a basis for ethical and just relations. So in a sense, landownership became equated with withholding.

For Odawa traditionalists, as with many American Indian peoples, upholding the integrity of ethical relationships typically is place or site specific (Michaelsen 1986:250). "In the end, from a perspective Native Americans and Anglos can both understand, the main issue in American Indian law is land. Property law is basic to Anglo American jurisprudence. Without law, property would not exist. With the advent of law comes regulation of property possession" (Loftin 1989:40). U.S. law identifies several aspects of property law, broadly divided into freehold estates and nonfreehold estates and largely based on and an extension of British Parliamentary Statute De Donis Conditionabilus, first established in 1285 (Smith and Boyer 1971).

Simply put (as I am neither an attorney nor a specialist in probate or property law), there are three typical cases of freehold estates: fee simple, fee tail, and life estate. A case of freehold estate in fee simple would be *A* to *B* and his heirs, which gives *B* a title to property in fee simple that leaves nothing in *A*. *B*'s estate is inheritable by either heirs who are lineal (i.e., in direct line of ancestry) or collateral (i.e., descent through marriage). Thus fee simple creates an unlimited inherited estate. A case of freehold estate in fee tail would be *A* to *B* and the heirs of *B*'s body, which gives *B* a title to property that leaves a reversion in *A*, so that *B*'s estate is inheritable only by *B*'s lineal heirs. Thus, unlike fee simple, fee tail limits the category of heir. A case of a freehold life estate would be *A* to *B* for life, which gives *B* a title to an estate for *B*'s life but leaves a reversion in *A* so that *B*'s estate is not inheritable.

Equally simplistic in its presentation, there are four typical cases of nonfreehold estates: estate for years, estate from year to year, tenancy at will, and tenancy by sufferance. A case of nonfreehold estate for years would be *A* to *B* for ten years, which gives *B* property title to an estate for a limited number of years and leaves a reversionary interest in *A*, so that if *B* dies during the ten-year period the balance of the term passes to *B*'s personal representative (e.g., an executor) for purposes of administration. A case of nonfreehold estate from year to year would be *A* to *B* from year to year, which gives *B* property title to an estate from year to year that leaves a reversionary interest in *A*, so that if *B* dies during the period of the lease, the balance thereof passes to his personal representative, the executor. A case of nonfreehold tenancy at will would be a property title passed from *A* to *B* so long as *A* wishes or so long as both *A* and *B* agree. This gives *B* an estate at will and leaves a reversionary interest in *A* so that either *B*'s or *A*'s death during the tenancy terminates the tenancy and *A* (if the survivor) has the right to immediate possession. A case of nonfreehold tenancy by sufferance would be the transfer of property title from *A* to *B* for two years in which, after the expiration of the two-year term, *B* would continue in possession of the land, having no title at all and without the agreement or disagreement of *A*. This last scenario of property law is especially pertinent when considering certain treaty stipulations, land claims, and federal "ownership" of traditional Indian territories. It also is relevant to the current land case that certain Odawa traditionalists are facing, which we will discuss in detail.

Our simplistic evaluation of U.S. property law allows us to begin to understand the traditionalists' perspective of the structure of the U.S. legal system. Their view is spearheaded particularly by Milner Ball's metaphor of U.S. law as "the bulwark of freedom" (1985:25). Elders warn of the hazards of such a defensive imagery, especially the right to collective religious practice at a specific place. As traditionalists understand it, non-Indians use the law to protect themselves—and their property—and to assert their own freedom and self-interest, most often at the expense of others.

Traditionalists understand U.S. law as being derived directly from the early Euro-American colonialist doctrine of discovery and conquest, which was based on the self-substantiating mandate of Manifest Destiny, to its present extension: ownership. The doctrine of discovery, conquest, and ownership rests on a distinctive Euro-American myth of progress. This myth of progress conflicts with the religious precepts structuring the Odawa traditionalists' ethos and worldview: personing, gifting, and empowering. For traditionalists, as we have seen, mediating disagreements through gift exchange unites people in dynamic relationships.

The assessment of U.S. law in terms of the metaphor "law as bulwark" expresses for these Odawa how non-Indian power rests on division, privatization, and accumulation. As with other American Indian peoples, for these Odawa traditionalists, fusion, not fission, creates sociocosmic harmony and justice (see Sanborn 1990). "The eagle feathers on the tribal flag at powwows remind us of the proper ways to be Odawa that guide our life," said Lone Wolf. "These ways of living keep us in harmony. They're not laws. They weren't created by people. They were a gift to us from the *manidos*, the powerful grandfathers. They bring us together." For traditionalists such as this pipe carrier, their power rests on the interpersonal connection and community that results from gift exchange and just reciprocity.

We have seen how and why traditionalists order and guide proper relationships by gifting, which they understand to be a continuum of sharing and reciprocity. They contend that they have given the United states all of their traditional lands without the United States' having reciprocated anything. Traditionalists interpret relations with the United States as completely asymmetrical and U.S. law as void of reciprocity: based on their experience, the United States has used its law to withhold and to own. For traditionalists, then, the paramount questions, according to Great Elk, are, "How do we respond to such unethical behavior?" and "How are we supposed to establish proper relations with [the United States]?" Echoing these questions, many traditionalists ask, Does federal statute and legislation apply to groups that are not under BIA supervision?

Addressing these questions does not require an exhaustive examination of Indian case law or belaboring the unequal and ethically unjust treatment of American Indians: Vine Deloria Jr., in particular, has done a far better and more comprehensive job of that than could be done here. It is enough simply to examine the absolute conflict between the metaphor structuring the U.S. ethos and worldview through a concept of law (*law as the bulwark of freedom*) against the metaphors orienting the Odawa traditionalists' ethos and worldview through a concept of justice (*time is a changer, life is fluid, purposes are destinations, events are actions*). The traditionalists' ethical system and concept of justice is similar on one level to a legal system as a way of maintaining order, but it extends to a broader plane of sociocosmic order that embraces the place of persons in it (including the ancestors and the *manidos*) and the people's collective duty to uphold it.

Generally, Odawa traditionalists do not approach justice as punitive or retributive, which they understand to be the perspective of U.S. law. Instead, justice is viewed as regenerative and a matter of personal and social healing. For example, besides all of his other activities, Lone Wolf visits a local prison, where he teaches traditional ways to the Indian inmates and conducts ceremonies such as sweat lodges and pipe ceremonies. He approaches this endeavor as being a guide for these young men's rite of passage to a new and invigorated identity and status. As he understands it, they have committed a behavioral breach that has hurt both themselves and their communities. Enacting justice thus becomes a ritual that reestablishes right and equalized relationships. Therefore, as with other rites of passage, including vision fasts and the quest for a revitalized collective identity itself, the individual is separated from the larger social group, secluded from a past identity during which a profound metamorphosis occurs in one's state of being, and then reincorporated into the social network with renewed purpose, status, and identity. "They die and then return a new person," as Lone Wolf put it. "I'm just there to help guide their transformation and help them heal themselves. No prison and no prison guards can do that."

These Odawa approach the mediation of disagreements and disruption caused by personal malfeasance and social transgressions not as a matter of legal *adversarial adjudication* but as just and consensual *negotiation*. I emphasize "adversarial adjudication" and "negotiation" because traditionalists view them as having conflicting intents. They interpret the U.S. legal system as having a fundamentally opposite purpose based on market exchange principles and "adversarial adjudication" as being the key concept that drives that legal system. To them, the "authority" of U.S. law is based on absolute rules and principles that govern by being meted out by judges and lawyers. For traditionalists, having the law—a humanly constructed abstraction—be the arbiter for settling disputes is not the same as negotiating. They understand ethical negotiation to mean conferring with others, including the *manidos*—the power persons—in order to reach a compromise or agreement. Traditionalists see that to non-Indian lawyers the law leaves no room for negotiation. Law, therefore, cannot operate in personalistic ways to mediate, which traditionalists understand as interpersonal consensus and intervention to produce agreement or reconciliation.

Odawa traditionalists approach the world through the principle of "Equal Law under Justice," not the opposite, "Equal Justice under Law," as does the United States, to which the motto's inscription above the entrance to the U.S. Supreme Court building testifies. For these Odawa, religiously prescribed justice—the ethical responsibility to perpetuate relations with each other, the ancestors, the *manidos*, and other people—cannot be subsumed under man-made laws. Conflict is bound to arise between these two diametrically opposed orientations and is unavoidable with such recent legislative actions as the Religious Freedom Act and the Graves Protection and Repatriation Act. Both acts affect the traditionalists' efforts at collective determination and are problematic for them. Traditionalists view them skeptically as failing either to be oriented toward interpersonalistic ways of mediating religious differences or to serve as ethical guidelines based on respect for others, which are what traditionalists expect of these acts and their application. Traditionalists, observing that both acts stress differences between their own and non-Odawa religious doctrines, feel they must respond collectively to uphold the integrity of their traditions and transform their social status. They fully understand that powerful actions can be used to mediate the intrusion of a law only if one recognizes an ethical foundation to the legal system.

As we have noted, acts of benevolence are the hallmark of the traditionalists' social activism. Today the call for social transformation, modeled by Nanabozho and voiced in ritual activities, especially *gi-be* feasts, informs the ability of traditionalists to overpower other people's malevolence and acts of malfeasance toward them, and to gain collective determination. This call also is heard in their narrative of the Seventh Fire, which conveys a model of constructive ways for producing social solidarity. Traditionalists manipulate power through purposefully constructive actions, and they focus on applying these actions for social justice. The ethics that orient the lives of traditionalists—personing, gifting, and empowering, which lead to *pimadaziwin*—are inseparable from all facets of their social experience. Therefore it is paramount that traditionalists apply those ethics to legal endeavors for gaining ethnic solidarity and collective determination. Yet First Amendment free exercise guarantees, legislation on sovereignty, claims to time-honored sites, and the Religious Freedom and Graves Protection and Repatriation Acts underscore the embattled concepts of law and justice between the non-Indian and Odawa cultures. Without benefit of BIA recognition (and therefore a tribal court), traditionalists cite resolving two questions, in particular, as being crucial to their future: (1) Do these congressional acts apply to non-BIA recognized communities of Odawa traditionalists? and (2) If they are "domestic dependents" under the U.S. protectorate, what trust responsibility does the federal government have? In answering these questions, traditionalists view rituals of authority (U.S. law) as competing with rituals of equality (Odawa justice).

Justice versus Law: Statutory and Legislative Bulwarks

Two cases adjudicated by the U.S. Supreme Court hold particular importance, generally, to Indian land claims, to sovereignty, and to the genesis of the Freedom of Religion and Repatriation Acts. The high court's decision in *Johnston v. MacIntosh* (1823) held that tribes cannot handle lands they inhabit without federal government consent. In *Cherokee Nation v. State of Georgia* (1832) the court held tribes to be domestic dependent nations under the legal jurisdiction of the U.S. Constitution, not sovereign foreign nations.

The case of *Johnston v. MacIntosh* involved the issue of conflict over property title: in one situation, the claimants argued that title to land was given by the Indians under British supervision at an open public sale; the competing claim was the superiority of a title to the same land granted by the United States through a sale by federal land agents. The issue before the court was not really a conflict between British-supervised and American-authorized land sales. The real question was: Do tribes have the authority to cede property directly? Chief Justice John Marshall's court held that they do not, interpreting as U.S. constitutional intent that only the federal government can alienate and allocate Indian lands: tribes could exercise rights over property only through the arbitration of the federal government. This was one means that the United States used to claim and dominate land through trust title; governmental prerogative that still exists (see Chaudhuri 1985:23–27; Ragsdale 1985:66–67; Deloria 1985:240, 245, 1992:299).

With the progressive expansion and establishment of states, the decision in *Johnston v. MacIntosh* theoretically held that the federal government has a fiduciary responsibility to protect tribes, and their reservation lands established through treaties, against property claims by states. In reality, this decision set case precedent for weighing subsequent American Indian title cases, and it spearheaded the conflict concerning Indian and non-Indian attitudes toward land (see Loftin 1989). The court held that tribes do not have the legal power to transfer title to individuals because of conflict of interest in settling competing non-Indian claims to lands ceded by tribes, especially through treaties before the U.S. Constitution (ratified in 1789) that fell to the jurisdiction of the Northwest Ordinance. The doctrine of discovery and conquest, on which the Northwest Ordinance was established, meant that the Crown possessed absolute title to all lands it occupied; tribes had right of occupancy only, subject to being overturned at any time by the authority of the Crown (essentially, nonfreehold tenancy by sufferance). James, a nontraditionalist Odawa attorney and tribal court member, told me: "The U.S. has always claimed to use the right to equal protection to support treaty arbitrations. However, if treaties were negotiated before the Constitution was implemented, then the relationship is bound only by the Northwest Ordinance." The Northwest Ordinance defines "property" based on the British Parliamentary Statute of De Donis Conditionabilus. James emphasized how it follows, therefore, that under the earliest treaties "lands could be claimed without equal protection and reimbursement." *Johnson v. MacIntosh* established the precedent that absolute right of ownership by virtue of conquest defined "title."

In *Cherokee Nation v. State of Georgia*, the Cherokee plaintiffs argued that they were a sovereign nation and therefore entitled to sue a state for usurpation of land under article 3, section 2, of the U.S. Constitution (Chaudhuri 1985:23–26; Ragsdale 1985:66, 67; McCool 1985:109, 110; Deloria 1992:288). Article 3, section 2 reads:

> The judicial power shall extend to all cases, in law and equity, arising under this Constitution, the laws of the United States, and treaties made, or which shall be made, under their authority;—to all cases affecting ambassadors, other public ministers, and consuls;—to all cases of admiralty and maritime jurisdiction;—to controversies to which the United States shall be a party;—to controversies between two or more States;—between a State and citizens of another State;—between citizens of different States;— *between citizens of the same State claiming lands under grants of different States, and between a State, or the citizens thereof, and foreign states, citizens or subjects* [emphasis added]. In all cases affecting ambassadors, other public ministers, and consuls, and

those in which a State shall be party, the Supreme Court shall have original jurisdiction. In all other cases before mentioned, the Supreme Court shall have appellate jurisdiction, both as to law and fact, with such exceptions, and under such regulations, as the Congress shall make.

Based on its interpretation of article 3, the Marshall court upheld the Cherokees' argument provisionally: instead of a "foreign" nation, the court defined the Cherokee as a "domestic dependent" nation under the protection of the United States. This decision set case precedent for a trust doctrine between guardian and ward: between the trustor (the doctrine of discovery, conquest, and ownership) and the land trustee (the United States), and between the land trustee and the beneficiary (the tribe). The Supreme Court unclearly differentiated between "foreign" and "sovereign" nations, however, so the issue of "trust relationship" emerged, and each subsequent case must reference jurisdiction. Though intended to define jurisdiction, this contractual relationship resulted in an overlap of jurisdiction between federal, state, and tribal powers, as "land trustee" became both federal and state governments.

With the widespread establishment of states during the nineteenth and early twentieth centuries, federal policy attempted to abolish traditional Indian "religions" and collective expression, especially through the control of land. By the 1930s, however, the Bureau of Indian Affairs softened its stance. In theory, when Indians were granted citizenship in 1924 (*American Indian Citizenship Act*), there was no need for special legislation to protect religious freedom because such rights were guaranteed constitutionally under the First Amendment. (The need for special legislation seems further unwarranted by Congress extending some of the Bill of Rights to Indian peoples in 1968 through the American Indian Civil Rights Act.)

Two cases in particular are noteworthy regarding the Supreme Court's interpretation of First Amendment free exercise claims: *Sherbert v. Verner* (1963) and *Wisconsin v. Yoder* (1972). In *Sherbert* the plaintiff, a Seventh Day Adventist, argued that her First Amendment rights were violated when she was fired for refusing to work on Saturday, her Sabbath, and denied unemployment benefits. The court upheld her argument: states can neither impose direct burdens (firing her) nor indirect burdens (denying her unemployment benefits) because of individual religious belief unless a compelling state interest justifies such activity (see Petoskey 1985:223–24, 230, 236). In *Yoder* three Amish parents claimed that sending their children to public school violated their constitutional rights (see Petoskey 1985:223–25, 230, 236). Based on answering the question "How serious is the incursion on religious freedom and how does the state's counter-interest weigh?" the court held that freedom of individual religious belief outweighed the state's interest in compulsory education. Especially,

> *Yoder* has proven to be a problematic precedent for Indian free exercise cases. Out of *Yoder* was fashioned the "centrality" standard which has dominated such cases. That is, unless a particular practice or, as in the case of sacred site claims, a particular place or area, can be proved to be "central and indispensable" to the religion of the claimants the claim cannot be sustained under the free exercise clause. (Michaelsen 1986:253)

Although these cases were critical to the outcome of future American Indian free exercise claims by individuals, neither specifically addressed the issue of collective religious attachment to a geographically specific place. The decisions in both *Yoder* and *Sherbert* theoretically established that the burden of proving that religious belief specifically would harm the state's interest falls to the government (Petoskey 1985:224).

In practice, however, federal and state officials and individuals with special interests—especially land developers—continued to deny Indian tribal members communal access to time-honored lands to practice collective rituals, despite supposed constitutional protections. Therefore in 1977, with the increased visibility of Indian activism and the civil rights movement in general, several senators responded by drafting Senate Joint Resolution 102 (see Craven 1983; Michaelsen 1984; Chaudhuri 1985:13; O'Brien 1985, 1988; Deloria 1992). The Carter administration voiced concern that the resolution conflicted with the First Amendment, asking whether the bill required federal agencies to protect Indian "religions" at the expense of public interest. For example, although First Amendment protections are reinforced in the Fifth and

Fourteenth Amendments, "property" remains ill defined, as does "just compensation" for the government's exercising its right of eminent domain, which is the Fifth Amendment power to take private property for public use. The administration also asked whether the bill would conflict with the Freedom of Information Act and, if so, how this might affect such federal agencies as the National Park Service (NPS), which acts both to "protect" sites and to allow the public to "know" them.

For example, the NPS, emphasizing the Freedom of Information Act over Indian religious free exercise, creates parks on time-honored Indian lands—even on reservations—allowing unsupervised public access to such Algonkian sites as pictographs along the north shore of Lake Superior, where people are free to inscribe their initials on the cliffs for posterity.[1] Algonkian leaders ask, Where is the protection in such action? "There is not unrestricted public access to Judeo-Christian churches—that is, buildings—which are protected for religious practices simply by locking the doors," said Brown Otter.

Congressman Morris Udall stated the issue on the floor of the House of Representatives: "For many tribes, the land is filled with physical sites of religious and sacred significance to them. Can we not understand that? Our religions have their Jerusalems, Mount Calvarys, Vaticans and Meccas. We hold sacred Bethlehem, Nazareth, the Mount of Olives and the Wailing Wall. Bloody wars have been fought because of these religious sites" (quoted in Echo-Hawk 1993:40). Despite Udall's foresight, with the threat of veto, the executive office insisted on amending Senate Joint Resolution 102 to read "nothing in this resolution shall be construed as affecting any provision of state or federal Law." Inserting this clause greatly weakened the bill for three reasons: (1) it opened the door for the federal government to violate its trust responsibility established by treaties; (2) it allowed the government to override earlier legislation and case precedent; and (3) it left the door open for states themselves to intervene (O'Brien 1985).

Senate Joint Resolution 102 finally was passed and became the American Indian Religious Freedom Act (AIRFA): A measure meant to affirm the federal government's fiduciary responsibility to maintain the ethnic identity and religious freedom of Indians.

Section 1 of the AIRFA states: "The United States [will act] to protect and preserve for American Indians their inherent right of freedom to believe, *express*, and exercise (their) traditional religions," especially by guaranteed right of access to sites, use and possession of ritual objects and the freedom to worship through ceremonies. Another section requires "an evaluation of federal policies and procedures, in consultation with native religious leaders, of changes necessary to protect and preserve the rights and practices in question" (*American Indian Religious Freedom Act*). For many Indian peoples, such as Odawa traditionalists, however, the act has proved to be toothless.

Free Exercise and Religious Freedom:
The Judicial Bulwark against Collective Action

Considering the First Amendment of the U.S. Constitution, why was the American Indian Religious Freedom Act necessary? The answer to this question is elusive, especially given that the First Amendment reads: "Congress shall make no law [1] respecting the establishment of religion, or [2] prohibiting the free exercise thereof." These two provisions, the establishment clause and the free exercise clause, define the relationship between church and state. Although written to limit congressional powers, these two religion clauses also apply to states through the Fourteenth Amendment's due process clause (ratified in 1868).

According to the establishment clause, Congress cannot pass laws "respecting the establishment of religion," thus calling for a broad separation between church and state. Neither the federal government nor a state can create a church, and neither can pass laws supporting either one religion or all religions or establishing preference for one over another. Theoretically, this clause set a barrier between church and state, an act consistent with the agenda to curtail the rise to political power of such religious organizations as the Church of England.

With the free exercise clause, the government cannot forbid religious services, punish individuals for having a particular religious belief, or exclude a member of a religious community from public service because such acts would limit religious freedom (see Ensworth 1983). Essentially, the free exercise clause was a direct result of and response to the European Reformation. It was intended as a measure to prevent discrimination against dissenting religious denominations, and to establish general freedom of individual belief.

Yet the free exercise of religion is not absolute: the clause creates exceptions for state regulations that serve secular goals. For example, in 1879 the Supreme Court held that Congress could outlaw polygamy among Mormons although for them the practice was a religious duty (*Reynolds v. United States*, 1879; *Mormon Church v. United States*, 1890). The high court held that special privileges cannot be granted because of religion if such waivers undermine public interests inherent to the law.

In theory only, then, the First Amendment is neutral and cannot be used to show favor or disfavor on religious grounds. But in practice, if the government can neither outlaw religious belief nor burden the exercise of that belief, then the courts must determine whether the asserted religious belief is held sincerely. If it is found to be sincere, the burden on individual worship is balanced against the state's interest in restricting the exercise of belief. If the state's interest is compelling, it outweighs individual interest. From the United States' perspective, the key words here are "sincerely" and "compelling." From the perspective of Odawa traditionalists, however, the key words are "individual" and "belief," and they ask, as does Lone Wolf, What about collective practice? The answer to this question remains elusive.

The courts have tried approximately twenty-four cases concerning the government's fiduciary responsibility to protect American Indians' free exercise of collective religious practice. Almost one-half of these cases address the issue of land use rights and Indian communal access to and protection of time-honored lands. Most of the decisions in these cases have overruled right of access and therefore dangerously threaten collective religious free exercise.[2]

For example, in *Sequoyah v. Tennessee Valley Authority* (1980) the Cherokee plaintiffs argued, based on First Amendment free exercise and AIRFA infringement, that the reservoir created by the building of the Tellico Dam prevented their use of time-honored sites, including ancestral burial grounds (see Petoskey 1985:225–26, 228, 233, 234; O'Brien 1988:13). In 1979 the Tennessee District

Court held that lack of land title overruled right of claims, and the case moved to the circuit court. The circuit court upheld the original ruling "but on substantially different grounds." The court decided that while a proprietary interest in property was unnecessary to the claim, "the plaintiffs . . . failed to prove that the geographical location was imperative to the practice of their religion. Rather, the Cherokees were expressing a 'personal preference'; their concern was with their tribe's historical beginnings and their culture, not their religious beliefs" (O'Brien 1988:13). The court decided that First Amendment guarantees were not violated, and federal authorization and funding for building the dam had preceded the enactment of the AIRFA.

In *Badoni v. Higginson* (1981) the Navajo plaintiffs argued that the federal government's creating a national monument on their time-honored land restricted both their access to this land and their ability to conduct ceremonies without disruption by voyeuristic non-Indian tourists (see Petoskey 1985:225–27, 229, 233; O'Brien 1988:13–15). Similar to the decision in *Sequoyah*, the Utah District Court held that neither First Amendment free exercise nor AIRFA guarantees had been infringed upon because the Navajo lacked land title (nonfreehold estate in tenancy by sufferance). Additionally, the court held that freedom of information and public interest outweighed the claim. The case moved to the Tenth Circuit Court, which "rejected the requirement of [property] proprietorship, but remained in agreement with the lower court's finding that the public's interest . . . superseded Indian religious rights. The plaintiffs' request to exclude tourists from the area during religious ceremonies furthermore would constitute the creation of a religious shrine and violate the establishment clause." The Court decided that the National Park Service did not inhibit the Navajos' religion and "dismissed the plaintiffs' reliance on AIRFA, stating that they had no arguments on the constitutionality of the Act's laws or regulations" (O'Brien 1988:14–15).

In *Fools Crow v. Gullet* (1982) the Lakota plaintiffs argued against the development of tourist accommodations at Bear Butte in the Black Hills of South Dakota, which is time-honored land in Lakota tradition (see Petoskey 1985:225–31, 233–35; O'Brien 1988: 16–18). The district court—and subsequently the circuit court—

held that the actions by the South Dakota Department of Game, Fish, and Parks did not violate Lakota First Amendment guarantees. The courts, basing this decision on the tribe's lack of property interest, emphasized the possibility of the infringement on religious belief over religious practice. Both the district and circuit courts reasoned that the right of non-Indian tourists to access state lands was equally important as the Lakota's right to freely exercise their religious beliefs. "Citing *Sequoyah* and *Badoni,* the [circuit] court pointed out that if the Cherokees' and Navajos' bar of access to lands . . . had not violated their first amendment rights, then certainly the state had not violated the Lakotas' rights" (O'Brien 1988:15). Furthermore, the court underscored that the Lakota claim, if granted, would violate the establishment clause. It also held that the AIRFA, "merely a federal policy statement," did not address issues at the state level that would provide for a separate cause of action.

In *Wilson v. Block* (1983) the Navajo and Hopi plaintiffs argued that the U.S. Forest Service would violate their rights to religious freedom if the bureaucracy proceeded with plans to expand a ski area in the San Francisco Peaks of northern Arizona, a time-honored site used for ceremonial purposes but located on federal lands (see Petoskey 1985:225–32, 234; O'Brien 1988:15–16). These mountains are significant to the Hopi because they are the home of the kachinas, powerful more-than-human beings who ensure tribal well-being by residing among the people for six months of the year. The Hopi feared that "If their [the kachinas'] sacred home [was] exposed to the type of development which tend[ed] to make the area even more of a public thoroughfare [the kachinas might] flee the area" and thereby disrupt communal well-being (Michaelsen 1986:249).

Similarly, the tribal medicine people representing the Navajo objected to "any digging or building on the San Francisco Peaks [as such actions] would constitute a threat to the health of Navajos as individuals and to tribal well-being in general" (Michaelsen 1986:249). The district court acknowledged the importance of the peaks to Navajo and Hopi religious "belief" but held that the expansion of an already existing public recreational area was not an infringement of free exercise. According to the court, to prohibit the development would violate the establishment clause. The case moved to the District of Columbia Circuit Court, which upheld the lower court's decision, arguing that the "indispensability" of the property to religious practice had not been proved and that the government's actions were merely "offensive," not intrusive, and therefore were permissible. Concerning claims under the AIRFA, the court held that the "AIRFA required only that the government had to fulfill three duties: to evaluate policies and procedures for protecting religious freedoms; to refrain from prohibiting access, performance of religious ceremonies, and the possession and use of religious objects; and to consult with Indian groups" (O'Brien 1988:16). The court's reasoning was that because members of the Forest Service had consulted with a few tribal leaders, it had complied with these stipulations.

The above cases serve as examples of claims to land use rights based on the AIRFA and the free exercise clause. The decisions in these cases illustrate that federal policy is defined nebulously concerning whether tribal land use rights are either statutorily or constitutionally bound. Further, these case decisions resulted in the Navajo, the Cherokee, the Cheyenne and Lakota, and the Navajo and Hopi, respectively, being denied communal access to use and protect sites under federal or state ownership. The *Badoni* case is especially disturbing; the decision implied that the American Indian Religious Freedom Act may be unconstitutional, particularly by "showing favor" and not upholding the First Amendment equal protection component (Petoskey 1985:227). Thus far, most cases related to the AIRFA are concerned with authority over property: tribal claims largely have been unsuccessful because the courts consistently have weighed the establishment clause over the free exercise clause.

These cases also illustrate the ineffectiveness—and Christian bias—of the judgments based on federal statute and legislation to uphold the right of American Indians to the free exercise of collective religious practices, which often include rituals to reaffirm kinship ties with the ancestors and power persons. "Most Anglo-Americans are Christian. . . . Christianity . . . is a 'Confessional' religion, one which is confessed. Their kingdom is not of this world. This difference leads to a number of legal problems for

Native Americans. . . . traditional Native American religions were practiced by everyone in the tribe, while Christianity is a religion embraced by individuals" (Loftin 1989:43). Denying the communal orientation of Indian people's religious traditions, especially as expressed by access to sites held under federal dominion, particularly burial grounds, breaks the collective ability to perpetuate cultural unity through ritual. Clearly, "the sacred site cases pose the question of survival in poignant fashion. While the general doctrine of broad applicability may be useful to [individual] American Indian free exercise litigants, there has been, among the various free exercise cases decided in the American courts, no exact precedent on which to rest [collective] Indian sacred site claims" (Michaelsen 1986:251, 252).

Case precedent regarding corrective religious practice on time-honored lands has not been established for several reasons. First, there is an absence of judicial and legislative consensus on whether the executive branch has to review federal procedures and make final decisions. Second, it has not been clearly established if collective claims are either constitutionally or statutorily bound. Third, there is no consensus about whether the federal government has a statutory trust responsibility to protect and preserve Indian peoples' religious practices and recognize them as inseparable from their traditional cultures. Two more recent cases crystalize the problem of the legal loophole that these inconsistent interpretations have created for American Indian collective religious liberty: *Lyng v. Northwest Indian Cemetery Association* (1988) and *Employment Division, Department of Human Resources of Oregon v. Smith* (1990).[3]

Lyng concerned the building of a logging road by the National Forest Service, the Gasquet-Orleans or "G-O" Road, across the Chimney Rock area in northern California. This area is claimed to be time-honored land used for ceremonial purposes by the Yurok, Karok, and Tolowa Indians. According to the *U.S. Supreme Court Reports'* summary of the case (99 L Ed 2d:534–35), the U.S. Forest Service planned to finish a seventy-five-mile road that was intended to connect two California towns by completing a six-mile span through an area within a national forest, and to develop timber harvesting with one-half-mile "protective" zones around specific sites. Before beginning the project, the Forest Service contracted an environmental impact study, which both acknowledged the significance of the land for the Indians and reported that "successful religious use of the land depended on privacy, silence, and an undisturbed natural setting, and constructing a road along any of the available routes would cause serious and irreparable damage to the sanctity of the area" (*U.S. Supreme Court Reports*, 99 L Ed 2d:534). These conclusions were overlooked, however, and road completion efforts continued.

Indian leaders from the three tribes, collectively challenging both the road-building and lumbering projects, brought suit against the secretary of agriculture. Their legal claim was both constitutional free exercise and AIRFA infringement. The U.S. District Court for the Northern District of California held that both actions by the Forest Service would violate the free exercise clause, the Federal Water Pollution Control Act (FWPCA; 33 USCS 1251 et seq.) and the National Environment Policy Act of 1969 (NEPA; 42 USCS 4321 et seq.). On appeal by the Forest Service, the U.S. Ninth Circuit Court of Appeals upheld the district court's decision and concluded that the government had not demonstrated a compelling interest in the road's completion (795 F2d 688).

The case went from the circuit to the Supreme Court. The high court majority (O'Connor, Rehnquist, White, Stevens, and Scalia)[4] reversed and remanded the lower courts' decisions based on their interpretations of several aspects of constitutional law. For example, the high court upheld the principle of judicial restraint in cases where claims of both legislative and statutory infringement are made.[5] This principle of judicial restraint requires courts first to establish whether a decision on the constitutional claim would allow for greater relief than that to which the claimants (in this case, the Indian tribes) are entitled under statute; if it does not, the court held, "a constitutional decision is unnecessary and therefore inappropriate." Looking to statute, the Court held that the Forest Service, by its environmental impact study and steps at protection of certain areas, was in compliance with the AIRFA. In deciding whether the Indians' claim of constitutional violation would provide greater "relief" for the claimants, the Court drew on

Constitutional Law 961 and held to a narrow interpretation of free exercise: protections against government programs apply only to rare cases in which such programs result in punishing a person for practicing religion, or in coercing a person into violating his or her religion. The Court stated: "Even if we assume that we should accept the Ninth Circuit's prediction, according to which the G-O Road will 'virtually destroy the . . . Indians' ability to practice their religion,' . . . the Constitution simply does not provide a principle that could justify upholding respondents' legal claims. However much we might wish that it were otherwise, government simply could not operate if it were required to satisfy every citizen's religious needs and desires." The Court decided that in this case neither punishment nor coercion were at issue (*U.S. Supreme Court Reports*, 99 L Ed 2d:537–41, 548).

Further, the Court held that "the Constitution does not, and courts cannot, offer to reconcile the various competing demands on government, many of them rooted in sincere religious belief, that inevitably arise in so diverse a society as ours." The Court reached this decision based on interpreting Constitutional Law 974 to read that "compelling interest" tests of "sincere" religious belief, and of which federal lands are "central" or "indispensable" to which religions, were both unconstitutional and contrary to court precedents (*U.S. Supreme Court Reports*, 99 L Ed 2d:548, 539–40). The Court majority's final holding was that the free exercise clause did not bar the federal government from allowing lumbering in or constructing a road through national forest area used for religious purposes by Indians. Justice Brennan, with Marshall and Blackmun, dissented.

In his dissent, Justice Brennan voiced an understanding and appreciation of the centrality of site-specific places in American Indian peoples' worldviews that is uncharacteristic of the Court members:

> Today, the Court holds that a federal land-use decision that promises to destroy an entire religion does not burden the practice of that faith in a manner recognized by the Free Exercise Clause. Having thus stripped respondents and all other Native Americans of any constitutional protection against perhaps the most serious threat to their age-old religious practices, the Court assures us that

nothing in its decision "should be read to encourage governmental insensitivity to the religious needs of any citizen. . . . " I find it difficult, however, to imagine conduct more insensitive to religious needs than the Government's determination to build a marginally useful road in the face of uncontradicted evidence that the road will render the practice of respondents' religion impossible. Nor do I believe that respondents will derive any solace from the knowledge that although the practice of their religion will become "more difficult" as a result of the Government's actions, they remain free to maintain their religious beliefs. Given today's ruling, that religious freedom amounts to nothing more than the right to believe that the religion will not be destroyed. The safeguarding of such a hollow freedom not only makes a mockery of the "policy of the United States to protect and preserve for American Indians their inherent right of freedom to believe, express, and exercise their traditional religion" [quoting AIRFA], it fails utterly to accord with the dictates of the First Amendment. (*U.S. Supreme Court Reports*, 99 L Ed 2d:564)

Brennan's dissent is a powerful statement that based on "the Court's toothless exhortation to be 'sensitive' to affected religions" (*U.S. Supreme Court Reports*, 99 L Ed 2d:562), the decision in *Lyng* made First Amendment and AIRFA guarantees for Indian peoples wholly inapplicable in situations concerning religious areas on federal property. Therefore, these federal laws are grounded not in what legal theorists refer to as "apodictic" law (meaning clearly demonstrated and unbendable) but rather in "casuistic" law (meaning their application to a specific situation by two or more parties presenting clever but conflicting reasonings and interpretations).

Instead of a claim to time-honored land, the issue in *Smith* was whether First Amendment and AIRFA rights extend to members of the Native American Church (NAC). According to the *U.S. Supreme Court Reports*' summary of the case (108 L Ed 2d:876–77), two members of the NAC in Oregon, who were employed as drug rehabilitation counselors in the private sector, were fired (arguably a direct burden; see *Sherbert*) because they used peyote as part of NAC ritual. Both individuals applied for state unemployment benefits but were denied by the Oregon Department of Human Resources Employment Appeals Board. The appeals board interpreted that they had been fired because of misconduct on the job. The case went before the Oregon Court of Appeals, which reversed the board's decision. The case moved to the Oregon Supreme Court, the state arguing that Oregon statute concerning the criminal nature of selling and using illicit drugs, which by state legal definition includes peyote, made no exception for the sacramental use of peyote, and that the NAC members' use of peyote thus fell within statutory prohibitions. The state supreme court held that prohibiting peyote use in religious contexts was a violation of free exercise protections and that the counselors could not be denied unemployment compensation for engaging in that religious practice as such action imposed an indirect burden (see *Sherbert*). Finally, the case moved to the U.S. Supreme Court, which reversed the state court's decision.

The high court majority (Scalia, Rehnquist, White, Stevens, and Kennedy) based their opinion on several aspects of constitutional law. For example, Constitutional Law 974 was interpreted to read that the free exercise clause allows a state to include religious use of peyote within the state's criminal prohibition against the drug's use if there is no evidence of infringement of religious belief. Constitutional Law 967 was interpreted to read that a state's denying unemployment benefits to any person who has been fired for religious use of peyote is consistent with the free exercise clause if state statute defines use of the drug as a criminal infraction. Finally, Constitutional Law 961 was interpreted to read that, under the free exercise clause, enforcing religion-neutral state criminal laws that burden religious practice need not be justified by a compelling state interest test.

In the majority's opinion, Scalia pointed out that Oregon classifies peyote as an illegal controlled substance, and that by state statute any persons knowingly and intentionally possessing this drug are guilty of a Class B felony (*U.S. Supreme Court Reports*, 108 L Ed 2d:882). Although acknowledging that the free exercise clause prohibits government regulation of religious belief (as established by *Sherbert*), Scalia said:

> We have never held that an individual's religious beliefs excuse him from compliance with an otherwise valid law prohibiting conduct

that the State is free to regulate. . . . Respondents in the present case, however, seek to carry the meaning of "prohibiting" the free exercise [of religion] one large step further. They contend that their religious motivation for using peyote places them beyond the reach of a criminal law that is not specifically directed at their religious practice, and that is concededly constitutional as applied to those who use the drug for other reasons. (U.S. Supreme Court Reports, 99 L Ed 2d:885)

Further, the majority argued that the only decisions in which the Court held that applying a generally applicable law burdened religious practice and therefore violated First Amendment protections were in cases that concerned free exercise infringement in conjunction with other constitutional protections (e.g., in *Yoder*; *U.S. Supreme Court Reports*, 99 L Ed 2d:887). This situation did not apply in this case. Finally, drawing on the *Lyng* decision, the Court overruled the constitutionality of a compelling state interest test in cases that challenge the government's ability to enforce laws that prohibit "socially harmful conduct" (ibid.:889–90). The Court majority concluded that "precisely because 'we are a cosmopolitan nation made up of people of almost every conceivable religious preference,' . . . and precisely because we value and protect that religious divergence, we cannot afford the luxury of deeming *presumptively invalid*, as applied to the religious objector, every regulation of conduct that does not protect an interest of the highest order" (*U.S. Supreme Court Reports*, 99 L Ed 2d:892).

Justice O'Connor, along with Brennan, Marshall, and Blackmun, dissented, especially on this last point. O'Connor wrote for the minority:

In my view, today's holding dramatically departs from well settled First Amendment jurisprudence, appears unnecessary to resolve the question presented, and is incompatible with our Nation's commitment to individual religious liberty.

. . . the First Amendment was enacted precisely to protect the rights of those whose religious practices are not shared by the majority and may be viewed with hostility. (*U.S. Supreme Court Reports*, 99 L Ed 2d:893–94)

The decisions in the *Lyng* and *Smith* cases prompted Senator Daniel K. Inouye, chairman of the Senate Indian Affairs Committee (SIAC), to propose a new statute regarding Indian religious liberty.

Between 1992 and 1993 a nationwide field hearing was held on Indian religious free exercise and resulted in a native coalition, which presented the findings to the SIAC. Working in consultation with the coalition, the SIAC drafted a bill to supplement the American Indian Religious Freedom Act with five additional protections:

> (1) protects Native American sacred sites through procedural and substantive legal standards; (2) protects Indian religious use of peyote by essentially codifying existing DEA regulations and making them uniform nationally; (3) protect religious rights of Native American prisoners; (4) protects Indian religious use of eagle feathers and other surplus animal parts in ceremonies by streamlining the present United States Fish and Wildlife Service permit system under existing law; and (5) establishes a private course of action to protect native religious practices under the "compelling state interest test." (Echo-Hawk 1993:49)

Senator Inouye and seven cosponsors introduced a bill, the Native American Free Exercise of Religion Act, in May 1993. As an additional measure to ensure the right of religious free exercise and collective practice, particularly, this new bill is being hotly debated at this writing.

Odawa Traditionalists and the Law

A case concerning land and water use rights in Michigan is noteworthy because of its implications for non-federally recognized Odawa traditionalists. In *U.S. v. Michigan* (1979) the United States enacted its fiduciary trust obligation established by treaties and represented an Ojibwe-Odawa group as its trustee for fishing rights against the state. On the Indians' behalf, the federal government argued that Michigan was violating the 1836 Treaty of Washington by regulating fishing and restricting water rights. This case resulted from the Michigan Department of Natural Resources' taking a water claim to regulate fishing by licenser in

1942. The federal government responded for the group, as it had been organized as a tribal government with a recognized land base in 1934, and argued that Michigan had no such authority and jurisdiction. The nonrecognized northern bands of Odawa, however, were not represented in the case because of lack of money, and because the United States viewed them as having been assimilated. The case moved to the appellate court, then to the Michigan supreme court in 1981. From 1981 to the present, debate has focused on the division of water rights between three recognized tribal groups in northern Michigan. And as Brown Otter commented, "This is basically Indian fighting Indian."

Odawa traditionalists interpret a self-defensive orientation of U.S. law throughout the above policy statements and especially in the Native American Graves Protection and Repatriation Act (1990). Based on several statements made during a session on repatriation between Odawa elders and non-Indian museum curators and archaeologists at the 1992 Michigan Museum Conference, the Odawa expressed two key concerns about the Repatriation Act.[6] Their first concern was that objects eligible for repatriation must be defined and inventoried and the information made available to Indian groups who may be interested in making claims within a five-year period, and that claims will be adjudicated by a seven-member board of Indians and non-Indians funded through the National Park Service (NPS). These Odawa understand this claims process to mean that the burden of proof for identification and reclamation falls to separate—and potentially competing—tribes and bands. The second concern was that regulations to proceed with the intent of the act will emanate directly from the Park Service, and more than one-and-one-half years into the program, the Department of the Interior, as an umbrella agency of the NPS and BIA, had yet to begin to seek funding. These Odawa argued that everyone, therefore, was on his own and must wait patiently.

At the meeting, two elders voiced questions about how the act is worded. They wanted to know what and how the credentials of the groups involved in defining objects of concern will be identified. They wanted to know whether a system ensuring equity of adjudication can and will be implemented. They wanted to know if the federal government has a fiduciary responsibility. They wanted to know, given that the NPS initially is responsible for funding, where available funding is located. They wanted to know whether the act applies to private collectors, and to burial sites under federal, state, and private dominion. Additionally, they raised questions about timing, what groups are eligible to make claims, what definitions apply, how the criteria for repatriation and graves protection will be balanced with the requests, and whether assurance of a balance of ideologies exists (i.e., between and within groups).

Many Odawa interpret the act to read that institutions have the responsibility to prepare inventories and make proper notifications so that Odawa groups can make claims. They do not see repatriation as a matter of legal arbitration. At the meeting, one elder said: "What we want is simple. We want the bones and associated grave goods of our ancestors to be returned for reburial—period. Artifacts taken by a non-Indian community that were not found in burials will be returned for our elders to use. The issue is central to our collective ability to determine our own identity and future. It's a means of retaining our traditions and of keeping our identity alive." This statement underscores how some elders interpret cultural and material artifacts "owned" by others as powerful agents for mobilizing Odawa communities. Repatriation of such materials is a significant part of the traditionalists' social activism for collective determination and sovereignty. However, a great deal of skepticism exists about whether the United States will give them what they want. "I'll believe it when I see it," said a second elder. "The government has made many promises and we've continually been disappointed. Another law. More big talk. But nothing ever gets done. I won't hold my breath about ever seeing our ancestors returned to the earth where they belong."

As with the above elders, no confusion exists among traditionalists about policy currently being debated in the arenas of the elected bodies and the courts. They know that policies not won in the legislature move to the courts, and that the court arena differs fundamentally from the legislative arena. Traditionalists clearly understand that in the U.S. system, court decisions are not by consensus and usually are adversarial. With this understanding, they have abandoned their strategy of invisibility and are asserting their integrity and what they regard as their newly empowered sociocultural status on the local, state, and federal levels.

Locally, Odawa traditionalists are actively engaged in constructing and asserting their physical presence. The council members of one band have gained grant support to acquire land and establish a community center, which offers such services as "meals on wheels," educational and vocational training, substance abuse counseling, and assistance with genealogical research for membership criteria. Also, this band recently acted to acquire from a local municipality the deed to a historic building that houses an Odawa museum, which the group supports with grants, donations, and proceeds from an annual powwow. Besides community sponsored powwows, the leaders of this band also organize annual elders' councils. Additionally, they are collecting a community-wide oral history, conducted among the elders by the elders. Perhaps the greatest attention currently concerns a conflict with the region's Catholic diocese and two local townships over the future of an early eighteenth-century mission church and adjacent Odawa cemetery (in fact, the place where the Odawa prophet The Trout originated).

Actually, this conflict has a long history, and its resolution largely relies on establishing whether statute and legislation—especially First Amendment free exercise guarantees, the Graves Protection and Repatriation Act, and the Freedom of Religion Act—apply both to property not under either federal or state domain and to non-federally as well as federally recognized groups, instead of individuals. Here is the scenario that traditionalists must address.[7] The Catholic diocese has protective custodianship of the church building and several platted parcels of land, which have been used as a cemetery solely for the Odawa since the church was built in the early 1700s. This property is located on the shores of Lake Michigan and extends approximately five hundred feet along the beach (for a variety of reasons, the exact dimension has not been established concretely). At current real estate value, the frontage is assessed at about two thousand dollars per front foot. Adjacent to the property, between extremely expensive non-Indian summer homes, are the remains of an Odawa settlement, which at one time numbered some five thousand people. The Diocese of Michigan faces increasing financial struggles, which have forced the closure of many parishes. With the threat of this one closing, several traditionalist Odawa leaders approached the diocese and, at one meeting that I attended, were assured that there was no such immediate intention. A verbal agreement was made that they would be notified if the diocese felt it necessary to take such action. These Odawa leaders underscored their ability to document the fact that their ancestors originally allowed the missionaries to occupy the land and use it for future Odawa generations but could reclaim the land at any time if the missionaries did not uphold their obligations to the Odawa community (in a sense, a nonfreehold estate in tenancy by sufferance). They expressed great concern about the status of the cemetery, especially since many people in several surrounding Odawa communities can identify ancestors' graves and have assumed that unused areas would be available to subsequent generations who wished burial in this place. This concern arose partly because the public has long used the property to access the beach. In doing so, however, people must walk through the cemetery grounds, and every summer grave markers are kicked down and used as kindling for beach fires.

Meanwhile, without the knowledge of these Odawa, the diocese discussed the sale of at least part of the property with the two adjacent township supervisors. The township supervisors proposed to protect the cemetery grounds by building outhouses, aboveground wooden walkways, and parking areas, and to include Odawa members in a long-term preservation program. Their real interest, however, was to acquire lakefront property to create a township beach for local residents. Without the Odawa's immediate knowledge, the diocese and respective townships agreed on the sale of one parcel immediately to the north of the cemetery plus the entire beach front. The sale price was approximately $950,000, which the supervisors planned to acquire through township revenues and state grant funds, and they submitted a proposal to the state to such an effect.

On discovering these events, some Odawa elders took action primarily because of concern that the entire area was filled with ancestral graves that no longer were marked or may never have been marked. (In fact, the area may once have been a Feast of the Dead site, which would explain why the missionaries were drawn to it in the first place.) Recently, with the diocese's knowledge, a number of elders, an Odawa archaeologist, and several non-Indian scholars (including myself) mapped the existing cemetery and tested the areas where unmarked graves were suspected. They established undeniably that the entire area, including the dunes along the beachfront, was filled with graves that represented both pre- and postmissionization periods. The Odawa leaders sent the state their findings, a summary report, and a proposal for protection, which included working to have the entire site placed on the National Historic Register (per *Public Law 89–665*, 1966).

Until very recently, the state had responded to neither the Odawa's nor the townships' reports and proposals. Several of the elders have been particularly uncomfortable with this situation, one commenting: "This isn't the first time that we've had to confront the interests of the local government, nor will it be the last. Can we really afford to alienate them from us or ourselves from them?" Implicitly, this question acknowledges that if the townships and the Odawa are to work together on this issue, then each side will have to compromise. Based on a telephone conversation with one of the members of this band's governing board, it was this elder's understanding that a satisfactory compromise had been reached: the townships would move forward with a proposal to purchase the beachfront only, which would be supervised by a committee composed of township residents, members of the diocese, and local Odawa.

But as it turns out, local government leaders have been unwilling to uphold this arrangement, and in fact, a township memo issued in August 1994 reported that the state had made its decision: funds would be granted to the two respective townships to purchase not only the beachfront but also the parcel of land that the Odawa had expected to continue to use for grave sites, and to support the establishment of the area as a park. At a subsequent meeting on the matter, which I attended, one township supervisor implicitly conveyed that the Odawa would be excluded from any involvement. It also was learned that the vast majority of local residents were wholly unaware of the actions by their elected township officials. This township supervisor reported that one stipulation of the state's funding was that the proposed park be public and under the supervision of the Michigan Department of Natural Resources, therefore essentially taking it out of local control. And in fact, being funded by state monies, it is unclear whether it would be classified a state park rather than a township beach.[8]

Odawa traditionalists identify a number of issues and questions here. Two questions these Odawa raise are whether they can retort by making a legitimate claim to the area and seek restitution by citing certain case precedents and the Freedom of Religion and Graves Protection Acts, and by insisting on the federal government's fiduciary trust responsibility to uphold religious free exercise.[9] Traditionalists cite at least nine legal issues:

1. State's rights versus constitutional protections (religious free exercise)

2. Place-specific religious free exercise and constant use of land (e.g., *Lyng*)

3. Lands held in perpetuity and the issues raised by property laws of freehold and nonfreehold estates

4. Fifth Amendment guarantee of equal and just compensation, when neither is equated by the people at issue with money or ethically reciprocal and just compensation

5. Jurisdiction (e.g., whether local government equals the state, and whether the Catholic diocese is above the law; e.g., *Cherokee Nation*)

6. Whether public interest outweighs Indian rights (e.g., *Badoni*)

7. Eminent domain

8. State intrusion versus state's interest (e.g., *Sherbert* and *Yoder*)

9. Whether proprietary interest and geographic location must be established as imperative to religious practice in order to make a claim (e.g., *Sequoyah*)

The solution to these and other legal issues inherent to this situation remain elusive to the Odawa, as they concede that no clear case precedent has been established. It is evident to them, however, that if a claim is made to the area's being time-honored, and an argument is presented for infringement of religious practice by virtue of the termination of the ability to bury their dead in the cemetery, that these Odawa would have to face several bulwarks based on prior case precedent.

For example, the Graves Protection and Repatriation Act applies to burials on federal lands but is ill defined about private lands. Although the elders deny it, the diocese claims it can establish title to the land and therefore can transfer it to another party at will. Even if these elders are correct, however, the decision in the *Sequoyah* case established that lack of title overrules right of claims. The Court decided in this case that while a proprietary interest is unnecessary to a claim, the plaintiffs (in this case, the Odawa) would have to prove that the geographical location is imperative to the practice of their religion. Yet unlike the situation in *Sequoyah*, in this case governmental authorization and funding have not preceded the enactment of either the Religious Freedom Act or the Graves Protection Act. Traditionalists argue that claims might be made on this ground and on the fact that neither the state nor the townships have complied with the three stipulations in the AIRFA, especially that government has refrained from prohibiting access. However, these Odawa also would have to face the decision in *Fools Crow* that the right of the public to access lands is equally important to the exercise of religion. They would have to prove the "indispensability" of the land to their religious practice, or at least the religious practice of some Odawa (i.e., those who practice Christianity.) Traditionalists regard it as possible, however, to make a claim based on the *Lyng* decision that the government has to demonstrate a compelling interest, which in this case neither the state nor local government has done.

Despite this disturbing situation, efforts by Odawa traditionalists are not restricted to the local level but extend to both the state and federal levels. On the state level, several bands have sought and acquired the recognition and support of the Michigan Commission on Indian Affairs (MCIA), which now acknowledges their groups' political legitimacy because of the constitutions each has established through their respective councils. The MCIA particularly is influential in helping to formulate and implement appropriate community development strategies. On the federal level, the council leaders of several groups have sought the political assistance of key legislators and the legal counsel of highly visible Indian attorneys in seeking congressional acknowledgment. To work through Congress instead of the Bureau of Indian Affairs requires that a group substantiate that its political legitimacy once was recognized by the government but is no longer. Several groups of Odawa claim they can do so, particularly because John Collier, then director of the BIA, recognized their ancestors' claim in the 1930s (see chapter 5), and because they once received government subsidies and no longer do.

Over the past few years, leaders from several bands have spent many hours in Washington, D.C., presenting their case to Congress. They aim for such acknowledgment to reinstate their federal status as legitimate organizations without facing the supervision of the BIA. In the past, however, tribal groups who have achieved this status have found that it requires a lengthy process of at least fifteen years, and they largely have to comply with BIA recognition criteria anyway. Additionally, few groups nationally have achieved such status, mainly because of shifts in federal Indian policy and interest associated with changing presidential administrations (which is predicated on whether the administrations voice federalist or nationalist politics). Whether all these groups of Odawa ultimately will succeed in achieving the sovereignty that they seek has yet to be fully realized.

As of May 1994, however, the claim by one Odawa band had passed the House, and by September 1994 it had passed the Senate as well. Additionally, in late September 1994 President Bill Clinton acknowledged four previously nonrecognized groups, two of which are Odawa (one with some five hundred members, the other with some fifteen hundred). This makes a total of eleven federally acknowledged groups in Michigan, seven of which are under the supervision of the BIA. The Clinton administration set certain criteria that have to be met before full recognition is granted to these four recent groups. First, within eighteen months each band must send membership rolls to be filed with the Department of Interior. Second, within twenty-four months each must hold elections for (new) constitutions. Third, each group must elect a governing body within six months of approving its constitution. Despite these seeming obstacles, Odawa traditionalists regard this action as a powerful first step on the government's part toward reciprocal gifting, and the transformation in collective esteem and worth—their congealing into a true and vital community—has been dramatic.

Conclusions

So where do the current activities of Odawa traditionalists and federal policy leave them? We can only begin to answer this question by appreciating the profound conflict between the United States' legal emphasis on the freedom of individual religious belief and the Odawa traditionalists' emphasis on the right of collective practice. We must also admit the impact on religious practice of the judiciary's bias toward the establishment clause over free exercise. And we must recognize the fundamental difference between the traditionalists' view of justice (as consensual negotiation based on apodictic rules of gifting) and U.S. law (as primarily casuistic and based on adversarial adjudication). If we accept the metaphor "law as the bulwark of freedom" as an accurate articulation of the intent of U.S. law, then we must acknowledge that it voices the hope of protection against danger, especially danger from threatening others. Odawa traditionalists understand this intent. But their goal now is to protect themselves from the system controlling them by working through that very system. How successful can they be when the essential battle in the courts concerning Indian cases is between law versus gifting as the source of protection against chaos? "Law as the bulwark of freedom" and its corollary, "Equal Justice under the Law," reflect a reality that conflicts absolutely with the reality voiced by the metaphors and ethics structuring traditional Odawa life as they form a system to mediate disagreements through acts of gift exchange. Traditionalists take action because of their conviction that, in a system in which justice is subsumed under the law, laws become the source of power behind that system: the more laws, the merrier the mighty. "Law is the means by which white society can dominate and suppress," said Brown Otter. This is the process that Odawa traditionalists are confronting directly today by relying on their ability to act powerfully to transform their state of being, both in personal status and in ethnic identity.

Understanding metaphorical reinterpretation and reapplication, and the transformative power of ritual action, the Odawa rework the central image of the American legal system and pluck that image from its context of "defender"; after all, for traditionalists *time is a changer, life is fluid, events are actions,* and *purposes are destinations.* They see that by rejecting a legal system that defends state interests conflicting with their own, they can initiate a gift cycle based on exchange between the religious sphere and the economic, political, and legal spheres. They understand that their Odawa world can be transformed if the aim of law is to mediate interpersonal disagreements and social distance, and to overcome a sense of "otherness": to mediate between disagreeing peoples through negotiation, as the councils did traditionally, following religiously set precedents, especially the moral gift of ritual established by Nanabozho, the Great Transformer. For traditionalists, if the legal system becomes a channel for proper ethical action and response to changing social situations, cultural plurality, and social identity, it can establish communication and therefore mediation. Such mediation can result in a reconstitution of traditional meaning, significance, and identity.

The precedent for traditionalists' just and ethical action to produce positive change is apodictically laid out in Odawa ritual and mythological discourses. In both discourses, fire always has been an image of energy and life. Today Odawa traditionalists interpret "fire" as the core designator of vital energy or power and by extension a reconstituted meaning of the relation between social structure and traditional ethics. For these Odawa, "fire" becomes a focal point for overcoming conflicts by law, which holds the potential of becoming a mediating and transparent medium— like fire—instead of a defensive and static arbitrating agency.

Just as the dominant metaphor *time is a changer* orients traditional Odawa life, the metaphor *law as medium* can be located within a family cluster. "In this cluster nature is gift and occasion for a gift cycle, a sharing of the advantages of time and earth. Politics is the action of forming, exchanging, and distilling opinion—the action of a body politic. And law is then a medium of solidarity (Ball 1985:123). The next and final chapter explores how the Odawa traditionalists have provided a model for this solidarity and have implemented it as a rite of passage that aims to revitalize their collectively determined sovereign identity.

The Three R's of Traditionalism
Religiousness, Rites of Passage, and Revitalization

Finding the center of strength within ourselves is in the long run the best contribution we can make to our fellow man.

Rollo May

At a powwow, Lone Wolf told me: "You know, we all gather here to become reacquainted with friends and to make new friends. There are a lot of people who oppose us. But here we're all brothers, and more important, we're all Odawa. We're all related that way." Contemporary Odawa traditionalists are transforming their identity by constructively using conflict to produce positive change aimed at solidarity. They also are realizing their goals by reaffirming Odawa "religiousness" as the most powerful means to solve problems of modernity.

Although they do not use the terms themselves, nonetheless we can understand the traditionalists' actions as a religiously informed process—a ritual rite of passage—that is directed toward social transformation. Viewing their own identity and social integrity as having once been vital but now dangerously in jeopardy, traditionalists charge themselves with adjusting their current status; metamorphosing their identity in the eyes of others who are not Odawa and in their own eyes. Within this transmutation of status a sense of nationalism appears among traditionalists. As authoritative people, the traditionalists drive their revitalization movement by calling for patriotism to traditional Odawa ways.

Our understanding of their efforts is aided greatly by considering their activities within a familiar theoretical framework, a theoretical base that has withstood the test of experience, if not time, and one that I argue still works. Such a consideration is the purpose of this final chapter. First, though, we must step away from the Odawa themselves and appraise how a humanistic sensitivity to religion affects a reassessment of some classic anthropological literature on revitalization and theories of ritual. During this brief detour, which is certainly not exhaustive, we also must consider whether common definitions of religion that strive for universal understanding are applicable to the Odawa traditionalist culture.

The traditionalists have shown that at least two critical flaws exist in striving for and applying a universal definition of religion instead of arriving at an understanding derived from indigenous cultural context. First, among traditionally oriented peoples such as these Odawa, the term *religion* does not work; generally, it is regarded as a cultural institution separate from law, politics, economics, and the like. From the traditionalists' understanding, however, no such demarcations and "institutions" exist. Second, these Odawa also have made clear that defining religion as an institution also is troublesome by overlooking "human religiousness," an idea emphasizing people's constructive actions and based on the action-oriented interconnection of ritual and myth over abstract beliefs.

Religiousness and Constructive Action

Many scholars today, especially anthropologists, follow Clifford Geertz's lead and approach the study of religion as a symbolic system that universally establishes seemingly real and indelible moods and motivations in people through their faith in an ordered existence, and then frames these beliefs as facts (C. Geertz 1973: 89–90). Often, it is accepted that to understand the activity thus motivated, "activity in which symbolism forms the positive content," one must approach "cultural acts, the construction, apprehension, and utilization of symbolic forms, [as] social events like any other . . . as public as marriage and as observable as agriculture" (C. Geertz 1973:91). In this conceptualization, the "watchword" of "the religious perspective" is "encounter," which happens as people enact mythically charged religious belief (C. Geertz 1973:112–13). This reinforcement of the belief system then becomes a medium of social change by locating the socially redefined person within the socially redefined group. Because enacting religious convictions provides a powerful psychological reorientation by fusing ethos (the ethical ideal of the universe) and worldview (the sociologically real), these reaffirmations serve as an agent of both personal and social change, and reality is redefined (C. Geertz 1973:216, 127, 112). This insight is important because it begins to define how ritual operates in general, and it also suggests that the focus can narrow to a consideration of what specific people's expressions of religiosity do for them. Surely this conceptualization leads us to a certain plane of understanding. Yet Geertz does not carry far enough the privileging of constructive action based on knowledge and motivations over abstract belief. The underlying attempt to arrive at a universal definition simply cannot apply totally. Insisting on the universality of such terms as *belief* and *faith* limits an understanding of indigenous meaning. Therefore we must find ways to appreciate religious action in more immediate cultural contexts.

The Odawa traditionalists' story provides us with the opportunity to grasp that, as with American Indian peoples generally, indigenous meanings of religiosity are actions and behaviors that are lived and experienced and grounded in constructive and creative observable behaviors (Gill 1982:9–12, 1987). Sam D. Gill provides insight into the need to interpret religiousness as driven by action, especially ritual performance, because doing so shows that what is significant in indigenous religious theory are "those images, *actions*, and symbols that both express and define the extent and character of the world, especially those that provide the . . . framework in which human life finds meaning and the terms of its fulfillment. . . . [and] those *actions*, processes, and symbols *through which life is lived* in order that it may be meaningful and purposive" (Gill 1982:11; emphasis added). This performative understanding of religion stresses action—and religious action is ritual—that may be altogether different from asserting abstract beliefs.

Also, it is uncritical and unfortunate to insist on Western categories of religion when considering the religious conceptualizations and practices of American Indians, primarily because doing so overlooks the essential value of attempting to understand indigenous perspectives of ritual, which Kenneth M. Morrison and Fritz Detwiler particularly spearhead (Morrison 1992a:202; Detwiler 1992:235–46). Both Detwiler and Morrison show us, for example, how for Indian peoples religiousness is reducible neither to a sacred/profane dichotomy, which scholars such as Émile Durkheim and Mircea Eliade propose as universal, nor to grace from on high as a source of empowerment based on belief in a supernatural as opposed to the natural, as Åke Hultkrantz argues (see Morrison 1992a:207–21).

Morrison identifies the challenge to understanding religiousness this way:

> The challenge consists of recognizing real cultural differences that a supernaturalistic understanding of religion misses. Hultkrantz's theory requires a cosmology in which vertical superiority privileges the supernatural. [Recent] works . . . suggest the need not only to understand [the] linguistic character of Native American ritual practices, but also the cosmic importance of ritual performance. . . . it is useful to understand Native American religions as the ways in which language creates, maintains, and shifts whole worlds of meaning. (Morrison 1992a:201)

The duality supernatural/natural and the notion of grace from above discount what religiousness is for American Indians: persons acting in creative contact with a vital sociocosmos in which all things are interconnected and mutually responsible as active participants.

> When the supernatural is re-examined in light of the view that language is powerfully generative—spoken in story and bodied forth in dance—an alternative theory of religious dimensionality emerges. Here the hard separation between the supernatural, natural, and the cultural vanish. In their place, reality becomes multi-dimensional, and microcosm and macrocosm become not the physical as opposed to the metaphysical, but dimensions on a closely related continuum. It seems that Native American cosmologies may be informed by existential principles which highlight the vitality of human expressiveness. (Morrison 1992a:202–3)

Morrison's insight suggests a causal significance for approaching ritual as people acting as ethical participants in a more encompassing, living, and equally active cosmos.

Fritz Detwiler, in his analysis of the Oglala (through a comparison of Hultkrantz and Hallowell), furthers our appreciation of religiousness as being action based in interrelational purpose: "The Oglala metaphysic is concerned primarily with understanding 'being' as characteristic of all aspects of reality [as Hallowell argues], rather than an ontologically different supernatural [as Hultkrantz argues]. Being manifests personal power and is experienced in interpersonal relations." For the Oglala, religiousness involves "awareness, potency, perception, conscience, behavior, will, and value," and ritual "is a quest for ethical responsibility through communicative action" (Detwiler 1992:244).

Conceptualizing Odawa traditionalists within this performative framework, we see that although the Odawa language lacks the word *religion*, fundamentally and vitally they are religious. Given their commitment to a moral and ethical responsibility to act, we can realize how both ontologically and phenomenologically the entire world for Odawa traditionalists—sociological and cosmological—is inherently religious: it lives, it acts, it conceives, it imagines. Traditionalists interact with the eventful rhythms of the world. What we need is a clear way to acknowledge the traditionalists' own understanding of the relational nature of the world and their place in it. This understanding is based on their particular practice of religiousness as fundamentally action oriented and future looking, as it is always concerned with social transformation.

Applying Religiousness to Social Transformation

Ritual theory in general provides a framework for grasping how Odawa traditionalists apply religiousness to their own collectively directed culture change. It also helps conceptualizing how Odawa rituals simultaneously engage the ethics articulated in myths as a change-provoking event.

Many scholars have discussed religious ritual (see, e.g., Turner 1969; C. Geertz 1973; Hultkrantz 1979; Grimes 1982; Bell 1987; Kertzer 1988; Bloch 1989; Driver 1992). Specifically, Victor Turner shows how rituals serve to justify "social drama" that leads both to splitting and separating some members of a group and to consolidating group membership and identity. Turner's (and Arnold Van Gennep's) focusing on ritual as a process illustrates that many rituals, as rites of passage, have three phases. Participants are first separated from their everyday world and secluded from their secular life, an act that leads to a profound transition before participants are returned and reincorporated into a social life with a new status or identity (Van Gennep 1909; Turner 1969). In the second phase of the ritual process, what Turner calls "liminal seclusion" and Van Gennep calls "transition," personal redefinition happens. To fully comprehend the powerful transformation that occurs during this second phase of antistructure, it is important to understand that "liminal" literally means a doorway, gateway, or threshold. Only by passing through the threshold of liminality can powerful shifts happen in one's self-orientation and relations with others—the former "normal" life has now been changed as a result of experiencing what Turner calls *communitas*.

The value of conceptualizing the fluid shifts in identity between the phases of structure and antistructure during the ritual process is that it supplies us with important distinctions between religion and religiousness. Some people, during the liminal phase of the ritual process, experience a tranformation in their orientation toward each other, resulting in a congruent cohesive identity. A unified group emerges with a collective thought world, or communitas: a community, to be sure, but an unstructured union of equalized people. People achieve communitas when they experience the implicit aim of ritual: *the restoration of the right relationship*. The ritual process frees the person from his or her position in the everyday social structure, with communitas annihilating all-differentiating categories of being. It is a period when the person bonds with others and each participant returns to everyday life empowered by the experience. People experience a sense of communitas during the ritual performance itself so that upon its completion they emerge with a new—or renewed—understanding of the relationship between social structure and traditional ethics, something people often forget in the hubbub of daily life. The ritual process—engaging religious action—is one meaningful way of addressing social fissure. The shift in orientation that each participant experiences results from a sense of separation or liminality from normally structured life to a sense of communitas, or an experientially grounded collective unity. Self-orientation powerfully flows from I to Thou (to borrow Martin Buber's formulation) and results in a powerful new voicing of We. The ritual process of liminality to communitas deviates from the structure of daily secular life and becomes a transformative and conjunctural event.

Besides having psychological and social aspects, ritual also has a powerful relationship to culture. David Kertzer (1988) and Maurice Bloch (1989) show how ritual meaning, correlated with a concept of history, can be manipulated by or applied to politics. Bloch, especially, shows that because ritual addresses power and history, ritual actors can transform adverse conditions (1989:1). Making the past immediately relevant and anticipating the future, ritual becomes a profound event in the present: the "now" and religious authority are linked conclusively, and the ritual event communicates and reaffirms the legitimacy of that authority. Authority, communicated through formalized ritual discourse, motivates and justifies social action because it communicates moral persuasion. Traditional ethics and their moral persuasion back the power of ritual action, which then takes on political dimensions, empowering leaders to guide communal destiny (Kertzer 1988:1).

Rituals become politically important since they link the person to a newly defined and consecrated social unit (Kertzer 1988:10; see also Turner 1969; Bloch 1989). By linking individuals as a unified group that shares a basic orientation to the world, rituals contribute to building political organizations and political legitimacy. Political competitors can use rituals in power struggles to defuse or incite conflict. In this way, ritual rites of passage especially can fuel social activism. When combined with an appreciation of religiousness as it shapes ethical behavior, this brief discussion of ritual theory helps us to begin to understand that positive ritual action drives the Odawa traditionalists' collectively directed socioreligious retention and adjustment—a fully revitalizing event.

Features of Revitalization

What is happening among the Odawa today, although expressed in their own language, conforms in some ways to classic anthropological studies of American Indian revitalization. But it also suggests that we must reconsider the issues underlying these studies because few, if any, fully explain the religious and ritual nature of revitalization. Virtually none explore these socioreligious movements as they are informed by a "relational" worldview, the ethics of which are enacted in rituals and articulated in myths. As Joel Martin has so poignantly put it, the studies that many scholars (especially anthropologists) have regarded as seminal to the study of American Indian revitalization movements and have relied on so uncritically "all imply at a formal level" that American Indian religiousness "belong[s] only at the beginning of the story of religion in America" (1991a:678). In suggesting that there must be more theoretical precision in describing these movements, I do not intend to supply an exhaustive evaluation of the literature. Such an undertaking is beyond the scope of this work, especially given the amount of recent material on revitalization theory in general. However, a brief critical examination of a few of these classic studies shows that a great many descriptive terms are used to refer to religiously informed social movements, and often interchangeably, fostering confusion. Descriptions include "religious resurgence," "religious militancy," "religious enthusiasm," "pietistic," "charismatic," "revivalistic," "millenarian," "nativistic," "crisis and response," and "liberation and independence." Each comes with its own theoretical baggage, which may or may not lend itself to an understanding of how and why Indian peoples such as the Odawa traditionalists seek viability through their religious traditions as responses to pressures created by the modern nation-state. Nor do they address the issue of whether a historical transformation has happened in either motives or strategies for revitalization.

Taken independently of each other, these standard studies have several drawbacks. None explains why people come to see their past as vital and their present as no longer so. None examines how people work constructively to rectify their crisis of meaning and reinvigorate relationships and therefore identity. Also, none of these studies tells us what correlation exists between a people's political, territorial, and economic displacement and their desire to return to traditional lifeways. Classic studies of revitalization movements overlook the central issue that motivates such social activism: pressures for sociocultural change, including but not limited to contact events, undercut social relations in ways that violate the moral authority of tradition. For example, in the case of American Indians, and certainly as the Odawa's story illustrates, Euro-American policy has been and continues to be the application of ways to keep people separated through actions that undermine and fractionate clan organizations and traditional boundaries (Dowd 1992). We need to understand, therefore, how revitalization movements reestablish meaning for people faced with liminal social conditions. What we see is the skill of people to "change in response to history [through] innovation, transformation, and resiliency"; to truly understand these conscious transformations calls for "new interpretive experiments that focus on internal dynamics and motives" (Martin 1991a:679, 680). The studies often drawn on as the starting point for revitalization theory do not understand liminality in its destructive mode as a crisis of meaning, and ritual liminality in its positive mode as a reconstitution of meaning by the restoration of right relationships. We need to pause and seriously consider the implications of these two understandings of liminality for the study of revitalization movements in general and for appreciating the Odawa in particular.

For our purposes it is needless to exhaust the abundant and increasingly growing body of literature on revitalization. Nor do we need to look at the authors themselves; the important task is to examine the issues that their works raise. Appraising a few of the key studies generally regarded as seminal to the study of revitalization, and as a series of works that build on each other structurally, reveals troublesome issues when using the Odawa as a case for analysis and comparison. I am not suggesting that these studies have nothing to offer, only that they must be read differently from how they have formerly been and with a more critical eye. For example, a predominant—and problematic—theme that courses through this literature is an emphasis on people's "political victimization," "economic deprivation," and lack of personal and social control. "Deprivation" and "victimization," restricted to purely economic and political meanings, produces an inadequate gloss—and a materialist one. In this restricted sense, "deprivation" and "victimization" may not be synonymous with the threat of total cultural decline and therefore identity. As the Odawa traditionalists' story suggests, the central issue that is elusive in the works that scholars have relied on in the past is whether "deprivation" and "victimization" describe the indigenous experience and appreciation of sociocultural liminality in its negative mode as a crisis of traditional meaning. Without a doubt, people aim for revitalization, viewing an adjusted way of life as more vital than the present, but economic and political deprivation or victimization is not the heart of the matter. As we have seen throughout their story, the Odawa traditionalists' case suggests that revitalization occurs from a sense that social solidarity is being threatened: in contrast to the accommodationists, the traditionalists' view of "deprivation" tends more toward the newer cultural understanding while the accommodationists' tends toward the classic materialist understanding.

Economic deprivation and victimization were first examined in the specific context of the 1890 Ghost Dance as a revitalization movement.[1] By 1890 the frontier phase of Euro-American history had ended and was replaced by widespread reservationism, to which many Indians remained unreconciled. Besides being physically and socioeconomically restricting, reservations were accompanied by other pressures that the Indians had to face and that forced them to deviate from traditional lifeways: pressures to become "civilized," especially by farming and herding; conversion efforts by Catholic and Protestant missionaries; removal of children to boarding schools, which eroded traditions, language, and clan-based kin networks; and factionalism within communities, especially caused by the forced conjoining of tribal groups— not all of which traditionally had particularly friendly relationships. In this study, the hypothesis is that revitalization results from the resurgence of what are regarded as traditional group beliefs, in decline because of culture changes resulting from Euro-American contact. Supposedly, the formal movement was a *reaction* to the demise of tribal economies, poverty, and oppression.[2] Framing the Ghost Dance as a reaction to the immediate experience of contact and economic decline pointedly raises the issue of whether economic "conditions," especially deprivation and victimization from a Euro-American perspective, are the proper focus. This focus overlooks indigenous conceptions of these events and proper actions in constructive response. Also, stressing the immediacy of Euro-American encounters cannot explain why similar responses happen well after the fact, and why many Indian peoples today—such as the Odawa—although having been in contact for over three hundred years, are engaged in similar activities.

> As the timing of these movements reveals, full-fledged prophetic [revitalization] movements almost never occurred in the initial encounter between Native Americans and Europeans. Several of these movements, particularly the later ones in the Eastern Woodlands [reviewed in chapter 3], happened in a context in which Native American groups experienced a severe depletion of marketable game and a rapid loss of land to Europeans. (Martin 1991a:683)

Besides erosion of traditional subsistence strategies and territories, Indian peoples over the course of several centuries faced decimation by alcohol and disease, threats to identity, and disrupted traditional clan relationships.

The Ghost Dance, as an example of a revitalization movement, also has been interpreted within a framework of psychological victimization that resulted from a crisis of sociocultural upheaval, which also defined the "origin of religion" (LaBarre 1970). The argument here is that "the innovator's ambivalence toward his culture, his tribe's ambivalence toward either native or alien culture or both, the crisis of cultural faith, and the psychological association of innovator and group" all became essential components in the Ghost Dance (LaBarre 1970:279). However, restricting the focus to "ambivalence"—having mutually conflicting thoughts—overlooks the possibility of actors behaving constructively and instructively for others, as with Odawa elders and prophetic leaders. It also overlooks the issue of how and why "time"—that is, cultural history and tradition—becomes perceived as disrupted or out of sync, and in response, some person or group becomes destined to set "time" right, as with Odawa traditionalists in general. This psychological approach restricts an appreciation of the religious and ritually driven character of these actions.

Other works not restricted to the Ghost Dance, or that use it to develop some universalist model, also focus on deprivation and victimization as the causes leading to revitalistic reactions. For example, this focus was applied to a study of the Northwest Coast Klamath, who in 1864 were thrust together on a reservation with the Modoc and two bands of Paviotso and were expected to overcome their traditional intercultural conflicts and live harmoniously. This study of the Klamath concluded that revitalization movements are reactions that arise among deprived groups following a shift in the group's value pattern. Further, the shift in value pattern results from suppression and domination, and the revitalistic reaction aims to restore traditional value patterns (Nash 1937). This analysis suggests a causal significance of "shifts in values." The study does not, however, identify and explain the differentiation between "shifts in values" and the retention of traditional ethics, located within a group of people's behavior, and the "suppression and domination," located outside. Based on the Odawa's story, it must be stressed that modifying ethical actions is a constructive way to counter socially disruptive influences and to arrive at new ways of understanding such encounters. We must acknowledge how these influences affect social behavior in ways that may depart from traditional ethics or that constitute some other theodicy that requires ritual intervention. As we saw clearly with the prophetic leaders of revitalization movements in chapter 2, it is crucial that we distinguish between creative adaptations and the decline of group ethics resulting from pressures for assimilation.

To continue our example of how to reread these texts on revitalization movements, an emphasis on victimization and deprivation also suggests that all such movements surface when culture change is directed by an outside group. This intrusion then results in economic and political dominance and cultural suppression of one group by another, and it produces disappointment with the new order and a sense of nostalgia for the past (Linton 1943). Odawa traditionalists, however, show how framing revitalization around "nostalgia for the past" is problematic because making "nostalgia," literally "homesickness," the cardinal component does not acknowledge the forward-looking religious and ritual confidence that drives their revitalization.

Other studies focusing on deprivation and victimization similarly have concluded that revitalization movements result from socioreligious reactions against new technological and cultural influences, especially economic subjugation through land control (e.g., those by Anthony Wallace).[3] This line of argument suggests that although protagonists are limited in their options, they do have and exercise choices within those options, and that the ultimate choice made provides the empirical evidence for characterizing all revitalization movements. The analysis raises several issues: Why are the options for actions limited, and if they are limited, what are they? Do protagonists view their options as limited; for example, would such Odawa prophets as Pontiac and The Trout have said so? This focus fails to explain how a particular choice of action, whether ultimate or not, becomes the principle empirical evidence for characterizing all revitalization movements. The Odawa's story suggests that the general purpose and proper course of action decided on may vary with specific circumstances and historical moments.

A narrower focus than the above studies are works on the rise and distribution of the Peyote Cult and the Prophet Dance as examples of revitalization movements (Aberle and Stewart 1957; Aberle 1959). These works regard the Peyote Cult as "a pan-Indian, semi-Christian, nativisitic movement," in that the leaders tended to "*favorably* contrast Indian and Christian orthodoxy and worldview[s]" (Aberle and Stewart 1957:1; emphasis added, as "favorably" is highly questionable, especially in light of debates about processes of syncretism). According to this analysis, the Peyote Cult spread because of profound economic disturbances, exhibiting differential growth that intensified during two time periods in which economic breakdown was particularly acute. During and especially after these periods of intensification, however, the cult had multiple appeals to its members. This first examination led to a second study that distinguished between movements that seek supra-individual change, which can be total or partial, and those that seek personal change (Aberle 1959). Within this framework, total change is the goal of transformative movements (e.g., the Chinese Cultural Revolution); partial change is the goal of reformative movements (e.g., child labor laws). Personal change can be sought on a total level, as in redemptive movements (e.g., medieval flagellants) or on a partial level, as in alternative movements (e.g., the dissemination of anti-birth control propaganda). Both studies stress that contact produces a revitalistic reaction to deprivation and victimization in a cause-and-effect manner, and therefore both victimization and deprivation create "a negative discrepancy between legitimate expectation and actuality, or between legitimate expectation and anticipated actuality, or both" (Martin 1991a:684). Neither conclusion, and particularly the latter, can account for the possibility that any given revitalization movement includes all the goals delineated in the typology presented, as is the case with the Odawa traditionalists.

All this literature emphasizes economic deprivation and sociopolitical victimization. With this focus, it overlooks people's own ingenuity in countering the threat of total cultural decline and the crisis of meaning and disrupted relationships that result. The focus is on abstract belief. As a result, these studies cannot offer an understanding of ritual as constructive action that uses positive liminality as a threshold through which to reconstitute tradition and therefore meaningful relationships and identity. This material systematically fails to appreciate ritual as the source for fundamentally positive action aimed at reconstituting meaning at the personal and group level. Particularly because they work outside a context of ritual rites of passage, these studies misinterpret processes by which people seek to transform society and its identity through ethical ritual action. Cultural contexts and theoretical approaches other than those focused on American Indians, however, acknowledge the critical need to account for ritual—human creative action—in understanding revitalization movements.

Studies of sociocultural conflict are a case in point. Such analyses suggest that conflict can become constructive and deliberate action that establishes, maintains, and changes social identity and ethnic boundaries (Coser 1956). Conflict with other groups reaffirms the primary group's identity by mobilizing its members and thus strengthening group cohesion. Embracing conflict constructively, embattled groups become intolerant of more than minimal departures from each group's central system of ethics, as do the Odawa traditionalists versus Odawa accommodationists. Conflicts in which participants represent the collective, fighting not for oneself but for the group's ideals and identity, tend to radicalism:

conflict tests ethnic power. Mediation can happen only if each group acknowledges the relative strengths of both parties. Although conflict analysis largely overlooks ritual, myth, and their interconnection as active religiousness, it can transcend the victimization/economic deprivation issue and provide a basis for identifying a basic element of revitalization: *Groups use conflict as a focus to counter crises of meaning and identity.* We have seen how Jonathan Z. Smith is informative about the religious use of conflict, especially his discussions of the rectification of ritual and myth, and his concept of a reinterpreted model, particularly through what he calls "situational incongruity," as their redescription during periods of cultural conflagration (see chapter 6; Smith 1982:94–95, 99–101, 36).

Besides illustrating a total phenomenon essentially rooted in positive protest, Kenelm Burridge's studies of revitalization movements in Melanesia highlight a fundamental question for participants: Is the individual worthy of playing an honorable role in redirecting society in association with other individuals?[4] With the purpose in mind to answer this question affirmatively, the movement becomes a collectively determined and creative means to structure social change and reestablish right relationships. Because such movements aim to create a future without threats to social cohesion, they are structured similarly: *The conjoined participants are dedicated to the proposition that power can redeem.* This redemptive process extends but is not limited to politico-economic processes, especially the prestige system of a specific culture. The focus is on gaining or retaining self-respect and traditional principles. As we have seen with Odawa traditionalists, the movement provides a framework for revitalizing the community by reconstituting measures of interpersonal integrity and meaning.

Revitalization movements that aim for cultural transformation and restructured social order come only with constructive collective action, whose actors share a common goal. Such movements fundamentally are protest and "may be regarded as a pattern of sustained social action stimulated by new . . . interpretations of contemporary processes of social change."[5] As the Odawa traditionalists' activism suggests, in these movements participants strive for complete redemption by acting cooperatively to save or generate a unique identity and way of life.

Read with a critical eye, the issues raised by these revitalization theories suggest that such socioreligious movements target some specific situations: intrinsic or extrinsic crisis; perception of disrupted time; redefinition of territory; new technological or cultural influences; shift in traditional patterns of ethical behavior associated with dominance and suppression; economic decline; loss of language and cultural identity; and threat of disrupted relationships and therefore identity and total cultural decline. These sociocultural circumstances produce the negative liminality—a crisis of meaning—of one group in relationship to another. This crisis can result from internal causes, external causes, or both, and it creates conflict in the relationships within and between groups. Here Victor Turner's (1969) concept of "social drama" crystalizes the conflict and disagreement, the divergence and incompatibility, in actually coping with social and cultural problems. As the Odawa traditionalists illustrate, a heterogeneous group many sustain many internal and external conflicts, and a liminal set of members may act to rectify the crisis of meaning. These actors advance several ethical responsibilities: charging a person or individuals with setting "time," or cultural history and identity, right; getting and maintaining power manifest in underlying ideologies; reestablishing a unique identity; linking ritual and myth with a preexisting apocalyptic tradition; and asserting traditional ideals and ethics.

These actions, aimed at reconstituting tradition, are examples of the conscious reinterpretation and reapplication of ritual and myth to changing cultural circumstances. That is, positive liminality is made the medium of reconstructing meaning. A reconstituted tradition decreases the influence of socially disruptive values, and it provides a positive future, the destruction or alleviation of the source of conflict, and group cohesion. Passing the threshold of negative liminality, these ritual rites of passage of revitalization seek social solidarity and renewed claims to cultural sovereignty.

These issues, reconceptualized, create a theoretical hypothesis:

If the standard feature of revitalization movements is that they are rites of passage that exhibit developmental processes of purposeful actions, then these actions must be ritually manipulated to produce specific, predetermined results: namely, to generate a new community, to seek salvation and retention of cultural identity and uniqueness, and to use conflict constructively to adjust to changing social circumstances.

Given this hypothesis, a general illustration of revitalization can be painted to use as a comparative base for understanding Odawa traditionalists (table 10.1). Viewing revitalization this way, we must distinguish between two socioreligious processes: first, *sociocultural liminality* as a crisis of social meaning, and second, *ritual liminality* that reasserts the traditional source of ethical behavior and reinscribes those ethics as personal and collective identity. Considering this illustration of revitalization within the Odawa traditionalists' context suggests that the traditionalists are engaged in a full-scale revitalization movement. Further, when compared with other studies, it suggests that the religious character of American Indian history is not well understood.

Table 10.1 further suggests that the Odawa traditionalists' revitalization movement is a pilgrimage, a rite of passage that anticipates periodic transitions in collective status and identity. However, the traditionalists' case extends the standard understanding of the ritual process because traditionalists recognize the important difference between real sociocultural liminality and ritually created liminality (in Van Gennep's and Turner's sense). The ritual process, as described in the standard anthropological model (again following Van Gennep and Turner), appears to ease, at least temporarily, the perceived disturbances in the social structure by framing chaos in the ritual setting. In this standard model, the ultimate result is a return to the original structure of unequal people. We have seen that for Odawa traditionalists and their predecessors, however, recreating an unequal social structure merely perpetuates the unacceptable present state of real sociocultural liminality. So they depart from the standard model of ritual process and rites of passage by attempting a renewed collective status. The goal is, indeed, a return to an "original" traditional structure of interpersonal relationships, but traditionalists consider that structure as social solidarity and sovereignty.

Table 10.1. Revitalization as a Rite of Passage

Tradition (Odawa) >	History (crisis) >	Action (ritual/myth) >	Purpose (meaning) >	Destination (goal)
Cooperative actions/relations Solidarity	Negative liminality (separation)	Positive liminality (communitas)	Reconstruction of tradition (reincorporation)	Cooperative actions/relations Solidarity

The Odawa traditionalists' revitalization ritual parallels the way American Indian peoples have negotiated and continue to negotiate other visions. For this reason, their movement becomes a road map for cultural and social transformation. Our illustration of revitalization can aid both this study and future studies if we remember that for many peoples, like American Indians, "the cycle of human life, the journey from birth to death, is brought into line with cosmology by being depicted as a process of movement within the landscape. Life is a road one travels . . . [which] is often described as an orientation" (Gill 1982:83) It is this "Right Path" to what the Odawa call the Seventh Fire that our reconceptualization of revitalization purposes and processes illustrates.

Conclusions

Examining the issues related to widely held definitions of "religion," theories of ritual, and rites of passage, as well as reviewing earlier studies of revitalization, has led us to an understanding that we must consider several largely unexamined factors, among them the following:

"Religion" recast as "religiousness" involves actively producing, maintaining, and transforming traditional meaning and significance.

The study of revitalization must be humanistically concerned with culture as meanings humanly constructed through ritual performance.

Revitalization movements seek to address both "inside" and "outside" conditions, to reconstitute tradition and meaning, and to transform the experience of negative liminality through ritual action (positive liminality).

The revitalization movement of the Odawa traditionalists extends or presents a variation of existing concepts of the ritual process and rites of passage. The standard anthropological model of ritual process shows individuals passing from individualism through liminality to participation in communitas and then returning to (perhaps a different) individualism. I suggest that this ritual process becomes a construct for social reality and constitutes a rite of passage that aims for total transformation of relational structure and collective identity that extends beyond the ritual setting itself. The traditionalists' ritual process of revitalization focuses on two planes: the person/group and the nation/world. On the person/group plane, the individual initially is removed from everyday existence. Simultaneously, on the national/world plane the group is separated from Euro-American-dominated society.

Cultural invisibility, seclusion from the outside secular world within the ritual setting, offers a unique space-time in which interpersonal differences are annihilated and conflicts mediated. Participants pass through this separation and become a harmonious unit, both with other ritual participants and with ancestors. This experience allows each person to return to mundane life with a powerful sense of renewal and allows the group to visibly announce its autonomy. Consequently, the micro-level of ritual separation–transition–reincorporation parallels, for Odawa traditionalists, the classic shamanic ritual process of suffering–death–renewal. The traditionalists' story reveals how in their revitalization movement, the implicit aim of ritual—the restoration of the right relationship—becomes explicit.

Afterword

The story of the Odawa traditionalists shows how and why they consciously reinterpret and reapply elements of ritual and myth during periods of sociocultural tension. Their actions strive to reconstitute tradition and identity (= positive liminality) and lead to the state of sovereignty and social solidarity, "communitas," remembered as Odawa status prior to disruptive events caused by other people's actions. Viewed in this way, the traditionalists' revitalization is a pilgrimage to renewed and invigorated social meaning.

Their story also shows how and why Odawa traditionalists use ritual as the most immediate way to generate positive transformation in social status by drawing on the performance's power to unify the socially redefined person with a socially redefined group. Since the ritual process leads to personal and collective change, traditionalists can redefine their reality. With this transformative purpose, their revitalization ritual assumes an element of power by being interconnected with historical encounters and applied to politics. Because of its political importance in linking the person— as an agent in society—to a newly defined and consecrated social unit, the traditionalists' revitalization ritual helps to build political organization and legitimacy. With this political characteristic of ritual, these Odawa use models from traditional rites of passage (e.g., vision quests and naming ceremonies) to fuel their social activism.

We should now appreciate the central ethics that inform the traditionalists' action: They hold that ethical persons give compassionately to others (personing), and that gratitude expressed as gift giving (gifting) is empowering. Powerful acts of ethical benevolence are the primary way to respond constructively to others who are threatening and dangerous. Personing for these Odawa entails shifting identity, which always includes elements of powerful behavior. The major goal of ethical behavior—engaging power constructively—is to perpetually extend one's own personhood and destiny through proper relationships; the individual is thus morally responsible for personal and group determination.

Gifting—enacting generosity—enhances social solidarity. Such displays of compassion mediate distance between the individual and other individuals, and between the group and other groups (e.g., by establishing trade relations with the Huron/Wyandot and with the French in the seventeenth century). Enacting generosity is life perpetuating (*pimadaziwin*) and results from powerful wisdom, especially that gained from ritual encounters with the *manidos*, or power persons (empowering). As the ability to gain wisdom through compassionate interactions constantly expands, so then does Odawa personhood, both individual and collective identity. Using this process, Odawa traditionalists are actors in history, not passive victims of history. Of course, others have tried to inflict a constrained sense of identity on them. It is to this point that the traditionalists most seriously direct their actions.

One way Euro-Americans have tried to constrain a dynamic and sovereign Odawa identity has been through treaties that limited mobility and action. Shifting federal Indian policies fueled intra-tribal and intertribal factionalism over proper responses, further threatening a cohesive Odawa identity. A second way Euro-Americans have tried to restrict a powerful collective Odawa identity has been through Christian conversion efforts. Being converted resulted in a new individualistic identity defined by the church in terms of hierarchical relationships and status, and not a relational identity based on powerful interconnections with many persons, human and otherwise.

The traditionalists' current revitalization movement, as a rite of passage, extends a long tradition of intertribal discourse, especially that which has resulted from Euro-American encounters. These encounters spawned a series of social movements, constructive actions countering the threat of total cultural decline—complete annihilation of a unique sovereign Odawa identity—owed to both the American government's Indian policies and Christianity. At the same time, these movements allowed some Odawa to act constructively within new cultural landscapes. The call to action was to redefine and expand a sense of ethical personhood and social relationships. Leaders of these movements, both historical and contemporary, have used and continue to use language that appears to be infused with Christian influences. These agents in society may have purposefully spoken and may continue to speak in terms identifiable both to non-Indians and to the next generations of Odawa facing continued inculcation of Christianity. Speaking in such terms means not that these actors sacrifice their personal integrity and worldview, grounded in ethical action, but that they bridge two cultural horizons, their own and the Euro-American. Through this discourse they present the possibility of expanded and ethical social relations.

Reflecting on the traditionalists' worldview as framed by the three interconnected ethics, personing, gifting, and empowering, has provided us with ways to appreciate their contemporary understanding of the moral gifts of ritual, and to understand the significance of certain mythic messages as they map their revitalization. The vision called forth is "Ki-je Manido," the focusing lens for ethical personing, which must be located in perpetually expanded and unified interpersonal relationships. The actions recounted in and further called for by some mythic messages echo the centrality of ethical personhood (life giving), gift (generosity), and power (wisdom). Traditionalists mirror two fundamental aspects of Odawa culture, which participants in their revitalization and collective determination consider their ethical duty to uphold during periods of profound cultural transition: the empowerment contained in ritual, and the significance of ritual contained in the formation of ethical personhood. This second principle most immediately returns us to the issue of the relational nature of the traditionalists' personhood and identity.

Traditionalists act to empower themselves, thereby strengthening fellow Odawa especially by calling on each person to enact the ethic of gifting. They reject an Odawa identity defined for them in Christian terms, based on abstract faith and established by grace from on high. Instead, they enact their Odawa moral responsibility to perpetuate an expanding and empowering identity, defined and continually redefined by ethical acts of giving as a means of mediating the threats of social disruption. Because enacting generosity is a gift to other people, traditionalists therefore expand relationships. They are indeed revitalizationists because they establish themselves as exemplars of ethical behavior and moral action. Furthermore, they call for future generations both to retain this Odawa cultural integrity and identity and to constructively respond to changed social spheres. A collective sovereign Odawa identity simultaneously emerges while being retained: using religious action, traditionalists work to reclaim the sovereign place and status that they regard as rightfully theirs.

The call for a revitalized Odawa identity largely has resulted from the central event in the traditionalists' contemporary cultural experience: their social liminality (liminality in its negative mode as a crisis of meaning). This liminality has prompted proactive reinterpretations and reapplications of ritual and myth (liminality in its positive mode as a reconstitution of tradition). Using questions presented in myths as a model, traditionalists subtly adjust definitions of themselves and other people. Through their actions, the Great Persons of mythology map definitions of ethical personhood, present the ethics that guide Odawa life, and inform a distinct Odawa culture and identity.

Traditionalists know that the world and their place in it are changing continually and that these changes transcend any one person's intentions. They see the constructive and creative importance of pooling the resources of the Great Persons of mythology for empowerment. This theme articulates the traditionalists' theory of cooperation, of ritual relations, especially between the living and the dead, and of processes for mediating socially disruptive differences. The major message that myths contain is that acts of cooperation form the core of ethical Odawa personhood. We have seen how Ki-je Manido acts in consultation with Nanabozho and how such cooperation establishes the goal of contemporary Odawa life as interpersonal solidarity—the expansion of personhood and identity. We also have seen how Nanabozho's most significant gift was to teach that living persons have the moral responsibility to periodically reaffirm kinship bonds with the ancestors—again, a reaffirmation and extension of personhood and identity.

Emulating the ethical acts of the Great Persons of mythology, traditionalists counter threats to their moral and social integrity by acting as the progenitors of their unique cultural history. Especially by charging themselves with the moral responsibility to uphold and create ethical relationships, traditionalists become the authorities of reinterpreting the religious ethics that underlie myths and of reapplying them to new cultural landscapes. With this understanding, we can better appreciate that the "text" of the Seventh Fire must be read as reflecting and articulating the impact of the changes in the Odawa traditionalists' social sphere resulting both from extrinsic encounters with others and from opposition due to intrinsic factionalism with accommodationists. The narrative reveals a powerful message of constructive ways of mediating interpersonal distance and methods of overcoming threats to identity, a message that traditionalists incorporate as part of their strategy for collectively directed social change. The myth illustrates how one should act as an ethical person and how so acting collectively generates solidarity and a constructively transformed social sphere—"Ki-je Manido" in the most comprehensive and ethical sense. When traditionalists reinterpret and reapply its allegorical component, the myth's message maps the way to their transmutation—the extension of personhood and identity through ritual action.

Just as our application of allegorical analysis as a heuristic device has helped explicate what is implicit in the Seventh Fire myth, our use of metaphorical analysis as a heuristic device to understand the *gi-be wiikonge* illuminates how traditionalists reinterpret and reapply ritual performances. They engage ritual as the most profound way to diminish differences between individuals and groups and to restore right relationships—another extension of personhood and identity. Because ritual action can restore proper interpersonal relations and create new relationships, it is fundamentally transformative. Recognizing the transformations in being that occur through ritual—a result of passing through the threshold of liminality—traditionalists structure their revitalization within the framework of ethical action.

Being fundamentally religious, traditionalists practice ritual beyond such settings as the powwow grounds and the dinner table.

Using these ritual settings as a focusing lens, they continually reassess and reaffirm the relationship between social structure and traditional ethics, and they apply this relationship to wider settings that we might call the secular arena, especially U.S. law. Today Odawa traditionalists know both cultures—their own and Euro-American—well enough to challenge U.S. laws and to ritually maneuver their way through the courts. How successful they will be in reclaiming the socioreligious sovereignty that they seek has yet to be fully established.

The story of these Odawa traditionalists invites continued investigation. As scholars, we may apply their model of collectively determined perpetuation to others. Many people currently are adopting similar actions and goals. Given the many little and big "nationalisms" apparent everywhere, we need not search far to find groups that seek sociocultural emergence and revitalized identity. The Odawa traditionalists have supplied us with a way to understand people's needs to reconstitute traditional meaning and significance, and to understand how and why people reaffirm the relationship between social structure and traditional ethics. Above all, they present us with a fundamental question: Is a person, acting together with select others, worthy of serving an honorable—and ethical—role in redirecting society? Based on the case of the Odawa traditionalists, we must answer yes. We should now ask whether other people pose the same question and give the same answer.

Notes

Introduction

1. George Tinker has extensively examined how past processes of cultural genocide have conditioned the present. We scholars are, ourselves, in the same situation—impressions and interpretations of cultural genocide still remain.

2. There is a rich body of literature on the relation between language, religiosity, and imagination; see, for example, Detwiler 1992; Pflüg 1992a; Irwin 1992, 1994; Brown and Brightman 1988; Johnson 1987; Gill 1982. My concerns with "imagination" were echoed by one of my American Indian students, who interpreted the term as being pejorative "if it's taken to mean unreal and therefore ineffective. For Indian peoples, what we dream, our visions, are the very essence of our being. They direct us to who we are." In this context, imagination should not in any way be construed to be a fantasy or untruth.

1. Maintaining an Odawa Identity

1. Here it is worth noting the achievements of postmodern ethnographers (such as Clifford and Marcus) in identifying and addressing the complex interpretive issues involved in linguistic and cultural translation.

2. Congressional acknowledgment, on the one hand, and BIA recognition with its bureaucratic control, on the other, are two entirely separate legal processes and ideological issues.

3. These terms may raise some controversy, especially among non-Indian scholars. Certainly, their are members of each faction in both BIA recognized and nonrecognized communities. However, the major philosophical split runs more along the lines of distinct communities than individuals.

4. Calvin Martin (1978) argues that Algonkians such as the Odawa's Ojibwe neighbors responded to the fur trade, Catholic missionization,

and decimation by diseases by reconceptualizing the breakdown of traditional relationships within the context of gift exchange as the most profound means to cure the threat of cultural decline. The essays in Krech 1981, however, are highly critical of Martin's argument, suggesting instead that commercial hunting did not stem from a decline of traditional ethics and that the fur trade did not oppose religious practices. Rather, the incentive to produce furs placed a high premium on those religious practices that enhanced the hunter's success. See also J. Martin 1991a, 1991b; Dowd 1992.

5. This is similar to the case of the Saint Croix band of Chippewa in Wisconsin earlier in this century (James Oberly, personal communication).

2. Making Meaning and Making Sense

1. Both Joel Martin (1919a, 1991b) and Gregory Evans Dowd (1992) refer to this idea of a separate creation as "polygenesis." I prefer "bigenesis" because the Indians did not seem to identify separate creations for the French, the British, and other Europeans; the separation appears to be distinctly between Indians and non-Indians. I might add that the idea of separate creations was an important concept for many European colonialists as well; see Hodgen 1964:230ff.

2. Although beyond the scope of this study, it is worth noting the plethora of literature by economists on the "irrational" behavior of the Indians in the fur trade. Assuming that the Indians had an understanding of capitalist economics, this material asks why they were not better economic players, or "monopsonists." For example, if they had restricted the output of furs, they could have both conserved the game supply and raised the prices of furs. It also addresses the issue that competition was created by having different buyers, when the system would have worked better with only one.

3. Claims of the deliberate spread of smallpox by the British at Mackinac are documented in Blackbird 1887.

4. The Trout, quoted in a letter from Capt. J. Dunham to Governor Hull dated 20 May 1807, in the Michigan Pioneer and Historical Collections; also in White 1991:486 and Dowd 1992:130. Note that this is similar to the southern Cherokees' turn away from deerskins.

5. The Trout, quoted in letter, Dunham to Hull, 20 May 1807.

3. Pimadaziwin

1. Hallowell 1942, 1947, 1955, 1960, 1967. Hultkrantz and Vorren (1982:163–86) do not agree with Hallowell's concept of personhood. Hultkrantz also disagrees with Hallowell's dismissing the distinction

between natural and supernatural, which Hultkrantz sees as a crucial distinction (Hultkrantz 1983:231–53, personal communication).

2. It is beyond the scope of this study to present an exhaustive analysis of the Midéwiwin. However, interested readers should consult such seminal works as Hoffman 1891; Landes 1968; Harrison 1982; Vecsey 1983; Ritzenthaler and Ritzenthaler 1970. The Algonkian scholars Harold Hickerson (1960) and Selwyn Dewdney (1975) agree that the Midéwiwin originated at Chequamegon or La Pointe as a response to the social upheaval and threat of total cultural decline—especially through disease—caused by the fur trade in the seventeenth century.

3. Actually, these pipe carriers interpreted the "offense" to have been my refusal to engage in sexual relations with an elder in exchange for his information.

5. Nanabozho

1. Morrison (1979:54) is referring to the Abenaki culture hero Gluscap, but with obvious Algonkian-based parallels with Nanabozho.

2. Just recently, well after this research was started, an elder reported that the MCIA has become virtually defunct.

3. This population figure is based on census data but undoubtedly is low, largely because of reticence to report among the broad Indian community.

6. The Seventh Fire

1. This is a concept first attributed to the Jewish exegete Philo of Alexandria, who in around 30 B.C.E. tried to mediate the tension between Hellenistic philosophy and Hebrew scripture. A good example is his allegorical designation of Abraham to mean both a historical figure and a representation of the soul, a designation that served to unite all Jewish people across time. This was the beginning of a philosophical system that eventually materialized as what scholars today call "hermeneutical prophecy."

2. It is interesting to consider the possible influence of Christian fundamentalist "Awakenings" here, or at least the coincidental parallel.

3. See, e.g., Russell 1978; Worsley 1957; Burridge 1960, 1969. It also has been shown to be a phenomenon not restricted to tribal societies. For example, Norman Cohn argued that apocalyptic/revitalistic movements arose in Europe between the eleventh and sixteenth centuries as a result of the "desire of the poor to improve the material condition of their lives," and that these movements "became transfused with phantasies of a new Paradise on earth, a world purged of suffering and sin, a Kingdom of

Saints" (1961:xiii). See also McLoughlin 1978 on revitalization, reform, and awakenings.

7. What Do We Do about the Others?

1. After seeing many pipes for sale at powwows, I asked several people, including a pipe maker, what they thought about just anyone—especially non-Indians—buying them. They assured me that the sacred and powerful pipes never were bought or sold. But I also was told that people who buy the pipes at powwows don't understand their meaning: "Folks who buy pipes usually just hang 'em on the wall or want them as a showpiece on their mantles."

2. See Whitehorse 1988 for a concise general description of the pancultural role of these events. *Powwow* is an Algonkian word that early Euro-American explorers associated with the healing rituals of shamans.

3. Benjamin R. Kracht, focusing on the Kiowa, has begun to explore this application (1993:471–72).

8. Invite the Others to Dinner

1. It is worth noting the possible correlation between prehistoric burial patterns, particularly ossuary sites, and the development of the Feast of the Dead in the Great Lakes area, especially as they reflect changing subsistence modes, settlement patterns, and social orientation. Looking at the primary archaeological variable—burial—by time sequence and subsistence mode suggests that the Odawa shifted their mortuary pattern with the newly adopted settled lifestyle associated with the fur trade. In the eastern woodlands, general trends in prehistoric burial patterns seem to shift from primary inhumations to cremation or secondary interment or both (with signs of systematic defleshing of the bodies) in mortuary mounds as settlement patterns became more sedentary (Pflüg 1987). Pilling (1982) is further enlightening on the possible expansion of burial patterns with intertribal contact and the development of multiclan settlements with the fur trade. By the late 1600s the Huron/Wyandot, to avoid Iroquoian threats, migrated with the French to the Michilimackinac area, around the Straits in Michigan. The Odawa and Ojibwe had long since laid claim to this area as at least a seasonal fishing rookery. By 1700 the Huron/Wyandot, Ojibwe, and Odawa had settled together at Saint Ignace, where they were pressured to move south to Fort Ponchartrain (later Detroit) to increase their contribution to the fur trade. By 1703 a number of multitribal villages were established around the fort that included Wyandot, Ojibwe, and Odawa residents. In 1782 Moravian missionaries in the Detroit area reported finding a site with "sixteen

baskets full of human bones . . . this reference is probably to a Huron [Wyandot] ossuary from one of their 'Festivals of the Dead'" (Pilling 1982:227). Pilling also reports that the Moravians had extensive contact with the local Ojibwe (1961:18). Additionally, Pilling reports several mound sites in southeastern Michigan as discussed by Samuel R. Brown in 1817 (1961:22–26).

2. See Nicholas Perrot's accounts in Blair 1911:86–88. Perrot's work was first translated and published in 1864 by Rev. Jules Tailhan, S.J., who notes accounts of "the great feast of the dead, among not only the Hurons [Wyandot] but the upper Algonkians," given by Champlain (*Voyages*, 303, 304); in the *Jesuit Relations* of 1636 (chapter 9) and 1642 (chapter 12); by La Potherie (*Histoire* 2:42); by Lafitan (*Moeure des sauvages* 2:446–57); and by Charlevoix (*Histoire* 3:377, 378); see Blair 1911:88, note 56. For additional sources, see Cadillac's observations of a mortuary feast performed by the Odawa at Mackinac (in Kinietz 1940:283–84), Brébeuf's account of "the solemn feast of the dead" in Thwaites 1959:10:279–311, and R. Mason 1981:384–89.

3. Jérôme Lalemont, in Thwaites 1959, vol. 23. Three Lalemonts were working as missionaries in the Upper Great Lakes and Saint Lawrence regions during the early seventeenth century: Jérôme, Charles, and Gabriel, who died at the stake with Jean de Brébeuf at Saint Ignace in 1649.

4. One of my former students, who is of Cherokee descent, has suggested that this combination of dancing and contest for prizes may present a historical forerunner of contemporary contest powwows.

9. Is Law a Medium for Collective Determination?

1. This assessment is based on a series of exchanges with NPS officials during a four-day job interview, as well as personal observation of such sites.

2. The most noteworthy of these decisions were the cases *Sequoyah v. Tennessee Valley Authority* (1980), *Badoni v. Higginson* (1981), *Fools Crow v. Gullet* (1982), and *Wilson v. Block* (1983).

3. For a recent analysis of the *Lyng* case, see Echo-Hawk 1993:8–11; Loftin 1989:56–60; Deloria 1992:74–83. For a recent analysis of the *Smith* case, see Echo-Hawk 1993:11–14.

4. Justice Kennedy did not participate in the case.

5. Courts 95.3—constitutional questions—avoidance—availability of statutory relief.

6. This summary is based on my attendance at the session, which I do not identify by specific date or place because of the inflammatory nature of the topic for both Indians and museum personnel.

7. This analysis is based on the following: my attendance at a meeting with the then-tribal chairman and the financial manager of the district of the diocese in question; further correspondence with the financial manager on my part and assistance to the tribal group with drafting a proposal for acquisition and preservation of the property; serving on the township's historic preservation committee and attending meetings with the township and tribal representatives; participation in the archaeological site survey project; and exchanges with a former township representative who allowed me to review the history of written correspondence between this township and the diocese.

8. Since the time the original proposal was submitted by the townships, the diocese has had an additional appraisal made of the property, independent of the townships, with a value of $1.2 million—a figure arrived at based on the possibility of there being four building sites on the property in question. Additionally, a newly created association of local residents also had their own appraisal made, which excluded all areas with known or suspected Odawa graves, which set the value at some $450,000. This group seeks either to have the townships purchase the property at this lesser cost or to lease it, taking similar "protective" measures as proposed by the townships and keeping control of the beach on the most local level. More recently, the January 1996 township newsletter reported: "Just as we were nearing the finish line for acquiring the church beach property from the Diocese . . . the unexpected became the expected. The Michigan Natural Resources Trust Fund (MNRTF) and the Townships . . . require a marketable title to the land. A request has been made to the . . . Title Company for title insurance for the subject property. In their examination of the property, they found that they could not provide title insurance. . . . The Diocese . . . has assured us that they will take what steps necessary to clear the title defect. In the meantime. . . . All plans . . . are strictly tentative and are . . . now slowed until the defect is corrected." One step the diocese took was to file suit against the immediate property owners for release of title to adjoining thirty-foot easements; the residents countersued, and the matter currently is stymied in the courts. Recently, however, members of the local association have taken their own action to acquire a parcel immediately to the north of the church building (for a proposed twenty-car parking lot) and the adjacent easement (for access to the beach), and at least one lot across the road from the church (for additional parking, outhouses, etc.). Title to this latter parcel is not at issue.

9. For a theoretical overview of the convictions that inform this Odawa stance, see Graber 1976.

10. The Three R's of Traditionalism

1. Mooney 1896. As a counter to Mooney, Joel Martin (1991a) reassesses the literature on the Ghost Dance and develops the hypothesis that revitalization movements among American Indians have been neither immediate nor passive ideological reactions to situations over which they had little or no control; instead, they are examples of Indian peoples perpetually acting in creative contact with history. Martin's argument, especially against victimization and lack of control, is suggestive and seems to be informed by a sensitivity to religion, as is, certainly, Gregory Evans Dowd's discussion in his *A Spirited Resistance* (1992).

2. Raymond DeMallie's (1982) revisionist approach to understanding Indian revitalization focuses on the symbolic facets of the Ghost Dance and argues that the Ghost Dance was a modification of the Sun Dance. In this reinterpretation, DeMallie suggests that the participants in the Ghost Dance engaged traditional ritual forms and mythological themes, reinterpreting them within a new socioreligious landscape.

3. Wallace 1956a, 1949, 1952a, 1952b, 1956b. As an important counter to Wallace's generalizations, see Kracht 1993. By analyzing the ritual symbols in the Kiowa Ghost Dance from 1894 to 1916, as these symbols show how the Kiowa saw themselves as actors, Kracht argues that this movement involved motives that the theories of deprivation/victimization and acculturation cannot explain. This work is suggestive in that it implies that neither contact nor politico-economic deprivation alone is the requisite event to precipitate revitalization.

4. Burridge 1960, 1969. The inherent questions that Burridge raises but does not answer are: What is "millenarian" about revitalization, and how is it a myth-dream? Discussing the transformation of myth into constructive action begins to get at what ritual is, but it does not explain what is efficacious about "physical activity."

5. Wilson 1973:1, 5–6. Although Wilson defines revitalization in thaumaturgical terms, I see the activities among Odawa traditionalists as a dynamic process of adjustment, involving both everyday activities and those Wilson would call thaumaturgical or magical and in a sense passive. The traditionalists are both ritualists and social critics who actively, as a group, work to restore the right relationship with the total social world, including the ancestors.

Bibliography

Aberle, David. 1959. "The Prophet Dance and Reactions to White Contact." In *Southwest Journal of Anthropology* 15.1:74–83.

Aberle, David, and Omer Stewart. 1957. *Navaho And Ute Peyotism: A Chronological and Distributional Study*. Boulder: University of Colorado Press.

American Indian Citizenship Act. 43 Stat. 253 (1924).

American Indian Civil Rights Act. 82 Stat. 73 (1968).

American Indian Graves Protection and Repatriation Act. Pub. L. No. 101–601, 104 Stat. 3048 (1990).

American Indian Religious Freedom Act. Pub. L. No. 95–341. S.J. RES. 102, 11 Aug. 1978, 92 Stat. 469 (42 U.S.C. 1996).

Andrews, Wesley. 1984. "Ottawa Mortuary Ritual: Belief and Practice." M.A. thesis. University of Chicago.

Auerbach, Eric. 1953. *Mimesis: The Representation of Reality in Western Literature*. Translated by Willard R. Trask. Princeton, N.J.: Princeton University Press.

Ball, Milner S. 1985. *Lying Down Together: Law, Metaphor, and Theology*. Madison: University of Wisconsin Press.

Badoni v. Higginson. 455 F. Supp. 641 (D. Utah 1977); 638 F. 2d 172, 180 (10th Cir. 1980); cert. denied, 452 U.S. 954 (1981).

Bell, Catherine. 1987. *Ritual Theory, Ritual Practice*. New York: Oxford University Press.

Bemister, Margaret. [1912] 1973. *Thirty Indian Legends Of Canada*. Vancouver, B.C.: Douglas & McIntyre.

Black, Mary B. 1977. "Ojibwa Power Belief System." In *The Anthropology of Power*, edited by Raymond Fogelson and Richard N. Adams, 141–52. New York: Academic Press.

Blackbird, Andrew J. 1887. *History of the Ottawa and Chippewa Indians of Michigan: A Grammar of Their Language, and Personal and Family History of the Author*. Ypsilanti, Mich.: Ypsilanti Job Printing House.

Reprint. Petoskey, Mich.: The Little Traverse Regional Historical Society, 1977.

Blair, Emma H., ed. 1911. *The Indian Tribes of the Upper Mississippi Valley and Region of the Great Lakes*. Vol. 1. Cleveland: Clark.

Bloch, Maurice. 1989. *Ritual, History and Power*. London: Althone Press.

Brown, Jennifer S. H., and Robert Brightman. 1988. *"The Orders Of The Dreamed": George Nelson on Cree and Northern Ojibwa Religion and Myth, 1823*. Winnipeg: University of Manitoba Press.

Burke, Kenneth. 1989. *On Symbols and Society*. Chicago: University of Chicago Press.

Burridge, Kenelm. 1960. *Mambu: A Melanesian Millenium*. London: Methuen.

————. 1969. *New Heaven, New Earth: A Study of Millenarian Activities*. New York: Schocken Books.

Chaudhuri, Joyotpaul. 1985. "American Indian Policy: An Overview." In *American Indian Policy in the Twentieth Century*, edited by Vine Deloria Jr., 15–34. Norman: University of Oklahoma Press.

Cherokee Nation v. State of Georgia. U.S. 1 (1832).

Clifton, James A., George L. Cornell, and James M. McClurken. 1986. *People of the Three Fires: The Ottawa, Potawatomi, and Ojibway of Michigan*. Grand Rapids: Michigan Indian Press, Grand Rapids Inter-Tribal Council.

Cohn, Norman. 1961. *Pursuit of the Millenium: Revolutionary Messianism in Medieval and Reformation Europe and Its Bearing on Modern Totalitarian Movements*. 2d ed. New York: Harper & Row.

Coser, Lewis. 1956. *The Functions of Social Conflict*. New York: Free Press.

Craven, Rex P. 1983. "The American Indian Religious Freedom Act: An Answer to the Indian's Prayer?" *South Dakota Law Review* 29:131–43.

Deloria, Vine, Jr., ed. 1985. *American Indian Policy in the Twentieth Century*. Norman: University of Oklahoma Press.

————. 1992. "The Application of the Constitution to American Indians." In *Exiled in the Land of the Free: Democracy, Indian Nations, and the U.S. Constitution*, by Oren Lyons et al., 281–316. Santa Fe, N.M.: Clear Light.

DeMallie, Raymond. 1982. "The Lakota Ghost Dance: An Ethnohistorical Account." *Pacific Historical Review* 51:385–405.

Densmore, Frances. [1929] 1979. *Chippewa Customs*. St. Paul: Minnesota Historical Society Press.

Detwiler, Fritz. 1992. "'All My Relatives': Persons in Oglala Religion." *Religion* 22:235–46.

Dewdney, Selwyn. 1975. *The Sacred Scrolls of the Southern Ojibway*. Toronto: University of Toronto Press.

Diamond, S., ed. 1960. *Culture and History: Essays in Honor of Paul Radin*. New York: Columbia University Press.

Dobson, P., ed. 1978. *The Tree That Never Dies: Oral History of the Michigan Indians*. Grand Rapids, Mich.: Grand Rapids Public Library, Native American Oral History Project.

Dowd, Gregory Evans. 1992. *A Spirited Resistance: The North American Indian Struggle for Unity, 1745–1815*. Baltimore: Johns Hopkins University Press.

Driver, Tom. 1992. *The Magic of Ritual*. San Francisco: Harper San Francisco.

Echo-Hawk, Walter R. 1993. "Native American Religious Liberty: Five Hundred Years after Columbus." *American Indian Culture and Research* 17.3:33–52.

Eggan, Fred. 1966. *The American Indian: Perspectives for the Study of Social Change*. Chicago: Aldine.

Eggan, Fred, ed. 1955. *Social Anthropology of the North American Tribes*. Chicago: University of Chicago Press.

Employment Division, Department of Human Resources of Oregon, et al., Petitioners v. Alfred L. Smith, et al. 494 U.S. 872 (1990).

Ensworth, Laurie. 1983. "Native American Free Exercise Rights to the Use of Public Lands." *Boston University Law Review* 63:141–79.

Ettawageshik, Fred. 1943. "Ghost Suppers." *American Anthropologist* 45 (n.s.): 491–93.

Federal Water Pollution Control Act, 33 USCS 1251 et seq.

Fogelson, Raymond, and Richard N. Adams, eds. 1977. *The Anthropology of Power*. New York: Academic Press.

Fools Crow v. Gullet. 541 F. Supp. 785 (D.S.D. 1982).

Foucault, Michel. 1972. *The Archaeology of Knowledge*. New York: Pantheon Books.

Freidl, Ernestine. 1950. "An Attempt at Directed Culture Change: Leadership among the Chippewa, 1640–1948." Ph.D diss. Columbia University.

Geertz, Armin W. 1994a. "On Reciprocity and Mutual Reflection in the Study of Native American Religions." *Religion* 24.1:1–22.

——. 1994b. *The Invention of Prophecy: Continuity and Meaning in Hopi Indian Religion*. Berkeley and Los Angeles: University of California Press.

Geertz, Clifford. 1973. *The Interpretation of Cultures*. New York: Basic Books.

Gill, Sam D. 1982. *Native American Religions: An Introduction.* Belmont, Calif.: Wadsworth.

———. 1987. *Native American Religious Action: A Performance Approach to Religion.* Columbia: University of South Carolina Press.

Graber, Linda H. 1976. *Wilderness as Sacred Space.* Washington, D.C.: Association of American Geographers.

Grimes, Ronald L. 1982. *Beginnings in Ritual Studies.* New York: University Press of America.

Gringhuis, Dirk. 1970. *Lore of the Great Turtle: Indian Legends of Mackinac Retold.* Mackinac Island, Mich: Mackinac Island State Park Commission.

Hallowell, A. Irving. 1942. *The Role of Conjuring in Salteaux Society.* Philadelphia: University Pennsylvania Press.

———. 1947. "Myth, Culture and Personality." *American Anthropologist* 49:544–56.

———. 1955. *Culture and Experience.* Philadelphia: University of Pennsylvania Press.

———. 1960. "Ojibwa Ontology, Behavior and World View." In *Culture and History: Essays in Honor of Paul Radin,* edited by S. Diamond, 19–52. New York: Columbia University Press.

———. 1967. "Ojibwa World View." In *The North American Indians,* edited by R. C. Owens, R. C., J. J. F. Deetz, and A. D. Fisher, 208–35. New York: Macmillan.

Harris, Grace Gredys. 1989. "Concepts of Individual, Self, and Person in Description and Analysis." *American Anthropologist* 91.3: 599–612.

Harrison, J. 1982. "The Midewiwin: The Retention of an Ideology." M.A. thesis. University of Calgary.

Hecht, Richard D. 1981. "Scripture and Commentary in Philo." *Journal of the Society of Biblical Literature*: 129–64.

Hickerson, Harold. 1960. "The Feast of the Dead among the Seventeenth-Century Algonkians of the Upper Great Lakes." *American Anthropologist* 62:81–107.

Hodgen, Margaret T. 1964. *Early Anthropology in the Sixteenth and Seventeenth Centuries.* Philadelphia: University of Pennsylvania Press.

Hoffman, William. 1891. "The Mide'wiwin or 'Grand Medicine Society' of the Ojibwa." *Annual Report of the Bureau of Ethnology* 7:143–300.

Hultkrantz, Åke. 1979. *The Religions of the American Indians.* Berkeley and Los Angeles: University of California Press.

———. 1983. "The Concept of the Supernatural in Primal Religion." *History of Religions* 22:231–53.

Hultkrantz, Åke, and D. Vorren. 1982. *The Hunters: Their Culture and Way of Life.* Oslo: Universitetsforlaget.

Hunter, Charles E. 1971. "The Delaware Nativist Revival of the Mid-Eighteenth Century." *Ethnohistory* 18:39–49.

Irwin, Lee. 1992. "Contesting World Views: Dreams among the Huron and Jesuits." *Religion* 22.3:259–70.

————. 1994. *The Dream-Seekers: Native American Visionary Traditions of the Great Plains.* Norman: University of Oklahoma Press.

Jacobs, Wilbur R. 1972. *Dispossessing the American Indian: Indians and Whites on the Colonial Frontier.* New York: Scribner's.

Johnson, Mark. 1987. *The Body and the Mind: The Bodily Basis of Meaning, Imagination, and Reason.* Chicago: University of Chicago Press.

Johnson v. MacIntosh. 21 U.S. 543 (1823).

Johnston, Basil. 1976. *Ojibway Heritage.* Lincoln: University of Nebraska Press.

Kenny, James. 1913. "Journal of James Kenny, 1761–1763." Edited by John W. Jordan. *Pennsylvania Magazine of History and Biography* 37:1–47, 152–201.

Kertzer, David. 1988. *Ritual, Politics, and Power.* New Haven, Conn.: Yale University Press.

Kinietz, W. 1940. *The Indians of the Great Lakes, 1615–1760.* Ann Arbor: University of Michigan Press.

Kluckhohn, Clyde. 1962. *Culture and Behavior: Collected Essays of Clyde Kluckhohn.* Edited by Richard Kluckhohn. New York: Free Press.

Kohl, Johann G. [1860] 1985. *Kitchi-Gami: Life among the Lake Superior Ojibway.* St. Paul: Minnesota Historical Society Press.

Kracht, Benjamin R. 1993. "The Kiowa Ghost Dance, 1894–1916: An Unheralded Revitalization Movement." *Ethnohistory* 39.4:452–77.

Krech, Shepard, III, ed. 1981. *Indians, Animals, and the Fur Trade: A Critique of "Keepers of the Game."* Athens: University of Georgia Press.

LaBarre, Weston. 1970. *The Ghost Dance: The Origins of Religion.* New York: Delta.

Lakoff, George, and Mark Johnson. 1980. *Metaphors We Live By.* Chicago: University of Chicago Press.

Lakoff, George, and Mark Turner. 1989. *More Than Cool Reason: A Field Guide to Poetic Metaphor.* Chicago: University of Chicago Press.

Landes, Ruth. 1968. *Ojibwe Religion and the Midewiwin.* Madison: University of Wisconsin Press.

Landy, David, ed. 1977. *Culture, Disease, and Healing.* New York: Macmillan.

"Letter from Captain J. Dunham to Govenor Hull, May 20, 1807." 1929. Michigan Pioneer and Historical Collections, 40. Lansing: Michigan Historical Commission.

Levi-Strauss, Claude. 1977. "The Sorcerer and His Magic." In *Culture, Disease, and Healing,* edited by D. Landy, 445–53. New York: Macmillan.

Linton, Ralph. 1943. "Nativistic Movements." *American Anthropologist* 45:230–40.

Loftin, John D. 1989. "Anglo-American Jurisprudence and the Native American Quest for Religious Freedom." *American Indian Culture and Research* 13.1:1–52.

Lyons, Oren, et al. 1992. *Exiled in the Land of the Free: Democracy, Indian Nations, and the U.S. Constitution.* Santa Fe, N.M.: Clear Light Press.

McClurken, James. 1988. "We Wish to Be Civilized: Ottawa-American Political Contests on the Michigan Frontier." Ph.D diss. Michigan State University.

McCool, Daniel. 1985. "Indian Voting." In *American Indian Policy In the Twentieth Century,* edited by Vine Deloria Jr., 105–34. Norman: University of Oklahoma Press.

McDonald, Thomas D., Robert A. Wood, and Melissa A. Pflug. 1996. *Rural Crimianl Justice: Conditions, Constraints, and Challenges.* Salem, Wisc.: Sheffield.

McLoughlin, William. 1978. *After the Trail of Tears: The Cherokee's Struggle for Sovereignty, 1839–1880.* Chapel Hill: University of North Carolina Press.

Martin, Calvin. 1978. *Keepers of the Game: Indian-Animal Relations and the Fur Trade.* Berkeley and Los Angeles: University of California Press.

Martin, Joel. 1991a. "Before and beyond the Sioux Ghost Dance: Native American Prophetic Movements and the Study of Religion." *Journal of the American Academy of Religion* 59.4:677–702.

————. 1991b. *Sacred Revolt: The Muskogee's Struggle for a New World.* Boston: Beacon Press.

Mason, Phillip 1978. *United States v State Of Michigan.* Civil Action no. M26–73. U.S. District Court, Western District of Michigan. Treaty of Washington, 1836. Summary Report no. 2. Detroit: Wayne State University Reuther Archives.

Mason, R. J. 1981. *Great Lakes Archaeology.* New York: Academic Press.

Mauss, Marcel. 1967. *The Gift: Forms and Functions of Exchange in Archaic Societies.* New York: Norton.

Michaelsen, Robert S. 1984. "The Significance of the American Indian Religious Freedom Act." *Journal of the American Academy of Religion* 52.1:93–115.

———. 1986. "Sacred Land in America: What Is It? How Can It Be Protected?" *Religion* 16:249–68.

Miller, Walter B. 1972. "Two Concepts of Authority." In *The Emergent Native Americans: A Reader in Cultural Contact,* edited by Deward E. Walker Jr., 565–83. Boston: Little, Brown.

Mooney, James. [1896] 1973. *The Ghost Dance Religion and Wounded Knee.* New York: Dover.

Mormon Church v. United States. 135 U.S. 1 (1890).

Morrison, Kenneth M. 1979. "Towards a History of Intimate Encounters: Algonkian Folklore, Jesuit Missionaries, and Kiwakwe, the Cannibal Giant." *American Indian Culture and Research* 3.4:51–80.

———. n.d. "Mapping Otherness: James Axtell, Myth, and the Interdisciplinary Study of Cultural Encounter." unpublished manuscript. Department of Religious Studies, Arizona State University.

———. 1984. *The Embattled Northeast: The Elusive Ideal of Alliance in Abenaki-Euroamerican Relations.* Berkeley and Los Angelels: University of California Press.

———. 1992a. "Beyond the Supernatural: Language and Religious Action." *Religion* 22.3:201–6.

———. 1992b. "Sharing the Flower: A Non-Supernatural Theory of Grace." *Religion* 22.3:207–21.

———. 1994. "They Act as Though They Have No Relatives: A Reply to Geertz." *Religion* 24.1:11–12.

Nash, Philleo. [1937] 1955. "The Place of Religious Revivalism in the Formation of the Intercultural Community of the Klamath Reservation." In *Social Anthropology of the North American Tribes,* edited by Fred Eggan, 377–442. Chicago: University of Chicago Press.

National Environmental Policy Act of 1969, 42 USCS 4321 et seq.

O'Brien, Sharon. 1985. "Federal Indian Policies and the International Protection of Human Rights." In *American Indian Policy in the Twentieth Century,* edited by Vine Deloria Jr., 35–62. Norman: University of Oklahoma Press.

———. 1988. "A History of the American Indian Religious Freedom Act and Its Implementation." Paper delivered at the Tenth Anniversary

Conference on the American Indian Religious Freedom Act, hosted by the National Conference of Christians and Jews, Inc., Newberry Library, Chicago, April 7–9.

Osoinach, Kirk. 1976. "Indian Politics and Culture Change in Rural Northern Michigan." Ph.D. diss. University of Michigan.

Otto, Simon. 1990. *Walk in Peace: Legends and Stories of the Michigan Indians.* Grand Rapids: Michigan Indian Press, Grand Rapids Intertribal Council.

Owens, R. C., J. J. F. Deetz, and A. D. Fisher, eds. 1967. *The North American Indians.* New York: Macmillan.

Paper, Jordan. 1988. *Offering Smoke: The Sacred Pipe and Native American Religion.* Edmonton: University of Alberta Press.

Peckham, Howard H. 1947. *Pontiac and the Indian Uprising.* Princeton, N.J.: Princeton University Press.

Petoskey, John. 1985. "Indians and the First Amendment." In *American Indian Policy in the Twentieth Century,* edited by Vine Deloria Jr., 221–38. Norman: University of Oklahoma Press.

Pflüg, Melissa A. 1987. "Survey of the Distribution of Mortuary Patterns in North American Prehistory." Unpublished manuscript. Anthropology Museum, Wayne State University, Detroit.

———. 1990. "Contemporary Revitalization Movements among the Northern Great Lakes Ottawa "Odawa" Indians: Motives and Accomplishments." Ph.D. diss. Wayne State University.

———. 1992a. "'Breaking Bread': Ritual and Metaphor in Odawa Religious Practice." *Religion* 22:247–58.

———. 1992b. "Politics of Great Lakes Indian Religion." *Michigan Historical Review* (December): 15–32.

———. 1996a. "American Indian Justice Systems and Tribal Courts in Rural Indian Country." In *Rural Criminal Justice: Conditions, Constraints, and Challenges,* edited by Thomas D. McDonald, Robert A. Wood, and Melissa A. Pflüg, 191–215. Salem, Wisc.: Sheffield.

———. 1996b. "'The Last Stand?': Odawa Revitalizationists Versus U.S. Law." In *Questioning the Secular State: The Worldwide Resurgence of Religion in Politics,* edited by David Westerlund, 75–95. London: Hurst; New York: St. Martin's Press.

———. 1996c. "Pimadaziwin: Contemporary Odawa Rituals of Community." *American Indian Quarterly* 20, no. 4, special volume edited by Lee Irwin.

Pilling, Arnold. 1961. "Six Archaeological Sites in the Detroit Area, I." *Michigan Archaeologist* 7. 3:18–26.

———. 1982. "Detroit: Urbanism Moves West: Palisaded Fur-Trade Center to Diversified Manufacturing City." *Michigan Archaeologist* 3.3:225–42.

Pommersheim, F. 1992. "Liberation, Dreams, and Hard Work: An Essay on Tribal Court Jurisprudence." *Wisconsin Law Review* 1992, no. 2: 411–57.

Price, John. 1975. "Sharing: The Integration of Intimate Economics." *Anthropologica* (n.s.) 17.1:3–27.

Pub. L. No. 89–665, 80 Stat. 915, 16 U.S.C. 470 (1966).

Quaife, Milo M. 1931. *The John Askin Papers.* Detroit: Detroit Public Library.

Quimby, G. 1967. "The Indian Tribes of the Upper Great Lakes Region." In *The North American Indians: A Sourcebook*, edited by R. C. Owen, J. J. F. Deetz, and A. D. Fisher, 576–80. New York: Macmillan.

Radin, Paul. 1914. "Religion of the North American Indians." *Journal of Folklore* 27:335–73.

Ragsdale, Fred L., Jr. 1985. "The Deception of Geography." In *American Indian Policy in the Twentieth Century*, edited by Vine Deloria Jr., 63–82. Norman: University of Oklahoma Press.

Reynolds v. United States. 98 U.S. 145, 25 L Ed 244 (1879).

Richard E. Lyng, Secretary of Agriculture, et al., Petitioners v. Northwest Indian Cemetery Protective Association, et al., 485 U.S. 439 (1988).

Ritzenthaler, R. E., and P. Ritzenthaler. 1970. *The Woodland Indians of the Western Great Lakes.* Garden City, N.Y.: Doubleday.

Russell, D. S. 1978. *Apocalyptic, Ancient and Modern.* Philadelphia: Fortress Press.

Sahlins, Marshall. 1972. *Stone Age Economics.* Chicago: Aldine-Atherton.

Sanborn, Geoff. 1990. "Unfencing the Range: History, Identity, Property, and Apocalypse in *Lame Deer: Seeker of Visions*." *American Indian Culture and Research* 14.4:39–57.

Schoolcraft, Henry R. [1856] 1984. *The Myth of Hiawatha and Other Oral Legends, Mythologic and Allegoric, of the North American Indians.* Au Train, Mich.: Avery Color Studios.

Sequoyah v. Tennessee Valley Authority, 480 F. Supp. 608 (E.D. Tenn. 1979); 620 F 2d 1159, 164 (6th Cir.); cert. denied, 449 U.S. 953 (1980).

Sherbert v. Verner, 374 U.S. 389, 407 (1963).

Smith, Chester H., and Ralph E. Boyer. 1971. *Survey of the Law of Property.* St. Paul, Minn.: West.

Smith, Jonathan Z. 1982. *Imagining Religion: From Babylon to Jonestown.* Chicago: University of Chicago Press.

Thwaites, Reuben G. [1896–1901] 1959. *The Jesuit Relations and Allied Documents*. 73 vols. New York: Pageant Books.

Torrance, Robert M. 1994. *The Spiritual Quest: Transcendence in Myth, Religion, and Science*. Berkeley and Los Angeles: University of California Press.

Turner, Victor. 1969. *The Ritual Process: Structure and Anti-Structure*. Ithaca, N.Y.: Cornell University Press.

United States v. State of Michigan, 471 Supp. 192 (1979).

U.S. Ninth Cir., 795 F 2d 688.

U.S. Supreme Court Reports, 99 L Ed 2d (1988).

———, 108 L Ed 2d (1990).

Van Gennep, Arnold. [1909] 1960. *The Rites of Passage*. Chicago: University of Chicago Press.

Vecsey, Christopher. 1983. *Traditional Ojibwa Religion and Its Historical Changes*. Philadelphia: American Philosophical Association.

Wagner, R. 1986. *Symbols That Stand for Themselves*. Chicago: University of Chicago Press.

Walker, Deward E., Jr. 1972. *The Emergent Native Americans: A Reader in Cultural Contact*. Boston: Little, Brown.

Wallace, Anthony F. C. 1949. *King of the Delawares: Teedyuscung, 1700–1763*. Philadelphia: University of Pennsylvania Press.

———. 1952a. "Halliday Jackson's Journal to the Seneca Indians." *Pennsylvania History* 19.2:117–48.

———. 1952b. "Handsome Lake and the Great Revival of the West." *American Indian Quarterly* 4.2:149–65.

———. 1956a. "Revitalization Movements: Some Theoretical Considerations for Their Comparative Study." *American Anthropologist* 58:264–81.

———. 1956b. "New Religions among the Delaware Indians, 1600–1900." *Southwest Journal of Anthropology* 12.1:1–22.

———. 1966. *Religion: An Anthropological View*. New York: Random House.

Warren, William. [1885] 1984. *History of the Ojibway People*. St. Paul: Minnesota Historical Society.

White, Richard. 1991. *The Middle Ground: Indians, Empires, and Republics in the Great Lakes Region, 1650–1815*. Cambridge: Cambridge University Press.

Whitehorse, David. 1988. *Pow-Wow: The Contemporary Pan-Indian Celebration*. San Diego State University Publications in North American Indian Studies, no. 5. San Diego: San Diego State University.

Wilson, Bryan. 1973. *A Sociological Study of Religious Movements of Protest among Tribal and Third World Peoples.* New York: Harper & Row.

Wilson v. Block, 708 F. 2d 735, 742, n. 3 (D.C. Cir. 1983).

Wisconsin v. Yoder, 406 U.S. 205, 214 (1972).

Worsley, Peter. 1957. *The Trumpet Shall Sound: A Study of "Cargo" Cults in Melanesia.* London: MacGibbon & Kee.

Wright, John. 1917. *The Crooked Tree: Indian Legends and a Short History of the Little Traverse Bay Region.* Harbor Springs, Mich.: C. Fayette Erwin.

Index